For Jacqui —
Let this be your
guide to the
money guide.
Judith Briles

ALSO BY JUDITH BRILES

The Woman's Guide to Financial Savvy

MONEY PHASES

The Six Financial Stages of a Woman's Life

by Judith Briles

SIMON AND SCHUSTER
NEW YORK

Published by Simon and Schuster
A Division of Simon & Schuster, Inc.
Simon & Schuster Building
Rockefeller Center
1230 Avenue of the Americas
New York, New York 10020
SIMON AND SCHUSTER and colophon are registered trademarks of
Simon & Schuster, Inc.
Designed by Irving Perkins Associates
Manufactured in the United States of America

1 2 3 4 5 6 7 8 9 10

Library of Congress Cataloging in Publication Data
Briles, Judith.
Money phases.

Includes index.
1. Finance, Personal. 2. Women—Finance, Personal.
I. Title.
HG179.B729 1984 332.024′042 83-20126
ISBN 0-671-45609-1

ACKNOWLEDGMENTS

No author ever completes a book without help, support and encouragement in completing the task. My warm thanks to Linda Rogers, my friend, my associate, who showed me the skill of writing and laughed at my zany anecdotes; to Louie Ward, who not only has the best typing skills of anyone I know, but also has the ability to deliver a joke better than anyone I have ever met; to Gayle Farrington for making me complete my eye therapy; to Everett Eaton and Keyvan Bahadi, who often left me in stitches at the most inopportune times; to Jacques de Spoelberch, my agent, for his continual guidance; to Patricia Soliman for her editorial suggestions and the fact that she would not let me get away with anything not done.

Special thanks are extended to friends and associates who read the original manuscript and offered recommendations and encouragement; Carolyn Morris, Jim Dolkas, Pat Port, Dick Clinton, Mary Ann Seth, John Wish and John Maling. Thanks should also go to my many clients and students without whom this book would have been impossible to complete.

To Josie, who is always there.

Contents

Preface: Minding Your Own Money 13

I. IDENTIFY THE ENEMY 15

II. DEVELOPING A PLAN 20
STEP 1—Identify Your Life Phase 21
STEP 2—Set Up a Personal Financial Profile 26
Evaluate Your Assets 26
Keep Records 28
Monthly Cash Flow (Chart) 28
Calculate Your Net Worth (Chart) 32
Determine the Break-Even Point 35

III. PULL THE TRIGGER 37
LIFE PHASE 1: 18–25 39
Contacts 40
Insurance Agents 41
Bankers 42
The CPA 43
The Tax Attorney 44
The Stockbroker 44
Real Estate Brokers 45
Property Managers 46
Financial Planners 46
Advisers or Investment Counselors 48
Live and Learn 48
Eliminate the Negative! 50
Keep Your Balance 50
Someone Else's Money 52
Credit Ratings 52
Take Credit Where Credit Is Due 53
Sources of Money 55

	Insure? Sure!	62
	The IRA Era	63
	To Market! To Market!	64
	To Collect or Not to Collect	72
	Pre-investment Questions	75
	Ms. Misc.	76
	Windfall!	76
LIFE PHASE 2:	25–35	80
	Chart Your Course	81
	Average and Save	82
	Liquidity	83
	Insurance—Disability and Life	84
	How Much Life Insurance Do You Need?	87
	Banks	88
	Stocks	88
	Options	94
	Mutual Funds	101
	Purchase of a Home	102
	Ms. Misc.	109
	Windfall!	110
	N.B.	111
LIFE PHASE 3:	35–40	111
	Add Venture	112
	Stock Up	113
	Do Your Own Thing?	116
	A Shelter for a Shelter	121
	Grab a Partner!	123
	Where There's a Will, There's a Way	130
	Ms. Misc.	135
	Windfall!	135
	N.B.	141
LIFE PHASE 4:	40–50	141
	Divorce Course	143
	Throw Me a Line!	143
	Don't Count On It!	144
	A Taxing Business	145
	Cash In Your Chips	146
	Avoid the Tax Bite	147
	Less Is More	148
	Some Growth, More Yield	152
	Too Good to Be True?	156
	New Directions	157
	Ms. Misc.	157
	Windfall	158
	N.B.	159

LIFE PHASE 5: 50–65 159
As You Owe, So Shall You Reap 160
Pain in the Joints 162
Watch the Underdogs! 163
Corporate Report Cards 163
Moving Down 168
Double Your Money 170
Home, Suite Home 170
Keep Growing! 171
Ms. Misc. 172
Windfall! 174
N.B. 175
LIFE PHASE 6: 65+ 175
"Win"come Deductions 176
Federal Estate Taxes 184
State Taxes 184
Inheritance Taxes 184
Federal Gift Tax 185
State Gift Tax 185
Trusts 185
Inter Vivos Trust 186
Testamentary Trust 186
Irrevocable Insurance Trust 187
Ms. Misc. 188
N.B. 188

IV. TAX FAX 189
Adjusted Gross Income 195
The Bottom Line 195
Keeping Track 196
Deductions and Exemptions 197
Charitable 197
Medical 198
Interest 198
Automobile 199
Business 200
Uniforms 200
Education 201
Alimony 201
Investment Counsel 201
Medical Insurance 202
Home Office 202
Moving Expenses 203
Dependents 203
Losses 204
Investments 204

Limitations on Deductions for Casualty Losses 205
Tax Credits 206
The Economic Recovery Tax Act of 1981 and the Tax Equity and Fiscal Responsibility Act of 1982 and Their Effect on You 207
Married Deduction 208
Indexing 208
Home Sale 208
Building Rehabilitation 209
Stock Options 209
Interest 210
Gifts and Marital Deduction 210
Dividend Exclusions 211
Withholding on Deferred Income 211
Retirement Dollars 212
IRAs and Keoghs 212
Tax Shelters 220
Afterword 231
Index 232

"The art of war is simple enough. Find out where your enemy is. Get at him as soon as you can. Strike at him as hard as you can and as often as you can and keep moving on."

—U.S. Grant, 1822–1885

Preface

MINDING YOUR OWN MONEY

PEOPLE love statistics. Statistics are respectable, they carry clout, they make us feel secure.

I can tell my daughter to clean her room or I'll cut off her allowance and her left arm, and she won't budge. But let me quote to her that "a recent survey of 100 ugly, bankrupt, social recluses indicated that 75 of them had messy rooms in their youth" and she can't get to the vacuum fast enough.

Statistics increase credibility and form a basis for mandates, predictions, and decisions. The obvious problem, of course, is that different people interpret statistics in different ways, depending upon—among other things—their "life phases." Don't panic: I'm no psychiatrist and this is not a book of psychoanalysis. I simply believe that there are physical, psychological and emotional circumstances that influence us as women in different ways and at different times in our lives. Because these circumstances help determine how we are likely to react to certain situations, any financial plan must take them into account.

Suppose, for example, the Consumer Price Index indicates that over the last twelve months the price of toothpaste has increased by 25 percent, while the price of shoe polish has shot up by only 5 percent. There are wealthy middle-aged women out there who would immediately decide that the answer is to buy a toothpaste company; while some young, poor, risk-taking "sister," faced with the same statistic, might start brushing her teeth with shoe polish.

Extreme? In the extreme! But it brings me to the point of this book. A woman, along with her ability to be independent, goal-seeking, and in charge of her own destiny, does tend to progress through life in phases. And recognizing current and future phases is an integral part of determining how best to react to current and future circumstances, conditions, and, yes, statistics.

In *Money Phases* I will cite only one major statistic. In the last 12 months, the consumer items most often purchased increased in price, on an average, by at least 10 percent—even when the inflation increase was less than 10 percent. I have written this book in the belief that the most practical way of dealing with the 10 percent–plus yearly inflation enemy is to devise a plan for increasing your income, net worth, and/or investible moneys by at least 15 percent a year.

How? Simply by doing the following:

1. Identify the enemy.
2. Develop a plan which includes the identification of your life phase and a personal financial profile.
3. Implement the plan by taking aim from the firing line of your life phase and pulling the trigger.
4. Keep abreast of Tax Fax (page 189) that may affect your plan.

Toward these goals, I have divided this book into four major sections. In the first, I provide a definition, a brief history, and an explanation of the enemy facing us—inflation. In the second I describe a plan for confronting and successfully conquering that enemy. In the third I address issues that are specific to your relevant life phase and critical to the implementation of your "plan." Finally, in the fourth section—Tax Fax—I provide tax information and updates and strategies that will enhance your ability to combat inflation successfully during your current and future phases.

Part I

IDENTIFY THE ENEMY

IT is said that one of the benefits of inflation is that kids can no longer get sick on a nickel's worth of candy. Despite this dubious advantage, inflation is still the most ferocious economic enemy we face today, and there is as yet no proven weapon to combat it.

During the 1960s, inflation did not particularly frighten politicians and economists, who occasionally even whispered that sometimes a little inflation was acceptable. Not until the 1970s and 1980s did people begin to read about it in their daily newspapers and come to recognize its dramatic effect on both a national and personal level. The eighties appear to offer both ups and downs in price movement, resulting in an overall increase—similar to a two-steps-forward, one-step-back approach.

The generally accepted method of tracking this is the Consumer Price Index, referred to by those who know it best as the "CPI." It is an annual listing of common consumer items along with their prices. So, by comparing the Consumer Price Index of 1972 with that of 1982, the astute consumer can, with the help of a calculator, get a rough idea of the inflation rate over the last ten years.

According to the CPI, the cost of living doubled in the 50 years between 1920 and 1970; but during the 1970s the Consumer Price Index doubled in approximately nine years. Two primary components of the index—food and home ownership—rose by more than 100 percent in the 1970s, and it is estimated that they could again double during the 1980s. Medical, fuel and utilities costs all increased by at least 100 percent in approximately seven years.

Although the Consumer Price Index has been the primary measure for both economists and the general population, it is not always the most accurate means of determining inflation rate. Why? First, it consists of items that many of us may not buy very often. If you hate cabbage and never cook it, its current price is irrelevant. Second, the CPI, as with many "across the board" measures, is a general reflection of the habits of males and females from approximately 18 to 72 years of age. As such, it is a less than accurate reflection of the buying habits of, and inflation rate for, say, the 26-year-old professional woman with a $30,000-a-year job, a husband, and one child or the 45-year-old widow with minimum income. In view of this, I recommend that, instead of using the "official" index, you put together one of your own. It should be composed of items that *you* purchase on an ongoing basis. By doing this, you will get a firm grasp of what *your* actual cost of living is each year, and you will see areas of significant increase or decrease. In the accompanying table I have listed several items, many of which a woman might purchase more than once a month, and their price increases since 1970. As you can see by the following table, the prices did not increase by just a few percentage points, but range from a yearly increase of 10 percent to 100 percent.

The last decade, then, has been an inflationary nightmare for most women, with average cost increases far in excess of 20 percent a year among their most commonly purchased items.

What does this mean to you? It means that your money buys less. In simple terms, inflation is a decrease in purchasing power. If inflation runs at 12 percent per year, for example, a thousand dollars' worth of purchasing power today will buy only $880 worth of goods and services at the end of 12 months. This decrease in purchasing power almost nullifies one of the oldest financial axioms of our society: "Save for a rainy day."

Historically, Americans have had very fundamental ideas about thrift and savings. They believed a certain percent of the paycheck in a bank or savings institution would insure a comfortable retirement. Unfortunately, most of today's savings institu-

SAMPLE PERSONAL CPI

	Actual Price						% Increase (Decrease)				
	1970	1975	1980	1981	1982	1983	1975 (5 year increase)	1980	1981 (1 year increases)	1982	1983
Single Copy Newspaper	.10	.15	.20	.25	.25	.25–.30	50	33	25	0	0–20
1 Gal. Regular Gasoline	.36	.57	1.22	1.30–1.50	1.30–1.50	1.21–1.40	58	112	16	0	(7)
Veterinarian Office Visit	9.00	10.	12.	13.	14.	14.	11	20	8	7	0
First Class Postage Stamp	.06	.10–.13	.15	.18–.20	.20	.20	50	20	11	0	0
Physician's Office Visit (brief examination)	11.	17.	20.	25.	25.	30.	54	17	25	0	20
Individual Flat Rate Telephone (residence)	4.65	5.7	7.	7.	7.	7.	22	23	0	0	0
½ Gal. Homogenized Milk	.89	.99	1.19	1.25	.99	.99	11	20	5	(−20)	0
Pair of Panty Hose (L'eggs)	1.99	1.99	2.49	2.79	2.79	2.29	0	25	12	0	(18)
Pair of Jogging Shoes (woman's)			25.	35.	38.	42.	—	25	40	8	11
Haircut (includes styling)	7.5	10.	12.5	15.	19.	23.	33	25	20	20	21
Movie Ticket	1.0	1.5	3.	3.50	4.–5.	4.–5.	50	50	16	20	—
Return Check Charge	.5	.5	3.	4.	7.	8.	50	50	16	20	14
Big Mac Hamburger	.55	.70	1.08	1.10	1.20	1.35	27	54	2	10	13
Boy's Haircut	3.	4.	5.	5.50	6.	7.	33	20	10	9	17
Whirlpool Washer (medium price)	239.	325.	391.	404.	445.	450.	36	20	3	10	1

tions, excluding the current money market funds, offer interest rates of only 5¾ percent or possibly a small fraction more. (There are some higher-yielding investment vehicles, but these generally have certain strings attached. Certificates of Deposit, which will return to the participant a higher percentage yield, have a penalty clause attached. If you should terminate the contract for the CD prior to the maturation date, the financial institution will charge back to the participant a prestated interest penalty. In the newer money market–related checking accounts there are penalties involved if your balance declines below a stated minimum and/or if you have more transfers of funds from your account than the monthly transfer allocation states. It has become difficult to salt away for that rainy day when savings are earning approximately 6 percent a year and inflation is eroding them at the rate of 10 to 15 percent per year.

Faced with this relatively new fact of economic life, many women have taken a self-indulgent approach to combating inflation. Spend it as soon as you get it, because tomorrow it won't be worth as much. As one humorist put it, "A study of economics usually reveals that the best time to buy anything is last year." This same program advocates borrowing as much as possible and paying it back with cheaper dollars somewhere down the road. Unfortunately, this approach to overall inflation may ignore some basic economic rules.

In previous times, after bouts with inflation an economic downturn occurred, resulting in an advantage for the person sitting around with the biggest stash of cash. During inflation, it does make sense to have some assets in a highly liquid form (in cash or in an investment that can be retrieved within seven days), since the woman who borrows to the hilt may eventually find herself in a tight situation. In addition, lenders attach a larger premium to the money they loan out during periods of high inflation. This premium comes in the form of higher interest rates. If both inflation and interest rates are at high-digit levels, the borrower and possibly the investor must receive a substantial return on those borrowed dollars in order to stay even or move ahead.

QUIZ

"Well," you might ask, "if it doesn't make sense to save money for a rainy day, and it is not always wise to borrow to the hilt, just what should I do to maintain and possibly increase my net worth during inflation?" The answer is:

(a) Fudge on your income tax.
(b) Rob your kid's piggy bank.
(c) Devise a financial *plan* to combat inflation.

If you answered (c), go on to the next section.

Part II

DEVELOPING A PLAN

THE enemy—personal inflation at the rate of 10 percent + a year—has been identified. It is a formidable enemy indeed. But human nature is such that even in the worst of circumstances the mere formulation of a plan helps diminish the terror of the situation.

Given the 10 percent-a-year inflation rate, the plan becomes one of increasing your income, net worth and/or investable moneys by 15 percent per year also. How to begin? To quote Alice in Wonderland, as she talks to the Cheshire Cat: "Would you tell me, please, which way I ought to go from here?" "That depends a good deal on where you want to get to," said the Cat. "I don't much care where—" said Alice. "Then it doesn't matter which way you go," said the Cat.

You can get a quick reading on what you'll need to protect yourself against inflation by using the following table. You can tell how much after-tax income you will need in future years in order to stay as well off as you are now. For example, if your present after-tax income is $25,000 and inflation drops to a 5 percent annual rate, you will need $52,000 ($25,000 × 2.08%) fifteen years from now to maintain your present standard of living.

You can calculate how your present net worth can grow if you increase it at an annual rate of 5, 6, 7, 8, 9 or 10 percent annually. For example, if your net worth is now $100,000 and it grows at 6 percent a year, you will have $240,000 in fifteen years' time

(100,000 × 2.4%). But if you can find a way to make it grow at an annual rate of 15 percent, you will have $813,000 in the same period of time (100,000 × 8.13%).

You can also find out how your savings and investments will increase at various annual rates. For example, the $5,000 you invest today at a 6 percent yield will grow to $6,700 in five years, $1,350 less than if you had earned a 10 percent return annually on the same $5,000.

STEP 1—Identify Your Life Phase

A few years ago my son came home sobbing, with deep teeth marks on his arm. The attacker, he revealed, was my neighbor's 3-year-old son. When I approached the defendant, inquired as to the motive behind such an act, and suggested that he would be unwise to repeat it, he stuck his tongue out at me, turned on his heel and walked away. Certain that the mother would be anxious to know of her child's potentially dangerous, antisocial behavior, I relayed the incident to her. She smiled knowingly, shrugged her shoulders, and said, "It's just a phase." Years later, when my 9- and 11-year-olds engaged in a breadstick sword fight in our town's finest Italian restaurant, I smiled at the waiter and said "It's just a phase."

Those magic words explained, if not excused, a variety of behaviors, from my teenager's inability to get up before noon on holidays to the latest fad diet. I noticed, however, that those "phases" mysteriously disappeared at around age 18. When I flunked my driver's license renewal test at the age of 25, the surly man behind the counter didn't smile and say, "It's probably just a phase." When I overdrew my checking account because I forgot to enter several checks, my banker didn't say, "It's just a phase." At that point I decided that it just wasn't fair. We all need phases. They were good for us as children. They provided us with comfy little identity slots. When we left one, either by change in age or behavior, we were immediately filed into another. It provided a real sense of security, and security is necessary at any age. So I am hereby reinstating phases.

Years from Now	Compounding Factor if Annual Rate of Inflation Is:										
	5%	6%	7%	8%	9%	10%	11%	12%	13%	14%	15%
1	1.05	1.06	1.07	1.08	1.09	1.10	1.11	1.12	1.13	1.14	1.15
2	1.10	1.12	1.14	1.17	1.19	1.21	1.23	1.25	1.27	1.29	1.32
3	1.16	1.19	1.23	1.26	1.30	1.33	1.36	1.40	1.44	1.48	1.52
4	1.22	1.26	1.31	1.36	1.42	1.46	1.518	1.57	1.63	1.68	1.74
5	1.28	1.34	1.40	1.47	1.54	1.61	1.68	1.76	1.84	1.92	2.01
6	1.34	1.42	1.50	1.59	1.68	1.77	1.87	1.97	2.08	2.19	2.31
7	1.41	1.50	1.61	1.71	1.83	1.95	2.07	2.21	2.35	2.50	2.66
8	1.48	1.59	1.72	1.85	1.99	2.14	2.30	2.47	2.65	2.85	3.05
9	1.55	1.69	1.84	2.00	2.17	2.36	2.55	2.77	3.00	3.25	3.51
10	1.63	1.79	1.97	2.16	2.37	2.59	2.83	3.10	3.39	3.70	4.04
15	2.08	2.40	2.76	3.17	3.64	4.18	4.78	5.47	6.25	7.13	8.13
20	2.65	3.21	3.87	4.66	5.60	6.73	8.06	9.64	11.52	13.74	16.36
25	3.39	4.29	5.43	6.85	8.62	10.83	13.58	17.00	21.23	26.46	32.91
30	4.32	5.74	7.61	10.06	13.27	17.45	22.89	29.95	39.11	50.90	66.21

As I mentioned earlier, I believe that there are issues and circumstances that influence us as women in different ways during different phases of our lives, and that our approaches to financial planning should take these into account. I have, therefore, taken the liberty of dividing your life into six phases: ages 18–25, 25–35, 35–40, 40–50, 50–65, and over 65. I will first describe characteristics and tendencies that I feel are specific to each group. Then, for each phase, I will (1) discuss specific financial areas that should be addressed; (2) relate a "windfall" scenario that will answer the question "What should I do if I were to receive a windfall during this phase?"; and (3) note how much money you would have accumulated to date if you had been investing $2,000 a year in an IRA (Individual Retirement Account) since age 18.

As you read the following phase outlines, I suggest you keep in mind that age is not the only criterion, that the phases are likely to overlap, and the fact that you are 39 years, 4 months old doesn't necessarily mean that you are in the 35–40 phase.

LIFE PHASE 1: 18–25

During this phase, you tend to make choices and decisions without a lot of experience to back them up. You are a builder setting foundations without really knowing the dimensions of the building. You make decisions which provide you with the information you should have had before making the decision in the first place. Most individuals in this group don't save a lot of money. They generally spend a great deal on personal pleasures and tend to ignore the fact that some day they will be in Phase 6.

It is during Phase 1 that you will probably establish a relationship with a bank and other financial contacts, borrow money for the first time and begin to establish your credit history.

The primary issues I will address in this phase are: establishing contacts, familiarity with financial terms, education, cash flow, record keeping, credit and credit ratings, borrowing, insurance, IRAs, money markets, and collectibles.

LIFE PHASE 2: 25–35

This is a time of decision making. By now you are likely to have completed your formal education and will probably have made some career decisions. You are also perfecting various skills and possibly experiencing healthy increases in salary that underscore the need for a financial strategy. You are becoming aware of tax obligations. You are extremely protective of your dependents. By this time you will probably have formulated a set of values that includes the importance of money and just how much of it is enough for you. Women in this phase are able to take risks; they can make substantial mistakes in career choices and/or investments and still fully recover and even turn those mistakes to their advantage. This also may be a likelier time to purchase a home as a personal residence.

The primary issues I will address in this phase are: tax advantages, income averaging, liquidity, life insurance, banking relations, stocks, and the purchase of a home.

LIFE PHASE 3: 35–40

By this time most of you will have achieved a sense of substance, will be fairly stable, and will have an overall understanding of where you are going. In addition, you are likely to be "tuned in" to your overall tax situation. You may even develop a sense of urgency to rectify it. This is also a period during which you are still able to take risks. As with the 25–35 age group, if you place your funds into an unsuccessful venture, it will probably not seriously dampen your overall investment and monetary confidence.

The primary issues I will address in this phase are: venture-capital opportunities, possible stock options, starting your own business, tax shelters, and wills.

LIFE PHASE 4: 40–50

This is a phase of reduced risk-taking and a time to assume a nonaggressive investment posture, especially as you reach the far end of the phase. This is usually not the time to go into venture-capital deals unless you are in a fairly secure and high-earning position.

This is often a critical time, especially in the family area. You may have adolescents who are "feeling their oats." You begin to realize that you are not immortal. It is also an age of abrupt reversals. In the previous phase there was a sense of stability, of substance, of knowing exactly who you are and where you are going. In Phase 4, however, unexpected changes are more likely to occur. If there is a dissolution in a marital relationship, it often occurs now, and can have a dramatic impact on your financial security.

The primary issues I will address in this phase are: lines of credit, Social Security, gifts and taxes, cash accumulation, tax obligations, short-term markets, trusts, change of residence, tax-deferred annuities and transfer of IRA monies.

LIFE PHASE 5: 50–65

During this phase, you find that there is less time to reap long-term rewards from investments, and you may look forward to retiring. You probably have felt you wanted to retire at some time during each one of the previous phases. (I wanted to do so at least half a dozen times in the 35–40 phase). You are now in a period of asset building and you become more conservative. You begin to eliminate activities and endeavors that are unrewarding. At this point you have acquired a great deal of knowledge and experience and can often use it to your best advantage. I often find that women in this phase are very philosophical about life and choose to share their experiences openly with the younger generation who, of course, are generally unwilling to listen . . . but that's "just a phase." In this phase, as well as the next, it is possible that you may become a widow. The economic impact of the death of a spouse can be disastrous, especially if you have made no plans for it.

The primary issues I will address in this phase are: undervalued situations, annual reports, possible change of residence, tax exempt bonds and annuities, home businesses, home equity, insurance and trusts.

LIFE PHASE 6: 65 AND OVER

This is generally thought of as the retirement phase. It should be a period of consolidation and comfort. It is no longer necessary or wise to make long-term investments, and the primary focus should be on liquidity (the ability to turn investments back into cash quickly if you choose) and using current funds as income to meet ongoing needs. This is often a time for having fun, and possibly even nurturing members of the younger generation through their own phases.

The primary issues I will address in this phase are: liquidity, money market funds, short-term certificates of deposit, Treasury obligations, municipal bonds, short-term bonds, utility stocks, sale of primary residence, and gifts.

Each life phase has a different challenge. As I emphasize throughout the book, you will make mistakes. There will be times when you lose money, energy and sleep. But I firmly believe that out of every negative situation there will be some positive result. You have probably noted, as you read through each of the life phase summaries, that they often overlap. These phases are not intended to be hard-and-fast divisions. They should be interpreted as loose guidelines—a way of identifying to some extent where you are, in order to determine where you are going and how best to get there.

STEP 2—Set Up a Personal Financial Profile

The first step in plotting a financial strategy is assessing your current position, not only personally, but financially. This means setting up a financial profile.

EVALUATE YOUR ASSETS

What are you worth? When the economy is stable—that is, when inflation and unemployment rates do not fluctuate drastically from year to year—it is not difficult to set up an intelligent financial program. Unfortunately, the last decade has not been terribly stable economically and taxes have become immensely complicated.

Perhaps, then, the best course to follow in establishing a financial program during unstable times is to focus on specific areas. For example, you might decide to concentrate on expanding your net worth, increasing your current income, or deferring any income until a later date. You are the only one who can decide your goals, your objectives and your ability to take risks, and only you can decide how any excess income is going to be used.

During times of inflation you must consider the cash value of everything you own, and ideally these assets should be appreciating (that is, increasing in value) as fast as, or faster than, the general inflation rate. As a rule, assets in that category include home, farmland, commercial property and collectibles.

A net worth statement is merely a statement of all your assets minus all your liabilities. The resulting number represents your net worth. Sometimes that number can actually be a minus. When I see a client in this situation, my attitude is that she herself is her best asset—it is her ability to work hard, to plan, to form strategies and to build or rebuild that ensure her financial security.

Most people have substantial assets with a total value that is difficult to determine precisely. For example, it is reasonable to have jewelry and fine art appraised and to get "second opinions" on questionable items. Often an auction can help determine the value of art and antique items.

Once you have determined, as accurately as possible, the value of your assets, you will be in a better position to cut your losses. By this I mean to keep track of funds or investments whose returns are negative or static—and ask yourself the economic reason for such unsatisfactory returns. One way of keeping track is to take a yearly financial inventory, including an examination and evaluation of interest and inflation rates. Such research takes time, but it is an essential process and a key element in the formulation of an effective financial program. Once you know where you stand, your annual update will be significantly easier. Your net worth statement coupled with a cash flow statement will give you a concise idea of where you are spending your money.

A cash flow statement will reflect all revenues and expenditures. You subtract your expenditures from your revenues to arrive at the amount you have left over on a weekly or monthly basis. If you actually find that your expenses exceed your revenues, then you must look into the expense section of your cash flow statement and determine what areas you can cut back on. Often I see people with very respectable incomes who do not know where that income is going. A hundred dollars here and a hundred dollars there add up to a substantial amount over a year's time.

KEEP RECORDS

Evaluating your position is no more important than keeping track of it. Record keeping is essential. The following tables will enable you to calculate your net worth, and determine your monthly cash flow. You will note that the net worth statement is broken down into three years so that you can do a comparison study. You will also see that there is a worksheet on inflation that will assist you in calculating how much after-tax income you will need in future years to assure the same buying power and stability you enjoy now. The inflation worksheet will also demonstrate how your present net worth must grow to match certain annual rates of inflation, and finally, how your savings and investments will increase at the various annual rates. This worksheet, coupled with your net worth statement and cash flow statement, should give you ample information about where you are financially.

MONTHLY CASH FLOW

The key to any plan for keeping ahead of inflation is knowing where your cash goes. Then you can make quick adjustments to your budget to cut down on frills, keep up with necessary expenditures without going into debt, and put money aside for investments.

Here is a monthly chart that can help you do just that. Make preparations for those months when you'll have bigger-than-usual expenditures—hence a need for more cash on hand—and, at year's end, you will have a valuable tool in reviewing how your beat-inflation plan is progressing.

	BUDGETED	ACTUAL
INCOMING:		
Alimony/Child Support		
Bonuses		
Capital Gains (the increase in value of an asset over purchase price at the time you sell it)		
Commissions		
Dividends		
Gifts		
Interest		
Other Income		
Rental Property		
Retirement, Pensions		
Salary		
TOTAL CASH IN		

	BUDGETED	ACTUAL
OUTGOING:		
Child Care		
Clothing		
Contributions, Dues		
Credit Card Payments		
Education (books, tuition, seminars)		
Entertainment		
Gasoline		
Gifts		
Groceries		
Home Furnishings		
Household Supplies		
Installment Payments		

	BUDGETED	ACTUAL
OUTGOING (*cont.*)		
Insurance		
Life		
Automobile		
Homeowners		
Medical		
Other		
Investments		
Loan Payments		
Medical and Dental		
Medicine, Drugs		
Mortgage Payments or Rent		
Personal Care		
Repairs		
Auto		
Appliances		
Home		
Other		
Savings		
Subscriptions		
Taxes		
Federal (withheld)		
Federal (quarterly)		
State (withheld)		
State (quarterly)		
FICA (Social Security)		
State Disability Insurance		
General Sales		
County or City		
Transportation		

	BUDGETED	ACTUAL
OUTGOING (*cont.*)		
Utilities, Gas or Oil		
Electric		
Garbage		
Telephone		
Vacation		
Other		
TOTAL CASH OUT		
Difference between cash in, cash out (plus or minus)		

No one enjoys completing net worth statements, but they are necessary to determine "where you are." Once you overcome the psychological obstacle of gathering all the data and putting it on paper, you will find it helpful and worthwhile.

Because of the different state laws governing assets obtained during a marriage, it is important for married women, or those contemplating marriage, to determine exactly how assets, income, and separate property will be treated. For example, in the community-property states (California, Idaho, Louisiana, New Mexico, Nevada, Arizona, Texas and Washington), assets that are acquired after the marriage are equally owned by both spouses. In addition, income that is earned during the marriage is equally owned. Income such as dividends or interest that is obtained from separate property owned prior to the marriage is clearly owned by the spouse whose name it is in. If you have separate property (that which you have earned or, in case you have received a gift or an inheritance either prior to a marriage or during marriage), make sure to keep it separate. Once assets are comingled, it is extremely difficult to unmingle them. I have seen many a woman inherit property, for example, put her spouse's name on it when everything is rosy, and, when the tide turns, find it extraordinarily difficult to validate that it was hers in the first place. In fact, many of these women give up after the hassle begins and walk away—only to have that asset thrown into the community pot for splitting. Keep in mind that separate property begets separate property. If your Great-uncle Waldo gives you 200 shares of IBM and you decide to sell that stock in order to purchase other stocks, the new stocks are still your separate property. A married woman's net worth statement will be partially determined by how the respective state laws view assets acquired during the marriage. Before you complete your net worth statement, determine exactly what share of these joint assets you are entitled to. If you have received separate properties during the marriage, of course all those should be placed and recorded on your individual net worth statement.

CALCULATE YOUR NET WORTH

	Dec. 31 1983	Dec. 31 1984	Dec. 31 1985
List exactly what you have in:			
Certificates of Deposit			
Checking Accounts			
Collectible Debts Owed to You			
Credit Unions			
Deposits with Utilities			
IRA			
KEOGH			
Money Market Funds			
Savings Accounts			
Tax Refunds			
U.S. Treasury Bills, Notes, Bonds			
Present cash value of your:			
Annuities			
Life Insurance			
Retirement Funds (Corporate)			
Stock Options			
U.S. Savings Bonds			

	Dec. 31 1983	Dec. 31 1984	Dec. 31 1985
Present market value of your:			
Bonds and Notes			
Business (if owned by you or spouse)			
Commodities			
Home(s)			
Mortgages you hold on others' property			
Mutual Funds			
Notes Due You			
Other Real Estate			
Stocks			
What would you get if you sold your:			
Boat, Motorcycle, Plane, Trailer, Bicycle			
Car(s)			
Horses, Dogs, Other Animals			
Patents or Publication Rights			
Sports or Photographic Equipment			
Appraisal or estimate on what you would get if you sold your:			
Collections (stamps., coins, etc.)			
Home Furnishings (including appliances)			
Household Valuables (paintings, silver, etc.)			
Jewelry and Furs			
Any Other Salable Property or Collectible Moneys			
TOTAL ASSETS			

CALCULATE YOUR NET WORTH (*cont.*)

Now list all:	Dec. 31 1983	Dec. 31 1984	Dec. 31 1985
Alimony and/or Child Support Owed by You			
Bank, Insurance Policy and Other Loans			
Credit Card Charges and Cash Advances			
Fixed Commitments (college tuition, etc.)			
Mortgages You Owe (in full)			
Payments Due on Purchases			
Taxes Due That Have Not Been Withheld			
Any Other Money You Owe			
TOTAL LIABILITIES			
TOTAL NET WORTH (assets minus liabilities)			

Generally speaking, your liabilities should be less than your assets, giving you a positive total net worth. If your liabilities actually exceed your assets, you may have a negative net worth. For example, you may be just starting out with a few charge accounts but no real hard assets, or you may have just come out of a divorce with minimal assets to your name, or you have spent the last few years studying in an educational institution to further your career. But all is not lost. Your best asset is yourself. Your ability to work hard and long toward an objective and the motivation to achieve that objective will probably outweigh any temporary negative net worth. Many highly successful women turned a negative net worth into a substantial asset.

Now that you have evaluated your assets and have determined

whether they have increased, decreased, or remained static over the preceding year, you probably have a pretty good idea what your financial weak points are, and want to know more about how to remedy them. I'll get to this—but before you undertake any financial investment, you must determine how it fits into your overall financial plan.

DETERMINE THE BREAK-EVEN POINT

One of the first things to consider is an investment's break-even point—that is: What percentage return must it provide in order to (1) pay the taxes on the gain, and (2) compensate for the loss in purchasing power due to inflation?

The following formula will help you determine that break-even point:

> Take the inflation rate you anticipate and divide that figure by the difference between 1,000 and the rate at which your gain will be taxed. (You can find your tax rate in the table in Tax Fax). When you multiply this result by 1,000 you will have the percentage gain you must make to break even.
>
> In other words, say your tax rate is 40 percent and the inflation rate is 9 percent . . .
>
> $$\frac{9}{1000-40} = \frac{9}{960} = .00937 \times 1000 = 9.375\%$$
>
> This is the percentage gain you must realize on your investments to break even.
>
> Now, say you were considering investing $1,000 in a passbook savings account that yields 5¼ percent. In one year that $1,000 would earn $52.50 in interest. But from using the above break-even formula you know that you must earn a 9.37 percent return to break even, or $93.75. By allowing your investment to earn straight passbook interest rates you would actually *lose* $41.24. If instead you chose a higher-yielding vehicle, such as a money market fund that yields 11.5 percent interest per year, you would earn $115, a profit of $21.30.

The required rate of return will always vary from person to person. One thing you will discover is that not all your assets will be increasing with the inflation rate. However, there are ways of improving the situation, such as putting more assets to work, improving the return on those you have now, or even reducing the taxes you pay on them. All these areas will be discussed in greater detail in a later chapter. The key is to be aware that not all your assets are going to increase in excess of your overall break-even point. Now you have identified the enemy (inflation) and defined a plan that includes the determination of your life phase and the development of a personal financial profile—but, as my Aunt Bertha used to say, ''It's not enough to buy ammunition, load the gun and take aim, you also have to . . . .''

Part III

PULL THE TRIGGER

IN this section I will address each of the life phases and explore various strategies for achieving financial independence within them. As you read this section, please keep in mind that the phases are not intended to represent absolute slots into which you fall solely because of your age. Phase I, for example, contains information that is pertinent and useful to the 18-to-25-year-old because the ideal is that every woman build the foundation for her financial well-being early on. It is entirely possible, however, that a woman could have reached the age of 40 or older without ever having set this groundwork. For this reason, I strongly recommend that you read Phase I regardless of your age. Some phases will have characteristics, and therefore recommendations, in common. I will base my recommendations on the dual goal of (1) increasing your income and net worth by 15 percent a year, and (2) reducing your overall tax obligation.

In making my recommendations for all six phases, I will refer to the following four basic types of income:

1. *Straight reportable and taxable*. These are the dollars you receive from various jobs you may hold, from dividends or interest, from notes or bonds, capital gains, distributions from partnerships, from pensions, and even withdrawal of funds from various retirement accounts.
2. *Tax-exempt*. This is the income that you would receive, for example, from a municipal bond. If you are in a 40 percent

tax bracket or higher and anticipate remaining there for a long time or retiring at that particular tax-bracket level, you may elect to have the greater part of your income fall into this category. Keep in mind that an individual in the 40 percent tax bracket who files a joint return will show taxable income in the area of $45,800. For a single woman, the taxable income will be in the area of $34,100. If you are working for an employer or are self-employed, of course you are going to be reporting your income on a gross (that is, pretax) basis. An individual who is able to achieve tax-exempt position has probably done so by investing funds that have already been taxed. These funds, then, will generate interest that is tax-exempt.

3. *Tax-deferred.* Tax-deferred income is something that may be generated from, for example, an IRA account or annuity. Funds are allowed to accumulate and taxes will be deferred to a later date when such funds are withdrawn.
4. *Tax-sheltered.* This form of income is often generated by investments that have special accounting provisions attached. Most often this involves depreciating the asset, be it property, equipment, etc., by reducing its estimated value due to wear and usage. For example, let's assume that you owned and rented out a house that originally cost $50,000. Let's also assume that 80 percent of the cost of the house was attributed to the actual house, and 20 percent of the cost to the land. Therefore, $40,000 (which is 80 percent of $50,000) would be depreciated according to the IRS formula for depreciation of rental property. With today's tax laws, a rental property that is used for residential purposes may be depreciated over 15 years. $40,000 divided by 15 is $2,666.60. So the IRS will allow you to take a deduction of $2,667 per year as your depreciation expense.

   Of course, you wouldn't want your property to actually depreciate in value. This is merely an IRS accounting tool that can save you, as the owner of the property, a substantial amount of money in tax liabilities each year. How? Let's continue with our illustration. Now that we have purchased the property and we know what our depreciation is, let's assume that we have a mortgage of $25,000 at 10 percent, or roughly

$2,500 worth of interest payments. In addition, there are real estate taxes, insurance, and some maintenance costs estimated at $1,000 annually, for a total actual expense of $3,500. If you were to rent the house for $400 a month, you would receive $4,800 over a year. That $4,800 would exceed your expenses of $3,500 by $1,300. When you take into consideration the $2,667 that you were allowed to deduct for depreciation, you will find that it actually exceeds the $1,300 in excess income over expenses. The $1,300 is, therefore, tax sheltered and you will, additionally, receive a write-off or deduction of $1,367 on your tax return.

Buy Rental House:

80% = building $40,000
20% = land $10,000

$50,000

Expenses

Depreciation:
$40,000 = $2,667 per year
15 years

Interest:
$25,000 mortgage at 10% = $2,500 per year

Taxes, Insurance, Maintenance = $1,000 per year

Total Expenses = $6,167
Total Write-off = $6,167 – $4,800 = ($1,367)
Actual Income $400 × 12 $4,800
Actual Costs $2,500 + $1,000 = $3,500
Actual Income Tax-Sheltered $1,300

Income

Rent = $400 per month
or $4,800 per year

If this seems confusing now, don't worry. I will discuss the various types of tax shelters in greater detail in later chapters and also in Tax Fax.

LIFE PHASE 1: 18–25

"Woman will always be dependent until she holds a purse of her own."

—Elizabeth Cady Stanton, 1860

Between 18 and 25 you are likely to be gathering a great deal of data, completing or upgrading your education, and/or entering the job market. You are probably more carefree than your older sisters and as much a risk-taker as you are ever likely to be. This is an exciting period of awakening to what money is and what it can do. You will make mistakes that you may forget or choose to ignore. But as you approach the end of this phase, you will have learned from those mistakes and will begin to understand and appreciate how money can work *for* you. Two major goals of this phase are to develop competent financial contacts and to establish a credit rating by doing what Americans do best—borrowing.

CONTACTS

The old axiom "It's not what you know, but *who* you know" is probably true to a certain extent. But it is also true that "Who you know can contribute to *what* you know," particularly in financial areas, where investment counselors, CPAs, bankers, tax attorneys, etc., can provide you with information that will help you to anticipate economic trends. If you had been aware, for example, that interest rates in March and April of 1980 were the highest they would be all year and would drop dramatically in the next three to four months, that information would have greatly enhanced your personal borrowing plans. Or if you had known that throughout 1979 and the early 1980s we would experience some of the highest inflation and interest rates in years and that a recession would follow, you could have planned your purchasing and borrowing to correspond with those trends. The key, then, is to determine and utilize the best information sources available.

As you explore these sources, you may find yourself inundated with information and confused by all the "experts" who have just the right theory for a particular moment. What you want is someone who is available, consistent, and reasonably experienced in business. When I say "available," I don't mean that he or she is able to pounce on the phone the moment you call. That's almost too available. Someone who is available will return your phone call and respond to your needs in a fairly short period of time—usually within the day. Consistent, in this case, means not oscillating with every new idea that comes along. You want someone who can evaluate a particular situation and make a decision and a recommendation to you. And given the complexity of today's financial arena, an experienced financial planner should be able to refer you to other experts when the need arises.

You should also keep in mind that when you deal with several experts in multiple areas, you may get conflicting opinions and recommendations from time to time, and the advice you have sought may turn out to be the absolute worst. Often, recommendations may be valid at the time they are given but turn out to be harmful in the long run. It is very difficult and costly to verify that a recommendation was inappropriate or due to negligence. Any kind of litigation costs a substantial amount and, in the majority of cases, the only person who wins is the attorney. Therefore, to help avoid such a pitfall, I recommend that when you sit down with the so-called experts, you obtain the following in writing: what a particular investment is all about, what the financial projections are in both the best and worst cases, who the principals are who will be managing and making decisions, and what the risks are. Finally, when seeking out experts, you should probably expect them to have been practicing their respective professions for at least five years. This, hopefully, will allow them to have already made and learned from their own beginner's mistakes. With these warnings in mind, who are the experts and what should you expect from them?

Insurance Agents

One of the first professionals you may encounter is the insurance agent. In the last few years insurance has gone through a major revolution and will probably continue to do so over the next five years or so. Insurance itself comes in all sizes and shapes. The most common is casualty insurance, which includes housing contents in a rental unit, homeowner's, automobile, jewelry or art, medical and dental, as well as life and disability insurance. Often, agents who specialize in the casualty area will offer their clients life insurance on the side. Brokers who specialize in life and disability insurance only will often refer casualty-insurance requests to other agents since it is a vast and complicated area.

Some insurance agents have expanded into financial planning, as well as selling mutual funds and public limited partnerships. I feel you often have an advantage if you deal with an agent who is able to offer you rates from several different companies.

The insurance industry's rates and products vary substantially from company to company. I recommend, therefore, that you review your policies at least every three years. Also, before you sign up for any insurance policy, make sure you fully understand its contents and limitations. Keep in mind that your needs will change through your life phases.

Bankers

Banking is an expanding field and the choice of a bank(s) is an important and integral part of your plan. Because of the rapidly changing economy and the tight dollars market, it might make sense to have more than one banker. In this instance, "a tight dollars market," also known as a tight money market, is one in which dollars are expensive to borrow. For example, in late 1981 and early 1982, interest rates were in excess of 20 percent. During such times your ability to obtain funds at a reasonable rate is substantially diminished, and banks and savings-&-loans institutions often curtail their lending activities for real estate. This happened in 1982 due to two factors—the inability of individuals to qualify for loans at such high interest rates, and what appeared to be a somewhat shaky time for real-estate values. Some areas of the country actually showed decreases in real property value. So you can understand why banks and savings & loans would be hesitant to make real estate loans, when the collateral for their loans could actually decrease in overall value.

Your banker should not be a junior member of a management team but someone who has spent several years with the particular institution you deal with—preferably not someone who has been transferred from branch to branch every six months while gaining experience. You need someone who knows you, will grow with you, and will be willing to work with you in the bad times as well as the good. Many of us merely have a checking or a savings account and never get to know our banker. Bankers are often very flexible and willing to answer questions and offer assistance over the phone. This, of course, will be the case only after you have established a relationship with them and after they know you as an individual.

The CPA

Unfortunately, most of us are obligated to pay taxes. Therefore a member of your team should be a good Certified Public Accountant. There are plenty of CPAs in the United States. Unfortunately many of them merely do bookkeeping tasks. You need someone who will plan and make recommendations that are appropriate for you no matter what your life phase is. There are accountants who specialize in certain areas such as the medical field, small businesses, or various forms of commercial real estate.

When you interview accountants, make sure you ask how they are compensated, what their areas of expertise are and what their tax-saving track records are for previous clients. For example, if a large percentage of their clients make between $85,000 and $100,000 and pay $25,000 to $30,000 in taxes, you have learned something significant. According to the current tax tables for 1983, a single person who has taxable income of $81,800 or more will be in the 50% tax bracket and have a minimum tax obligation of $30,373 (this, of course, does not include any state obligation, which could substantially increase the overall amount). Often, when individuals are paying what the maximum rate would be if they didn't have deductions, that can mean one of two things. Either they are unwilling to risk money on investments that might provide some tax deductions, or they are not aware of various deductions currently available to them. It could also mean that their accountant is merely doing bookkeeping, not tax counseling. Today it seems that the tax laws change annually, so it is important to deal with a professional who not only keeps up with such changes but is alert to any advantages to his clients that may result from these.

It is also important to know whether or not your accountant will stand by you in the case of an audit and/or appear in your behalf. One final question you may want to ask potential accountants is the annual number of audits their clients face. If they have a significant number of clients audited—40 to 50 percent—you should be cautious. This is a substantially higher percentage than the norm and it could be that the IRS is monitoring this particular accountant, possibly due to poor tax-return work.

The Tax Attorney

If you have had any large windfalls or make a significant amount of money, you would be well advised to consult a tax attorney. In addition to a knowledge of law, this individual should have the expertise of an accountant. He/she should know how the tax laws apply to you specifically, as well as how they are likely to be interpreted in a court of law.

The Stockbroker

If you are contemplating the purchase of stocks or bonds, you may engage a stockbroker. As in the case of insurance, the securities industry has gone through a substantial revolution over the last decade. The stockbroker's primary function is the selling of stocks and bonds, but some have branched out into the tax-shelter area and are selling public limited partnerships. (For greater detail on public limited partnerships, see Tax Shelters in the Tax Fax section.) Some have even entered the insurance area and are selling not only life insurance but also annuities. Many large brokerage firms have purchased insurance companies over the last few years and have developed products specifically for their brokers to sell to clients.

Some brokers specialize in specific industries. For example, a friend of mine is recognized as one of the top experts in the technology-related area. Any time I consult with a client who is interested in technology-related companies, I refer them directly to my friend.

Some brokers merely mimic what their particular parent firm produces in investment recommendations. It is important to understand that if you keep your eyes open and look at what is going on in the supply-and-demand area, you can often make stock-purchasing decisions on your own. For example, in 1982, one of the hottest industries was electronics—particularly video games. Two of the companies that were the most visibly involved in video games—Warner Communications, which owns Atari, and Bally Manufacturing, which manufactured the equipment that housed the Pac-Man game (also conceived and produced by Atari)—would have been a good choice if you felt there would be a continued demand for this type of product. Both companies, Warner Communications and Bally Manufacturing, enjoyed significant increases in the market values of their respective stock. Unfortunately, what goes up often comes down, and in this case, when Warner Communications reported dismal earnings for Atari, the market value of its stock plummeted. It appears that the general public has become somewhat bored with the first generation of video games and was ready to move on to the next.

Stockbrokers get paid by commission, so if you are demanding a substantial amount of their time and producing few results in the form of income, they may soon lose interest in you. There is also a substantial amount of turnover within brokerage firms, so it is highly recommended that you deal with someone who has been in the business for several years.

If you feel you do not need a broker to assist you in selecting particular issues to invest in, then consider a discount brokerage house (one that offers reduced commissions to its customers when they buy and sell securities). There are many fine discount brokers in the country and they often clear their transactions through the large houses such as Merrill Lynch. In addition, they provide the same insurance coverage on your accounts. The primary difference is that you are not inundated with all kinds of investment recommendations and you may actually save around 50 percent on the commission charged by a full-service brokerage house. My experience suggests that with a little bit of reading and understanding, you can make investment choices as poorly as most of the professionals, possibly better.

Real Estate Brokers

If you are considering a commercial real estate investment, deal with someone who has considerable experience in real estate, specifically in the commercial field. There are many areas in real estate and there are specialists in each. If you want to buy single-family houses, condominiums or townhouses, there are people who specialize in such packages. If you are considering small commercial buildings that might be appropriate for professional offices, then you want to deal with someone who specializes in that area. If you have the financial resources and the nerve to invest in large shopping centers or even in developmental deals, there are also brokers who focus on these areas. Each of these investments will have different tax consequences as well as financing packages. If you choose to involve yourself in these "big deals," you should be aware that it may be necessary to follow through with additional money after the initial commitment. With the ever-changing economic environment, a financial package that is put together by what was considered a "friendly" bank may, in fact, fall through. As a consequence, you may not be able to do the construction that was planned and may have to contribute additional funds to carry the project until another source is obtained.

Property Managers

If you own or are a partner in complexes such as apartment buildings, it may make sense to hire professional help in the form of a Certified Property Manager. Many people may state that they know how to manage property, but it is indeed an art that demands years of experience and know-how. Firms that handle several thousand units are often very efficient because they spread their costs and have extensive computer resources. As a result, you can get ongoing income and expense statements that will allow you to keep up to date on your property, noting any irregularities as they arise.

Financial Planners

Another member of your "competent contacts team" is the financial planner. This professional has enjoyed increased attention in recent years. In fact, professionals with a major research firm on the West Coast did a study on financial planning in the 1980s and were so impressed with the results that they terminated the relationship with their firm and opened up a financial planning practice. As I mentioned earlier, in order to get anywhere tomorrow you should have a clear idea of where you are today. When it comes to determining where you are financially, planners can often be of help. They will consult with other specialists such as attorneys, accountants, and insurance brokers in order to give you a comprehensive view of your present and future financial status. While planners may not provide a tax reduction and increase in both net worth and income all at once, they can contribute necessary advice that may help you to define and/or realize some of your objectives. In addition, most financial planners have a variety of licenses that qualify them to sell and analyze numerous products that are available on the market. These products could include the purchase and sale of mutual funds, limited partnerships, stocks and bonds, insurance, precious metals and commodities.

Most of the major brokerage firms, insurance companies, banks, and accounting firms offer some form of personal financial management. Often, however, their recommendations in planning are geared only to the financially substantial individual. Therefore it is recommended that those of average means should seek some of the independent financial counseling services available throughout the country. If you are unaware of them, or don't have anyone to give you a recommendation, you can contact the International Association of Financial Planners at 5775 Peachtree-Dunwoody Road, Suite C120, Atlanta, GA 30342. The IAFP consists of over 8,000 members. In addition, the association may have local chapters in major cities close to you. If you cannot find any in your Yellow Pages, contact the Atlanta office directly. This organization is comprised of accountants, bankers, real estate and securities personnel, money managers, financial consultants, attorneys, and insurance agents.

Once you have chosen a planner, it is best to determine from the start exactly how he/she wishes to be compensated, since they are paid in a variety of ways. The majority of planners charge a fee for the consultation and also receive a commission for any products bought through them. Some, however, charge by fees only, and still others may have no fees except those generated from commissions. These commissions, of course, are incurred when you purchase specific products that the planner recommends. My personal preference is for someone who operates on a fee basis only and will refer you to competent and qualified individuals who can assist you in the implementation of specific investment recommendations.

Advisers or Investment Counselors

Registered Investment Advisers or investment counselors are registered with the Securities Exchange Commission (SEC) for the purpose of administering investment-related advice. Unless an individual or group has been in the investment-advisory field for a number of years, I would not attach a lot of significance to this particular license. It does not require the testing or knowledge other licenses do, and it is not difficult to obtain. If you are adept at filling out government forms (which, I will admit, does deserve some commendation) and can come up with the required fee, there is a high probability that you will be able to obtain a license as a Registered Investment Adviser.

LIVE AND LEARN

Phase 1 is probably the phase during which you will seek an education. I don't mean simply college or graduate work; I also mean an overall awareness of what is going on in your financial life. If you are in college or thinking of returning, why not add to your schedule some basic accounting classes that deal in tax matters? This will familiarize you with some of the tax jargon you will be exposed to throughout your life. There are also other ways to become educated. In the community college classes I teach, as well as in my lecturing across the country, I recommend various free seminars that are sponsored by brokerage firms—even though the purpose of these seminars is often to pitch a specific product. It could be real estate, it could be oil and gas, it could be stocks in general. Brokerage firms hope to bring in new clients this way. At the seminar they will often ask you to supply your name and address and both the day and evening phone number where you can be reached. A broker may then call and encourage you to invest your money according to his/her recommendation. So if you do not wish to be contacted, politely refuse to give your address and phone number or, if pressed (and sometimes you will be pressed to reveal that data), merely give incorrect numbers and move on. When the broker tries to contact you, and that is usually within a week's period of time, he or she will discover that somehow the numbers were transposed and their lead is invalid. It is highly improbable that you will hear any further from them.

After you have attended several such seminars, you will begin to notice similarities. For example, in the case of real estate, most of the limited partnerships offered will have the objectives of preserving your capital, giving you tax-sheltered income, reducing the mortgage payments and/or obtaining capital appreciation. (A limited partnership is merely the pooling of many investors' funds for the purchase of certain items.) Of course, there is no guarantee that any of the above will be realized. You will hear terms like "depreciation," "accelerated depreciation," "recapture," "cost basis," "phantom income," "minimum tax bracket," "acquisition costs," "speculation," "high risk," "raw land," "developmental," "commercial buildings," "triple net lease," "adjusted basis," "leverage," and "non-recourse loans." Relax—these terms will not gobble you up. They may be intimidating at first but with a little time and effort you will soon be familiar with them.

In addition to seminars, most junior or community colleges offer investment courses taught by qualified professionals covering such topics as financial planning, beginning investments and the stock market. These classes will acquaint you with financial terms and practices, give you examples of various investment opportunities and discuss such things as taxes, interest rates, etc. Just remember when you have a lot of new data thrown at you, you may not be able to absorb it all. So don't be afraid to take the same class a second time. I know plenty of financial planners who spent two years in kindergarten!

Your "education" in financial matters should also include a close look at how you spend your own money. The cash flow chart on pages 29–31 will give you a good idea of where your dollars go. Most of us are spenders rather than savers or planners. Many of us seem to think that we are immortal. But as my Aunt

Bertha always said, "There are three sure things—death, taxes, and arthritis." And as I always say—"Good money management just might help you face all three."

What else should you keep abreast of? Everything else. By this I mean local and world events, conditions, trends, and changes. Impossible? Not really. Most of us read a daily newspaper. Continue to do so, but in a more analytical manner than you may have done in the past. Take note of such things as declining interest rates, devaluation of the dollar, crop failures and the toppling of governments. These events, although they may seem irrelevant to you on a day-to-day basis, will affect your investments.

ELIMINATE THE NEGATIVE!

On pages 29–34, there are tables for calculating income and expenses, as well as net worth. Those of you in the 18–25 phase may find that your calculations result in a negative net worth. You may have had to borrow for educational costs or for the purchase of an automobile, and you probably haven't yet acquired assets to offset those debts. Not to worry! If your net worth is negative or minimal, it's no big deal at this stage in your life. It is, hopefully, just a phase, and it is your ability to motivate yourself, set defined objectives and go forth that will help you reach that coveted destination called "positive net worth." If, however, all of your income becomes "outgo" and you can't identify its destination—it's time to do a little detective work.

Most of your income will, of course, be used for ongoing living expenses. But, when you examine those expenses, you should find a certain balance. One thing I notice time and again about women in this phase is that they spend excessively on clothing. This is one of the first areas I monitor when counseling a new client who can't seem to figure out where all her money is going.

KEEP YOUR BALANCE

If you have not already opened up a checking account by the time you are 18, you should do so immediately. A checking account tells a financial institution that you have ongoing income being deposited and that you meet your various obligations. The fact that you are able to keep your checking account in balance —which is really not too difficult with the assistance of a good calculator—tells the bank that you are careful in the way you manage your money.

Many of today's checking accounts offer a special feature called the NOW Account. What this means is that, if you maintain a specified minimum balance, you will be entitled to a normal passbook interest rate on your balance and also may be entitled to other perks that the financial institution can offer such as free checking, free Mastercard/VISA, etc. A word of caution should be offered here—if the particular institution you deal with requires a minimum balance of, say, $1,000 and you can earn 5½ percent or $55 a year if you maintain such a balance, remember that the interest is taxable.

In addition, if you have an ordinary checking account that doesn't require a $1,000 minimum balance but that has a monthly charge of anywhere from $3 to $8 it might make more sense for you to take that $1,000 and transfer it to one of the higher-yielding accounts such as a money market fund. These funds over the last few years have paid anywhere from 6 percent to 17 percent on day-to-day accounts. Taking the low 6 percent figure, your $1,000 would have earned approximately $60 a year—which is a little better than the $55 that you would get from your NOW account. For example, if it earned on the high side of 17% (which is how high some of the money market funds were in 1982), $170 is far better than $55. So you would be better off paying for the monthly service and investing those funds in another area.

If you are beginning to build a relationship with a bank, it may be wise to place your excess funds into a savings account there —at least temporarily. Then if you have to borrow funds or participate in other services the bank may offer, you can verify that you are a bona fide customer and actually have funds on deposit with them.

QUIZ

If you hear, on Monday morning, that high cold winds and hailstorms are approaching the southeast coast of the U.S., and, barring dramatic drops in wind velocity and direction, will hit Florida by Friday evening, what would you do?

(a) Sell your 50 shares of Sunnyside Orange Juice immediately.
(b) Cancel your Miami vacation.
(c) Send that portable heater in your attic to the Miami chapter of the Citrus Fruit Growers Association.
(d) Buy orange juice futures (a commodity contract).

If you chose (d), go to the next section; if you chose (a), you should have first determined that Sunnyside had no other divisions that could be considered profit centers and could offset any negative impact a freeze would have on the Florida crop. (c) is incorrect unless you verify that the Citrus Fruit Growers Association is a charitable organization, thereby allowing you to take a tax deduction for your generosity.

SOMEONE ELSE'S MONEY

All of us, at one time or another, will have to acquire money from an outside source; and we can use it to improve our situation, provided we act wisely and make good use of another economic phenomenon: borrowing.

Borrowed money can be used to purchase anything from new clothes to a long-awaited home. But it can also be used to make more money—that is, to purchase something with someone else's money, let it appreciate, then sell it for a profit.

This has been done most commonly and effectively in real estate. It is well documented that in the 1970s people purchased multiple units (apartment complexes) and single-family residences for as little as 5 percent to 10 percent down, rented them out for close to the cost of the mortgage, and eventually sold them for a substantial profit.

This assumes that the investor was able to borrow enough money to make the purchase in the first place. But in order to borrow, it is important to know what your credit rating is.

CREDIT RATINGS

If you are serious about borrowing money, it is important for you to determine your overall creditworthiness. The detailed cash flow chart you have completed on pages 29–31, coupled with the net worth chart on pages 32–34, will give you an idea of what kind of cash is available for supporting any kind of debt. It is one of the primary areas any banker will look at in determining whether or not you can make good a loan obligation.

It would be wise, also, to check with a local credit-reporting agency regarding your overall creditworthiness and exactly what is being maintained in the computer banks under your name. TRW, Inc., which is the largest credit-reporting agency in the United States, has branches in all major cities and is probably one of the best sources of credit information. If, on the basis of such an agency's credit report, a company has denied you credit in writing within the previous six months, the credit-reporting agency must supply you with a copy of your credit-history readout. If you have not been denied credit, you may merely write the local credit bureau, usually giving your name, address, and social security number, and they will forward your history. Most agencies charge for this, so check with them first about the cost.

If you find a mistake in your credit report—and this is not uncommon—it is important that you notify the respective agency of the error. It is then their obligation to contact the various entities that have seen your credit report and to correct the record if necessary. Once a mistake is made, it sometimes takes several months to unravel it, so if you are borrowing money, check into your credit rating before you apply for your loan.

TAKE CREDIT WHERE CREDIT IS DUE

Once you have borrowed money, you have begun to establish a credit rating. If you are employed by a corporation that has a credit union, you can often borrow money at a lower rate and earn on passbook savings at a higher rate than at most financial institutions. One thing you should be aware of is that often credit unions do not report your good pay-back ability to credit-reporting agencies.

If you don't have a credit rating or if the computer indicates insufficient information for one, contact your bank and ask for assistance. Bankers are basically flexible individuals and as they get to know you and watch you grow and become successful, they will be available to meet your needs. If you have had a checking account and possibly a savings account, or have participated in other products at the lending-institution office, you should apply for either a Visa or MasterCard account. Most financial institutions now offer those to their customers. The banker should be able to tell you up front whether or not your application will be approved. From then on, assuming that you pay your bills within the proper time and don't abuse your card privileges, you will establish a credit rating. And since your good credit habits are reported to a central agency when you apply for credit with other establishments, they will be able to verify that you are certainly a good risk. (The Bank of California puts out an informative brochure called "Women: Credit Where It's Due." American Express also provides a booklet called "The Credit Handbook for Women." Both are excellent sources of information on all aspects of credit and should be part of your financial "library.")

Remember that lenders are really concerned about only one thing when they lend you money—they eventually want their money back and they prefer to have it back on the terms originally agreed upon. If, for some unforeseen reason, you run into a problem and get behind on your payments, don't feel that you are alone. This can, and does, happen to many. If so, you may attempt to reduce some of your outgoing expenses in order to meet your loan payments on time. Sometimes that form of cutback will not be enough and you will have to tell the bank officer that you are having problems making the full payment, but that you can make a portion of it. Whenever you have a problem in meeting an obligation, approach the institution that lent you the funds *before* the problem goes totally out of control. Although it is not going to be fun when you have to sit down and tell the bank you can't meet the obligation you originally agreed to, quite often it will be willing to renegotiate the terms in order to bring you up-to-date. The key here is communication.

Finally, as with the yearly evaluation of your net worth and cash income-expense statement, it is a good idea to make a yearly check into your credit rating.

SOURCES OF MONEY

The next question is, Where do these borrowed dollars come from?

Banks: Banks offer the most services of all the money-related organizations. They make a variety of loans, and if you have a creative banker—one who does more than make car loans and approve MasterCard or Visa applications—he or she may be very helpful in putting together a package for you.

If you have placed money in higher-yielding vehicles, such as money market funds, and you need to borrow money, you should be aware that some trade-off may be necessary. After all, why should a banker go out of his way to make an attractive offer to you when you have all your liquid dollars in another entity? It makes sense to move some money over to a bank before you ask for any of its services. Then, depending on what you actually negotiate for, you can either place those dollars in a higher-yielding vehicle at the bank or move them back to a money fund where the return may be more attractive and more liquid. If you have in excess of $2,500, regulations that became effective in 1983 allow banks and savings & loans to pay money market fund rates. Take advantage of this.

Not having a bank is a mistake. We all need one at some point. It is better to have the relationship established before the need arises. Often bankers can make decisions very quickly if they already know you personally and financially.

Of course, in the last analysis, the best source is the one that offers the cheapest available loan. The table below will be of assistance in determining that loan. Take into consideration that both interest and earning rates vary and that the collateral sources listed are not the only ones that can be used. The table also establishes some relative costs for borrowing in a variety of ways.

Savings & Loans: If you are attempting to borrow money on your signature alone, without offering any collateral, you will not be able to deal with a savings & loans institution. At this writing they can only lend dollars with a piece of real estate or a Certifi-

TABLE I—RATING LOANS BY NET COST—OR GAIN

Collateral	Maximum Loan	Loan Period	Interest Rate	Earned Return on Collateral	Net Cost or Gain
Life Insurance (policies, pre-1978)	90%–95% of cash value	Unlimited	5%–6%	Money Market Rates 10%–12%	+5% to +7%
Life Insurance (policies, post-1978)	"	"	7%–10%	10%–12%	+2% to +5%
Bonds	75%–90%	Renewable (depending on market value)	9%–12%	7%–9%	−2% to −5%
6-Month Savings Cert.	Up to 100%	Renewable	11%–12%	10%–11%	−1%
Stocks (banks) (brokerage firms)	65% 50%	Renewable (depending on market value)	13%–15%	4%–6%	−9% to −11%
Your Signature (educational loan)	$20,000	Up to 7 years	10%–12%	—	−10% to −12%
Your Signature (banks, finance companies)	$10,000 $15,000	Up to 7 years	12%–18%*	—	−12% to −18%**
Real Estate	80% of appraisal value	Up to 15 years	10%–15%	—	−10% to −15%**

* Rates can go higher in some states.
** Returns vary substantially and will depend on use and eventual return.

cate of Deposit or passbook account as collateral. On a home-improvement loan you must have a trust deed against your home as collateral. A trust deed is a note recorded as a lien against the particular property it is owed on. This means that if you do not pay the monthly payments or the principal amount in full when it is due, the holder of the trust deed can actually take action against you and force the sale of the real estate that it is recorded against. This is known as a foreclosure proceeding. Savings & loans are not full service, and therefore are limited in what they can do for you.

Credit Unions: If your company has a credit union or you have access to one, you may be able to borrow up to a stated amount unsecured. Rates are often a little better than with other financial institutions and credit unions will often lend at a higher value than brokerage firms against the company's underlying stock. A catch here is that if money is tight, the credit union is often one of the first places to restrict loans.

Financial Thrift Institutions: If you are contemplating borrowing from a financial thrift institution, be aware that you may pay the highest rate of interest there. By the time you get the loan paid off, you may find that the interest you paid was almost 50% higher than if you had borrowed from a banking entity. This kind of loan is often one made in desperation and should be sought only as a last resort.

Stock Market: One borrowing source may be the stock market. If you have a regular brokerage account, you can sign the appropriate forms allowing you to borrow from the firm. This is called a margin account. If you do this, you must remember that you do owe the brokerage firm money for purchasing the stock and they will monitor on a daily basis the overall value of the underlying stock that you've purchased, as well as any other stocks that you have in the margin account. If the stock you purchase declines in value, or if any other stocks used as collateral decline in value, the brokerage firm will demand that you put up additional dollars to support the debt in your account. Also, interest rates are never at a set price in a margin account and will vary at what is known as the "broker's call rate."

Here's how a margin account works. As you can see in the illustration that follows, if you were to pay cash for 100 shares of Profits, Inc., stock at $40 a share, it would cost $4,000. If the stock had increased four points in value when you sold, you would make a $400 profit or 10 percent over your original cash outlay. If the stock declined four points to 36, if you sold it you would take a loss of $400, or roughly a 10 percent loss.

Buy 100 shares at $40 per share of Profits, Inc.
Total cost = $4,000*

1. Profits, Inc., increases to $44 per share
Total proceeds on sale = $4,400 or +400
400 ÷ 4000 = +10%
2. Profits, Inc., declines to $36 per share
Total proceeds from sale = $3,600 or −400
400 ÷ 4000 = −10%

* Does not include commissions

If you bought the stock on margin, you would buy it at the same price of $4,000, and you would be required to place 50 percent, or $2,000, in a margin account, borrowing the remaining $2,000 from the brokerage firm. If the stock went up four points and you sold it, you would make a $400 profit. Based on the initial $2,000 you invested, this gives you a 20 percent profit. Conversely, if the stock declined four points and you sold it, taking a $400 loss, the loss would be calculated with your $2,000 initial cost and equal to a 20 percent decline.

Buy 100 shares at $40 per share of Profits, Inc., on margin
Total cost = $4,000*
Margin requirement = $2,000
Borrow $2,000 from brokerage firm

1. Profits, Inc., increases to $44 per share
   total proceeds on sale = $4,400 or +400
   Pay brokerage firm $2,000
   Return = $2,400
   400 ÷ 2000 = +20%

2. Profits, Inc., declines to $36 per share
   Total proceeds from sale = $3,600 or −400
   Pay brokerage firm $2,000
   Retain $1,600
   400 ÷ 2000 = −20%

* This does not include commission costs or margin interest—the longer you hold the stock position on margin, the greater amount you owe the brokerage firm.

In this phase, one of the most common reasons for borrowing money is the purchase of a car. This loan will either be obtained through your bank, the financing company used by the dealer you are working with, or your credit union, if you belong to one. If you are a member of a credit union, it is probably best to borrow there. My experience has told me that most credit unions offer lower new-car interest rates than do dealers or other traditional financial institutions. (Of course, there are always exceptions. In 1983 when the economy began to turn around, all the major automobile companies were offering financing well below what was considered normal for the market. This was done as an inducement to bring new customers through their doors.) One of the reasons credit unions traditionally offer lower interest rates is that they are nonprofit organizations. Finance companies have been known to charge rates in excess of 18 percent.

Why would you go to a finance company or a dealer instead of a credit union or a traditional bank? It could be that you have no credit rating. Some people have credit ratings, but they are not good and therefore a bank would probably turn them down. If this is the case, these individuals would more than likely turn to a finance company who would lend them the money, but with a higher interest charge.

If you are borrowing funds for the first time, there are several areas to consider. The first one, of course, is the interest rate. Car loans can vary anywhere from 36 months to 60 months. I have even seen one for seven years. Ask the individual with whom you are dealing what the total interest over the term of loan will be. Add that to the amount you are paying for the car and you will obtain your total purchase price.

This is the time to sharpen your pencil. It is important for you to know what your tax bracket is because interest on the loan is tax-deductible and you can determine how much in actual tax savings you will receive from the interest deduction. You can then calculate your effective total cost with the tax savings included. If you are able to receive some tax benefits from the use of your car in your line of work (this does not mean simply driving to and from work: it means, for example, that you have a sales job that requires you to call on various customers), then you will receive various tax deductions for the operation of your car.

After you have calculated your tax savings, you will be able to determine your real monthly cost by dividing the tax savings or interest deductions by the number of months your loan is in effect. Whenever you borrow, it is important to determine exactly how much you can afford in payments on a monthly basis.

Educational loans still exist, contrary to popular opinion. With the Federal Government cutbacks in the early 1980s, many thought that educational loans were a thing of the past. This is quite untrue, and, in fact, numerous newspaper articles have attempted to inform the public of the availability of educational loans. Interest rates carried on the loans will vary depending upon your needs. Your need will be determined primarily by the adjusted gross income recorded on your tax return of the previous year. (Remember that the adjusted gross income, or AGI, is merely the number derived after all your sources of taxable income are taken into consideration and adjusted by various additions and subtractions, including such items as partnership losses, IRA contributions and capital gains, to mention a few. The AGI is the number just before excess deductions are subtracted. If you did not file a tax return for the preceeding year, then merely state that you had no taxable income.)

Often interest on an educational loan is deferred until you graduate from school. Those rates average 9 percent at this time, and are, of course, subject to adjustment by Congress. How do you find out what is available? Merely by checking your financial aid office at the university or college you are attending. Of the several programs, you will more than likely find one that will fit your needs.

Other loans that you apply for, which you might not even consider as loans, are credit cards. When you ask for credit from a retail establishment, you are asking them, in a sense, to extend you a line of credit. This allows you to charge and pay back the money within a 30-day period (thus avoiding most of the interest) or over whatever length of time the store requires.

There are two really important things I did for my children when they turned 16. The *first* was to put them on one of my MasterCard accounts where each individual's name appeared directly. They were then given a credit card. My job was to monitor them closely, and, if they made any charges, to make sure that each paid his or her share. By adding their names to the account, they would establish their own credit file, which was my primary objective. Every time a payment was made, they also got credit for that. The secondary objective was to familiarize them with money management. When something was purchased, it had to be paid for—"Those who play, have got to pay." In our house, that particular MasterCard was known as the "kid's account" and the adults did not use it. When one of the children abused the privilege by overcharging beyond the limits, the card was immediately taken away. I, of course, as a parent, had to make good the funds that were charged. If I did not, then I would have jeopardized the other siblings who had been meeting their obligations on time (I had three teenagers during this training period). The *second* thing I did was to introduce them to my banker when it was time for them to buy their first car. We went through the whole pretense of making a loan application in his or her respective name. I, of course, had to guarantee the transaction, with my name being added to the loan documents after my son or daughter completed them. As far as they were concerned (and what the bank and I led them to believe), the loan was in their name and there was an obligation to pay the monthly payment. If it wasn't paid, the bank would take the car back. As monthly payments were made, the bank reported the transaction on the individual child's credit rating. These two incidents significantly increased my children's awareness of what credit and money were all about. When my oldest daughter turned 18, she actually received an invitation to get her own Visa card. This was one of my goals for each of the kids—to be able at some point in time to begin their credit lives on the right foot. As each son or daughter turned 18, the bank released me as guarantor on the remaining loan balances, if any. During the entire period, loan payments were made from their checking accounts, never mine. There were some rough spots—like the fact that their checkbooks never balanced in the beginning—but they learned. One time, the final resolution was to close an account and open a new one—just to know exactly what the beginning balance was!

Other forms of borrowing could include the purchase of your first home or subsequent homes. When that time comes, it is essential for you to have a clean bill of health on your credit report. Today there is a significant demand by the general public for mortgage money. When the time comes for you to apply for a mortgage loan, it is important to put your best foot forward with a clean and established credit report or rating.

As you progress, you will find that you may have to borrow at some time to pay taxes, to cover a vacation, or even to start an IRA. Whatever the purpose is, make sure that you have all your ducks lined up—that your credit rating is in order, that you have the ability to repay and are realistic about your needs.

INSURE? SURE!

In this life phase you may begin to explore different insurance products and programs. Those of you who have dependents should analyze your life-insurance coverage. In my opinion, life insurance should be purchased to protect those who are dependent upon you. If you have no dependents at this time, it may make sense to bypass the purchase of life insurance; but take a look at acquiring a reasonable disability policy. While most of us are covered by some form of state disability insurance, be aware that the money you are likely to draw from such insurance will not carry you through if you are injured and out of work for a long period of time. You may feel that you are young and healthy and that nothing can happen, but accidents do occur. The time to prepare is before the calamity. And as part of your preparation make sure you compare several companies. Compare, for example, the premium cost for a 30-day, 60-day, and 90-day waiting period before commencement of funds.

Because of your age, insurance costs, particularly in the automobile area, are extremely high. You are encouraged to shop around carefully in this area, as well as in the area of homeowner's or renter's insurance.

THE IRA ERA

Assuming that you will be employed at some time during this life phase, I strongly recommend that you begin an IRA account that has an average growth of 12 percent per year. If you were to deposit $2,000 a year into an IRA account over the next 40 years your hard investment, that is, actual dollars deposited, would be $80,000. Your accumulated total by the time you reach Phase 6 (65 years old) would be $3,821,179.60. This, of course, assumes that you have earned a minimum income of $2,000 for each of the years in which you make the contribution and that the investments made with your funds will give you a 12% return. If you earn less than that you will not be able to contribute the full $2,000 that is allowable under current law. I also suspect the $2,000 limit will be increased over the next few years, particularly as social security continues to have problems. (The how-to's of all this are discussed in greater detail in the Tax Fax Section.)

Because you have a substantial number of years ahead of you, I would recommend that instead of starting your IRA in a savings institution or an annuity, you consider placing your funds with either a quality mutual fund, a limited partnership that invests in long-term real estate, or (if you are savvy enough to select your own stocks or have the fortune to establish a relationship with a good stockbroker), a self-directed account that invests in stocks and other security issues.

If you are self-employed, or contemplating becoming self-employed, you can participate not only in an IRA but also in a Keogh account. A Keogh account is for those individuals who have not been covered by any profit and/or pension sharing program from their employer and are, in effect, their own employer. At this time the government allows you to place up to 15 percent of your net earnings (your earnings after all expenses, including taxes, are paid) into a self-directed Keogh plan. "Self-directed" means that *you* decide what to do with the moneys you contribute. The ceiling on a Keogh plan is $30,000 per year—significantly higher than the maximum in an IRA contribution. In addition to the Keogh plan, you can also initiate an IRA, which would allow you to place up to $32,000 in retirement programs. If you are married and your spouse does not work, you can place up to $250 per year in a Keogh plan for him. As in the IRA account, there is a limitation on the maximum age in which contributions can be made. As of this writing, it is 70½ years. Both IRAs and Keogh plans are discussed extensively in the Tax Fax section.

TO MARKET! TO MARKET!

There are many areas in which cash assets can be placed that are attractive to the 18-to-25-year-old, as well as older persons. The most common is the passbook savings account. This can be obtained from any financial institution, with a minimum interest earned of 5¼ to 5½ percent. A passbook account allows you to deposit and withdraw funds on a daily basis. The interest rates will not vary and you can call your bank or savings & loan and ask them to transfer funds from your passbook savings account into your checking account if the need arises.

As you begin to accumulate cash, other alternatives become available to you. If you have, for example, $1,000, you could purchase a Certificate of Deposit or a time deposit. As explained in greater detail further on in this section, a Certificate of Deposit merely means that the financial institution in which you have deposited your funds will pay to you a higher interest rate than that paid by a normal passbook savings account. The reason is that when you sign the certificate, you agree to leave your funds for a specific time—longer, of course, than a period of one day.

If you accumulate $10,000, you can purchase Treasury bills or participate in what is known as a "T-bill account." A Treasury bill is a United States Government obligation which is also guaranteed by the Government and can be purchased from a Federal Reserve Bank, through a stock-brokerage firm, or through a savings & loan or a commercial bank. To participate in this market you must have $10,000 on deposit with the particular entity with which you are dealing before you instruct them to buy the T-bill. A Treasury bill is issued for a minimum of $10,000 with increments of $5,000. The maturity date of a Treasury bill is one year or less from the date of its original issue. Usually they come with three-month, six-month, nine-month, or one-year maturity. Proceeds from Treasury bills are used to finance the day-to-day operations of the U.S. Government and are one of the primary monitors of what is happening in the interest market. If interest rates on recently issued Treasury bills begin to increase, there is a general consensus that interest rates overall are headed higher. On the other hand, if the interest rates on the new bills decrease or stay at the same level as the preceeding issue, then overall rates may continue to decline or will stay at the current, or what is known as a flat, level.

A T-bill account with a financial institution is merely an account with $10,000 in it that pays a fixed interest rate and is usually for six months, very much like a real Treasury bill—but it is not backed by the U.S. Government.

Another area that is attractive to the 18-to-25-year-old is the money market fund. In fact, I recommend that women in all life phases put their liquid dollars into such funds. Bear in mind that interest rates will vary and there are minimum dollar requirements for most of these. Those of you who are just beginning to save should open a savings account first, and, as you build up your account, transfer most of your savings to instruments such as money market fund, leaving only what you may need for an emergency in your savings account.

Although there are money market funds that have no minimum requirement, I strongly recommend that you start a savings account with a bank in any case. There are times when you will need a bank's services, and by having an account already established, although not necessarily significant in funds, you will be validated as a customer.

One fund that does not require a minimum amount to start is Alliance Capital Reserves. The Franklin Money Market Fund has a minimum requirement of only $500. Funds such as Capital Preservation and Dreyfus Liquid Assets have minimum requirements of $1,000 and $2,500 respectively. Brokerage firms such as Merrill, Lynch, Pierce, Fenner & Smith and E. F. Hutton also have money funds, often with initial minimum requirements in excess of $10,000.

As a rule, a money market fund allows you to write checks against your balance, but these often have to be for a specified minimum amount. You may make additional contributions to your fund, depending upon the stated minimum for that particular one. It offers liquidity in that you can retrieve your money on a daily basis without any penalty, and, if interest rates in general continue to go up, there is a high probability that the interest yield on your particular fund will also increase. On the other hand, if interest rates deline, then the interest paid by your fund will also decline.

Money market funds are basically mutual funds that purchase only money instruments. They are not guaranteed by any Federal agency. You can obtain a prospectus or offering memorandum from the funds by contacting them directly. If you scout the newspapers you will find several advertisements for local and national funds. Most of them indicate "800" numbers which you can call directly to request a prospectus and ask questions.

As I mentioned earlier, money market funds are viable instruments to use in each of the life phases. In 1982 alone, there was more than $200 billion in over 160 different money market funds. With that much money, you would think that everybody would know about them, but even today, only about half the American population is really aware of what money funds are and what they can do.

Money funds exist for two primary reasons. The first is inflation. In prior years most of us were willing to accept the saving passbook rates of 5¼ percent and 5½ percent. The Federal Reserve prohibits savings institutions from paying returns in excess of 5½ percent on passbook savings accounts. This is known in the industry as "Regulation Q." With the advent of the money market funds in the early 1970s, the small investor or saver was able to get a far more reasonable rate of return and keep up more consistently with inflation rates.

When money funds first appeared, they were not offered by thrift institutions or banks and were therefore not subject to the "Regulation Q" rates ceiling. They are, in fact, regulated by the Securities Exchange Commission and various laws of the states in which they are sold. Money market funds grew slowly, but in the late 1970s investor participation escalated dramatically.

The money fund consists of small amounts from thousands and thousands of savers. The total fund is then used to purchase very high-yielding but short-term money market instruments, such as Treasury bills. Treasury bills have a maturity date of anywhere from three months to one year. When interest rates are oscillating as they have been over the last few years, the Treasury bill is probably the most drastically affected financial instrument. Treasury bills are auctioned on Mondays and are quoted in your afternoon newspaper or the following morning's paper.

Money funds can also be placed in commercial paper. Commercial paper is an instrument in which a corporation such as General Motors literally goes out and borrows money from the general public as an unsecured line of credit. GM's good name will attract dollars. Commercial paper often has a minimum investment of $100,000 and can mature, for example, in 30 days. Most of us cannot participate in minimums of $100,000, but several of us can pool our funds in order to participate. Thus commercial paper has gained a strategic foothold and is a cornerstone of many money market funds.

Another commonly used instrument is a banker's acceptance. Banker's acceptances are often used in import and export businesses and are basically collateralized loans arranged through a bank for a fairly short period of time. The collateral offered is a specific inventory of the entities issuing the banker's acceptance. For example, let's say that General Motors is importing a tremendous shipload of steel. The cost of the steel is in excess of their current cash reserves. The company expects to have all necessary funds within two months from the sales of their new line of automobiles that are expected. A bank lends them the necessary funds to bridge the shortfall needed to pay for the steel. The bank may sell a portion of the loan to another party (or bank), hence the term "banker's acceptance." Keep in mind that the loan is secured not only by the importer (GM in our example), but also by the steel inventory, as well as by the bank that originally accepted it. If the company that borrowed the funds cannot pay the loan off, there are two other sources to cover the debt: One is the actual inventory, in this case steel, and the second, the accepting or issuing bank. Because of your ability, if you are a participant in a banker's acceptance, to collect on a bad debt from three sources (in our case GM, the steel inventory, or the issuing bank), the banker's acceptance is considered as having a high degree of safety—certainly above that of commercial paper and just below a Treasury obligation.

Another instrument that is very common in money market funds is the certificate of deposit, commonly known as the "CD." CD is a buzzword that gets thrown around rather loosely in financial circles. It refers to savings that are deposited in a bank or savings & loan for a specific period of time. For individuals such as you and me, CDs are usually issued in minimums of $1,000 denominations. To participate, you would simply place your funds on deposit and sign up for the various programs that your particular financial institution can offer. The time frame could be as little as 30 days or as long as eight years. For example, you, as a depositor, could leave $1,000 with your bank and receive a certificate that guarantees 8 percent interest for eight years, as opposed to 5¼ percent per annum. The difference is that to earn this higher rate of return, you have to leave your funds there for a longer period, and if you change your mind, which you are allowed to do, you have to pay a penalty. The penalty could be as much as six months' interest.

Before you sign any documents, make sure you understand the pros and cons. In the case of money market funds, CDs that are held with the fund often mature within a very short period of time and involve huge amounts of money (amounts in excess of $100,000). Because money market funds purchase so many different types of CDs, with varying maturity dates (it is unusual to see a money market fund purchasing CDs with maturity dates in excess of six months), you will not be penalized when you withdraw funds from a money market fund that purchases CDs as you would be simply as an individual who had purchased a CD and then wished to withdraw the money. This is because there always appears to be a portion of the money market fund's portfolio maturing on any given day, as well as new funds invested from new shareholders. If, for example, you examine the prospectus of the money market funds, you might notice $20 million in one particular certificate of deposit with Bank of America. As a rule, the certificate of deposits that money market funds purchase are only those of substantial-sized financial institutions. Money funds will enable you to earn a high rate of return while keeping your funds in a liquid state. This is very important with the ever-changing market conditions and the volatile inflation and fluctuating interest rate common over the last few years.

There are three basic categories of money market funds. The first is one that a brokerage firm may sponsor for their specific customers. Merrill Lynch, for example, has a fund called Cash Management Account (CMA), which requires you to place a minimum of $20,000 and provides you with a Visa debit card at the same time. A Visa debit card is somewhat different from a regular Visa card or a MasterCard. When you use a regular Visa card, you receive a monthly statement with your various charges. You can choose to pay the balance off in full or you can pay it over a period of time with a minimum monthly payment plus a finance charge.

A debit card, on the other hand, is one in which the issuer, in our example, Merrill Lynch receives the bill directly from Visa and automatically debits your account for the entire amount.

The second type is an institutional fund, which only services investors of very large institutions.

The third fund is a general-purpose fund and is the one I recommend that you participate in. These funds provide an anonymity to the investor that other funds do not. Anonymity has two advantages. The first is that it allows you to bypass a standard brokerage house and not reveal your cash reserves. The second is that, if you are with a brokerage, you are now a customer or client with cash. Don't be surprised if you receive a call from a broker recommending the purchase of a stock—after all, he knows you have the cash to pay for it. There is minimal probability of anyone discovering that you have placed money in a general-purpose dollar-market fund. These funds, as mentioned above, are sponsored by mutual fund organizations and open to anyone who meets their minimum requirement. In a money market fund, interest is credited to your account daily and a statement is issued monthly or quarterly, depending upon the policy of the particular fund. You can instruct that dividends be mailed to you or you can have them reinvested in order to accumulate more. When you wish to withdraw funds you may do it either by writing a check (as a rule, for a minimum of $500), or you can send a letter directly to the fund telling them that you want to terminate your account or that you wish a certain amount to be mailed to you.

Before placing your money in a money market fund, an important area to consider is maturity. In this case, I am referring to the maturity of each of the instruments the money market fund purchases. In times of rising interest rates, you would like to have very short-term maturities. Maturity means the date on which the money market instrument is cashed out. For example, let's say your fund's management had $10,000,000 in Treasury bills with interest at 7 percent due on January 15, 1984, and today is August 12, 1983. August to January is five months, a reasonably short period of time. Let's assume that interest rates begin to rise and some economists estimate that interest rates will go even higher. Because the Treasury bill matures in a few months and will pay off, the fund management can then invest the cash in higher-yielding new Treasury bills. On the other hand, when interest rates are beginning to decline, you want long-term maturity.

A high-yielding fund is not necessarily the one for you. Before deciding, make sure you analyze the fund's objectives and what type of money market instruments they purchase. Money market funds do not have commissions, but the management of the fund receives a percentage of the operating expenses and management fee. It then distributes the money to its shareholders with interest earned daily.

In conclusion, I repeat that money market funds are excellent instruments and should be used not only in this particular life phase but in all of them.

William Donoghue and Thomas Tilling's book *The Complete Money Market Guide* (Harper & Row, 1981) can be of assistance in describing the various categories of funds. In the appendix there is a partial listing which includes the address, minimum requirements and phone number of each fund for your reference.

It took almost a decade for the American public to be aware of money market opportunities. In January 1983, a whole new item was introduced through the nation's banks and savings & loans. It was the money market checking account, the primary purpose of which was to trap all those billions of dollars that found their way into market funds. Basically, a money market fund checking account is offered by a bank or savings & loan, allowing you to place funds on deposit, usually a minimum of $2,500, and earn ongoing rates equivalent to the already established money market funds. You are now aware that the money market funds, as a rule, allow you to transfer funds or write checks for a minimum of $500. These new money market checking accounts do not normally have the $500 minimum rule but they do set a maximum amount you can transfer or write checks for. If you are security-conscious and need to know that they are backed by federal insurance up to $100,000 per account, then such a fund may be the right place for you. Even so, we do not recommend that our clients close out their existing money market funds but that they initiate an additional money market checking account if they have the $2,500 as the minimum deposit. If you fall below $2,500 they will let you participate in the interest-bearing checking account, which is limited to 5¼ percent or 5½ percent—again, provided you meet their minimum-balance requirement. This amount will vary from one financial institution to another. If an institution does not offer a checking account with an interest that meets your initial amount, then keep those funds in your money market; if you do have the $2,500, keep both accounts intact. This will allow you to take advantage of increasing interest rates or of any variance in interest that the accounts offer.

Since the majority of us write in excess of three checks a month and a majority of those are going to be for less than $500 each, it is necessary to have a regular checking account. I recommend that on a monthly or semimonthly basis, you merely transfer the funds from the higher-earning interest account to your regular checking account and then proceed to pay your usual bills.

With the availability of these new accounts, and banking institutions being full service, your bank can offer you far more when you need to negotiate loans and other services that they offer. If you are maintaining significant deposits with a financial institution and you apply for any of their available loan packages or services, it is highly probable that you will get preferential treatment. Why? Because they like to take care of their own before bringing in new and unfamiliar accounts. Before long, banks will be involved in all kinds of financial areas, including stocks and bonds, and someday even commodities. With the recent acquisition of a major discount firm by one of the largest banks, the beginning is here. In addition, the brokerage firms are going the other way. When Sears purchased Dean Witter, they were dubbed immediately "Stocks and Socks." Now that does seem to be full service!

TO COLLECT OR NOT TO COLLECT

If you enjoy collectible items such as gemstones or antiques, you may find that you can begin to acquire a few pieces during this particular phase in life. But be aware of the drawbacks. The gem market, for example, is extremely complicated. It is definitely a "buyer beware" market. Before you purchase gems you should know something about them yourself—even before you choose an expert to assist you. One of the more solid and more readable publications is *The Gem Kingdom* by Paul E. Desautels (MacDonald; London, 1971).

There are four areas to consider in purchasing gems. The first is color; the second, clarity; the third, carat weight; and the fourth, the actual cut. Before you purchase a gem, especially one that has already been evaluated by a Certified Gemologist, check with another Certified Gemologist as to the accuracy of the appraisal for the stone you are considering. The Gemological Institute of America (GIA) located in Santa Monica, California, is the most respected of the various appraisal groups. The GIA verifies the authenticity of the stone. If it does not put a dollar value on it, an individual Certified Gemologist should. Gem investment is considered very long term and it is recommended that you hold gems for a minimum of five years. If you choose to set your gem in a piece of jewelry, be aware that you may actually decrease its value and it can often be damaged when set. It is also more tempting to a thief. On the other hand, you will be able to admire your investment when you wear it, wherever you go.

In the case of antiques, be aware that they are a poor investment if you are looking for a quick profit or the ability to cash out and receive your funds back within a seven-day period.

The value of collectibles depends on the economy and market conditions. An advantage in the antique area is that you can begin with an inexpensive item. You would do well always to buy the best you can afford. One terrific piece will be likely to appreciate at a far greater annual rate than several ordinary ones. Buy conservatively and stay away from speculative or fad items such as jukeboxes and slot machines. It is important to be knowledgeable. It would make sense to develop friendships with dealers. Not only can they be an important source of information, but they can also be instrumental in locating a special piece you may not find on your own. As in all areas, you can't know everything about an entire field. In purchasing antiques, it often makes sense to specialize. Select a period that appeals to you, or concentrate on collecting one particular type of item, such as silver or quilts. There are several publications that will assist you not only in evaluating some of the pieces you begin to assemble, but also in determining whether you have the "real thing." At this point a visit to your public library or a well-stocked bookstore may be in order. There are innumerable titles that include both general coverage and specific periods.

Well-made, attractive collectibles tend to stay ahead of inflation. Over the last decade, items such as clocks, Tiffany lamps, English desks, and Chinese porcelains have all appreciated by approximately 25 percent. However, in the recession of 1981 and 1982, several of the collectible areas, including gems, declined substantially in overall value. But such a decline provides an opportunity for the astute investor to add to her investments at bargain rates, and the nostalgia or mystique associated with another era seems to keep collectibles ever popular.

Finally, collectibles are tangible items, and people like to be able to see what their money is buying. When you are able to contemplate a beautiful article in your living room, you are reaffirming that you not only have an investment but also a distinctive addition to your decor.

QUIZ

A man in a green leisure suit and dollar-sign tie tack approaches you and offers you "the chance of a lifetime." He gives you a one-inch-thick proposal that says "confidential offering memorandum." You take it home to read, and it replaces Aunt Martha's sleeping potion. You obviously need help to figure out what it says. You should consult:

(a) A Berlitz School of Languages
(b) A banker
(c) A financial planner
(d) An attorney
(e) A CPA

If you chose (c), (d) or (e), go on to the next section—but first be aware that an attorney should not necessarily comment on the overall merits of the investment. What he/she should be able to comment on is whether or not the investment has all the data and disclosure necessary for you to make a decision. If you answered (e), be aware that a CPA should also comment on whether or not the financial projections are realistic. If you answered (c) be aware that if you take a proposal to a financial planner and he/she immediately tries to sell you another product, you may be dealing with a "commission only" person. It might be better to contact someone who is operating on a fee basis and is not trying to sell you something that would be financially beneficial to him or her.

In Part II, on page 35, you learned how to determine the break-even point for any potential investment. In addition, you should consider the following before embarking on any new investment plans.

PRE-INVESTMENT QUESTIONS

1. Will my potential investment keep me ahead of inflation, return enough to offset any tax obligations resulting from a gain, and/or allow me to pay any interest on a loan if I borrowed funds to make the investment, as well as the principal payment when the loan matures? If you are thinking of borrowing for the purpose of purchasing municipal bonds, for example, think twice. The IRS has stipulated that there is a penalty on any transaction in which you borrow for the purchase of municipal bonds. The IRS will disallow the interest deduction for Federal income tax purposes on such a loan.
2. What are the opportunity costs of my potential investment? Since borrowed money must eventually be repaid with interest, it can be more expensive than using your own funds, so be careful to weigh what the opportunity costs are. Could you use the same amount of money to make an investment that has a greater potential for return? How much time and energy are you going to have to put into this investment? Would it be better to make 15 percent per annum return versus an 18 percent per annum return that would require a great deal more of your time and energy?
3. Does this investment provide enough liquidity? Remember, my definition of liquidity is the ability to get your money out within seven days. As a rule of thumb, you should have salted away approximately three to six months worth of after-tax money for current living expenses. This, in my opinion, is what all of us should have as liquid assets. If you are borrowing from any lending institution to purchase something in the fine arts, jewelry, coins or any other collectibles, you should know that often these investments do not have the liquidity of stocks, bonds and other cash-oriented instruments. Therefore, while you are waiting for someone to buy the collectibles at an appropriate price, you should have enough liquid assets to keep up your loan payments, plus interest.

Once you have borrowed the money, keeping current on your loan payments is especially important, since your ability to continue borrowing money hinges on your credit rating. As Earl Wilson so aptly put it, "If you think nobody cares if you're alive, just try missing a couple of car payments."

MS. MISC.

You can purchase both stocks and mutual funds with minimal dollars. Look for stocks in the high-growth areas such as technology and genetic research, and purchase only "no-load" mutual funds (funds that require no commission payments).

At this time, you should probably shy away from tax shelters. It is unlikely that your present income will qualify you to participate in most tax shelters and your moneys are, frankly, better off invested elsewhere. Besides, a participation in an IRA account offers not only tax-shelter advantages but also a tax deferral on the income or gain that accumulates over a period of time.

If you are employed and are considering a career change or a job switch, related moving expenses can count as reasonable and certainly legitimate deductions. For those of you who are continuing or completing your education and have a part-time job in addition, you may have legitimate educational and automobile deductions. This is not the time to panic over what your current tax obligations are, but it is the time to become fully aware of what tax deductions and/or credits are available to you so that you may take advantage of them. (See Tax Fax for more on possible tax savings.)

During this phase you may purchase your first home. If so, you need to deal with the fact that you will probably not be able to move into the quality and style of home that you had hoped for. It takes a while to build the funds and assets necessary to acquire the house of your dreams. But there are several homeowning opportunities even with the current interest rates and high housing costs. Keep your eyes open. In the following life phase, I will discuss in detail and analyze the purchase of a house not only as a residence but also as a possible investment.

WINDFALL!

One day I received a call from a prospective client in her early 20s who had just received a $100,000 award for medical damages.

As we talked, it became obvious that she was concerned that she would spend all the money and someday wake up asking where it had gone.

We sat down and devised a general plan whereby she would continue to hold a substantial amount of funds in liquid form, such as in a money market fund. At that time, money market funds had a substantial yield and were, in my opinion, a safe investment. She then said that she would like to place anywhere from $10,000 to $20,000 into real estate. Since the real estate market had been a fairly attractive way of hedging against inflation, it seemed to be a reasonable game plan. We discussed purchasing a residence, a condominium, or pooling funds with other individuals. Because she did not want to own a house directly and be responsible for its upkeep, she elected to place $5,000 in each of two partnerships. They both involved the rehabilitation of older buildings. In pooling her funds, she would be going into a limited partnership. A limited partnership allows an investor to participate in a passive role, with a general partner managing the overall project. The limited partner's liability, as a rule, is therefore confined to her original investment. She does not have any management responsibilities nor does she participate in any of the day-to-day decisions related to management of the partnership's assets.

A limited partnership can take two forms. It can be a public limited partnership or a private limited partnership. A public limited partnership has in excess of 35 individual limited partners. A private limited partnership has fewer than 35 individual limited partners. In the case of a public limited partnership, there will more than likely be as many as 4,000 partners, even more. Some public limited partnerships raise as much as 100 million dollars. As a rule, the minimum investment is $5,000. If you divide $5,000 into $100 million, you will find that there could be 20 thousand individual partners. Public limited partnerships are sold through brokerage firms and many financial-planning companies. Private limited partnerships are not usually offered by brokerage firms, but are available through many financial-planning companies.

There are pros and cons to both types. If a change of management is needed in a private partnership, it is often easy to assemble at least a majority of the limited partners to vote any necessary changes. Four thousand partners, however, will be difficult to gather for a vote. Private limited partnerships often invest in just one item such as a small commercial building. Public partnerships, on the other hand, generally invest in such things as shopping centers, commercial buildings, apartment houses. Because public limited partnerships often raise millions and millions of dollars for later investment into a number of areas, such partnerships are also known as "blind pools." And because they are raising so much money, they usually will not put any deposits on properties until a certain percentage of the funds is raised. As a rule, public limited partnerships have a bigger reserve fund to set aside for problems than private ones do. Problems could be as simple as replacing a roof, or as extensive as repairs of earthquake or flood damage.

My client decided to wait a while before investing the remaining $10,000 of the $20,000 she had allocated toward real estate investments. She also wished to purchase some growth stocks of a company in the high-technology area. Although high-technology stocks can return substantial rewards to investors, they also carry with them a higher degree of risk. Therefore I recommended that she put half her remaining funds in the money markets and the other half in Treasury bills. I also told her to advise me if and when she went back to work so that we could, if necessary, readjust our recommendations. Several months went by and we did not hear from her and found it difficult to contact her. Finally her mother called and the story unraveled—she had contacted the stockbroker we referred her to. She did invest a few thousand dollars in the stock that was recommended, as well as in one that a good friend of hers told her was a "sure thing."

The funds that were to go into the Treasury bills, however, never made it, and, in fact, only $30,000 was left of the entire $100,000. It is hard to believe that so much money disappeared so quickly. She had lent money to friends, and would probably never see it again. She had purchased a new car, since she had always wanted a Porsche and thought that she had earned it. She had also enjoyed some extensive trips and met many new friends on her travels.

You may be thinking that it was her money and she had a right to do what she wanted. Sounds good—but how many of you will ever receive a lump sum such as $100,000 and have the opportunity to use it to build for your financial security? One of the problems of the young is that they are under the impression that they will live forever and never have to retire.

This is one of the myths that begin to evaporate once you're past the age of 45. Our young friend still thinks she will live forever, but she can't imagine what happened to all her money. She would have been far better off if she had taken 5 to 10 percent of her settlement, classified it as "kiss-off dollars" and done whatever she wanted with it. The remaining 90–95 percent should have been placed in solid long-term investments.

Further checking revealed that one of the buildings my client had invested $5,000 in had been sold and she would receive back approximately $9,000 in a few months. She could hardly wait.

How would you like a windfall? Let us say that your grandfather has left you $10,000 when you come of age. Most people immediately think about a car, but this is not necessarily an investment—unless you are involved in collectibles or very expensive foreign models.

Any windfall demands that you place those funds in a liquid asset until you have had an opportunity to explore your alternatives. A bank or savings & loan savings account or a money market fund is an appropriate place to begin. The next step is to determine what your objectives are, and maybe go back to school. That is a great way to invest, as nothing returns more than investing in yourself. Perhaps you have already finished your education or you are tired of school; it is time, you feel, to have some fun with investments. Where can you start? Because of your age, you are in a position where you can take a great deal of risk. Although you will not live forever, according to the actuarial tables, you do have many years ahead.

If you are interested in the stock market, the fastest-growing area, and probably the "blue chips" of the 1980s, will be in the technology area. Subscribe to magazines like *Venture* and *Money*. Learn about the new companies coming onto the horizon. Any day the next IBM could appear. Remember that there is always high risk in technology and in the stock market and, if you need the funds, you can instruct your broker to sell and send you the proceeds. Again, there are no guarantees that you will have what you started with. You could have less, but you also could have more. If you are willing to tie up your funds for a while, you could consider some fine collectible pieces or art, but remember that you are not going to be able to sell these unless there is a ready buyer there. You can't liquidate them as you can stocks. You may be working and have a reasonable income coming in—that $10,000 just might be the amount that you could put toward your first home.

If you had started your IRA at the age of eighteen and contributed $2,000 per year, earning 12 percent, at the end of this life phase its accumulated value would be $22,459.40.

QUIZ

Your Aunt Harriet dies and leaves you $75,000. You have three children under ten years of age. What is the first thing to do with the money?

(a) Give it to your ex-husband because money scares you.
(b) Buy 180,000 jars of peanut butter.
(c) Put it in a high-yielding, principal-guaranteeing account like a money market fund.

Answer: The money market fund is a good temporary place to put dollars while deciding how the money should be invested. Do not jump into anything. Take the next six months to explore your options and then make investments. If you answered (c), go on to the next section.

LIFE PHASE 2: 25–35

"I do wish that more women would become owners of the soil."
—Amelia Bloomer, 1855

You have completed your education but you may actually be considering adding to or building on existing skills. This is an exciting time in which you are truly on your own, personally and financially, and are probably turning your labor into money. You have become your own person. You make firm decisions in your personal life, as well as in your career. Women in this life phase do a significant amount of job hopping in order to advance their careers, and often become involved with professional groups and networks.

If you have not already married, you are statistically most likely to do so in this phase. If you were married in your early twenties, these are apt to be your childbearing years. If you are married, it is highly probable that both you and your spouse work. This will allow for accumulation of savings and the purchase of a home, often a primary objective in this life phase. Not only are you aiming for a high comfort level in your career choice, but you are also beginning to develop some solid financial skills. As a consequence, you develop a strong interest in tax savings. You should be aggressively building up your net worth, which will be the basis for what you do in the future. A growing net worth will assist you in procuring loans and purchasing a home, and will give you some freedom. This is a period when record keeping is essential. It is also a period in which you may tend to be impulsive in your financial habits. Sometimes it pays off, sometimes it doesn't. If you make a mistake, you may go through a retrenchment period as you gather up your financial and emotional strengths to go forward again.

CHART YOUR COURSE

In the first few months of each year you should sit down and map out your objectives and plan what you can realistically accomplish by year's end. In addition, you should reevaluate your overall tax obligation, if you had one in the preceding year, and do some rough estimates of where you may be spending your money and what tax benefits might be derived from it.

It is easy for money to slide through your fingers here and it is important to get a fix on your cash flow and to label areas where you spend money frivolously. Two repeated temptations are eating out and buying clothes. If one of your primary objectives during this particular phase is to purchase your own home, then curbing excess spending will be crucial to achieving that goal. Of course, there are always some who will receive a windfall or have the ability to borrow funds from relatives at attractive interest rates which will enable them to purchase a home without going through a lot of the belt tightening and cutbacks necessary for most of us. Be aware of your present tax bracket, especially if your goal is home purchase—the rent you pay plus tax savings via mortgage payments may make the impossible possible.

During this phase many women will find they are receiving tax refunds. This may seem like a nice bonus for quick spending, but that is not really the most efficient use for your money. Besides ongoing savings, one of the most consistent ways of getting started on asset accumulation is to look closely at your tax situation and, hopefully, to reduce your withholding—allowing that base to begin building up. After all, why allow the government to use your money, interest free, when you could be investing it elsewhere?

AVERAGE AND SAVE

As you earn during this phase, you may find your income increasing by more than 10 percent a year. If so, one of the best methods for legally reducing the amount of tax you pay is to average your income. Under income averaging, part of your income, which the IRS will call your "averageable income" will be taxed as if you had received it in equal slices over a five-year period, and that period is calculated from the current taxable year. The best way to determine whether or not you qualify for income averaging is to add up your taxable income for the preceding four years (do not include the current year), divide that number by 4, and multiply the result by 120 percent. If your current taxable income tops this figure by at least $3,000, you are a candidate for income averaging and should consult an accountant to make sure your calculations are valid. In calculating your taxable income, both for past years and the current year, make sure to include all your salaries, dividends, any commissions, bonuses, consulting or referral fees, interest, long-term gains, income allocated to partners, as well as taxable gifts and inheritances. Income averaging will not save you a fortune, but it could save you hundreds of dollars.

LIQUIDITY

During this phase, and throughout the remainder of the life phases, I recommend that you maintain some form of liquidity for emergencies. As a rule of thumb, three to six months of after-tax income is generally sufficient. This, of course, is over and above funds you will invest in stocks, mutual funds, real estate, IRA accounts and any other investment opportunities that may come your way. Liquidity refers to the ability to terminate your investment position within seven days and receive the market value of your cash back. Bank accounts, money market funds, tax-deferred annuities, Treasury bills and some of the Government-guaranteed bonds, which were discussed under Phase 1, are all liquid.

When we look for liquidity, we are looking for items that have principals guaranteed and/or very minor likelihood of change in their value. Some items have strings attached, however. If you have to terminate your position in an annuity, for example, there may be a slight penalty on the interest. Certificates of deposit and time deposits also have penalties if you terminate before their maturity date. Many consider stocks, mutual funds and IRA accounts liquid, and indeed they can be terminated with proceeds in your hands in a fairly short period of time—in seven days, as a rule. The string attached here is that there is no guarantee of the value of the principal in the case of mutual funds and the stock market. They will oscillate—both the stocks you own outright and the mutual funds that invest in them. Bonds can also change in value, again depending on interest rates and the quality of the company. Depending upon where you place your IRA funds, some can be quickly liquidated and some can't. Before you place funds in any investment, you must know what will happen if you need them in an emergency. If you can't get them within a seven-day period and you have no other available funds for emergencies, forget it!

INSURANCE—DISABILITY AND LIFE

One thing many women don't think about is disability insurance. No matter what your occupation is—secretary, nurse, doctor, manager or CEO—if you get sick or require major surgery that will keep you out of the office earning stream for more than a few weeks, disability insurance becomes essential.

There are three different definitions of "disabled" that the insurance companies use in their various policies. The first one is "totally incapacitated and confined to bed." The second is "unable to work at any occupation." This does not necessarily mean that you are bedridden. And the third is "unable to work at a specific occupation."

The primary purpose of disability insurance is to replace lost earnings. As a rule, the sooner the payments begin the more expensive the policy. I recommend you explore disability policies that commence 90 days after you have been incapacitated. In addition, the more extended the coverage, for example several years, the more expensive the policy. As of this writing, there is no disability insurance available for a woman employed inside the home as a homemaker.

Often, when someone becomes ill, not only does her income decrease, but her expenses increase. For this reason it is always advisable to have that minimum of three to six months' worth of assets in a fairly liquid form to supplement your disability insurance. It is also essential to have the appropriate savings and health insurance to protect you and your family until disability payments begin.

Now, how much do you really need? If you purchase disability insurance directly and pay for the premiums with your after-tax dollars, any benefit that you receive will be nontaxable. On the other hand, if you receive disability insurance and your employer pays for the premium, then any proceeds you receive during the convalescence period will be taxable. If you are dealing with nontaxable dollars, then you will probably need 60 percent to 70 percent of your current annual income after taxes. If you make $25,000 a year, 60 percent of your income after taxes will be approximately $13,000. Seventy percent will be approximately $15,000.

The next step in your calculations is to determine how much income you will receive from any savings or investments on a monthly and annual basis. How much income, if you are entitled to any, could you receive from social security disability benefits? How much income, if you are entitled to it, could you receive in a work-related injury from Workmen's Compensation? How much income would you receive from any employer providing disability benefits? After you have totaled the amounts that you would receive from other sources, deduct that amount from your estimated annual needs. This will give you the total amount of coverage you will need to carry. If, after checking all your sources, you determine you will receive an additional $3,500 annually, deduct that amount from the $13,000 that was your minimum requirement, divide the remainder ($9,500) by 12, and you can determine that you will need additional coverage of $792 per month.

Your next step is to get a quote from an insurance broker who deals in long-term disability programs. Because rates vary from company to company, it is a good idea to get quotes from at least three. An insurance broker who represents several different companies will best be able to assist you. If you deal with an individual who represents only one company, you will not get comparative estimates.

There are many advocates of the theory that life insurance isn't necessary. It is extremely difficult, however, to defend that stance to a young family that finds itself without a breadwinner. Even if the decedent carried a minimum group term insurance policy of $10,000—which is quite common—the proceeds would probably not sustain an average family for longer than a few months.

Inflation has increased the need for adequate protection against sudden loss of an individual's or a family's income, and life insurance is usually the primary source of cash following a death. Anyone buying insurance should, of course, seek the most protection for the least money. This is certainly appropriate when you have young dependents who have several years to go before they complete their education. In the last few decades, the life span of the average person has increased substantially. Therefore the mortality tables that insurance premiums are based on are out-of-date and will probably be modified soon. When they are updated, you will find that the premiums, or the cost of carrying insurance, should be reduced. So, the insurance you carry should be reevaluated at least every three years. It makes sense to shop the various agencies for the most appropriate policies. When you do, you will find that the annual premium for basic insurance will vary substantially from one company to another.

If you are in an industry that encourages job movement or if you are planning to make several promotional changes over the next few years, it is certainly wise to have your own insurance in addition to the group insurance usually offered by an employer. This way, if you terminate a job and are waiting for another, or your life style changes, or for unforeseen reasons you lose your group policy, you can still maintain proper coverage.

In determining your life-insurance needs, there are several areas to consider. For example, should your spouse die, you may have accumulated debts that should be paid off, as well as initial administrative funeral and estate costs. If you have children, you should take a close look at your current annual living expenses. This, of course, should be adjusted for other current sources of income. Whatever the proceeds are, the beneficiary will more than likely put them to work in order to achieve some economic growth. Unless the proceeds from a policy are extremely small, it is improbable that the beneficiary or the surviving spouse will immediately spend them all. But beware—many widows are approached to "invest" their insurance proceeds in a whole gambit of "opportunities." Mistakes are made, often to another's benefit (i.e., commissions), during times of emotional stress.

My experience has shown that women who become widowed will more than likely enter the work force within a few years. Even though this may be the case in your particular situation, it is important for you to consider—especially in the purchase of life insurance—that you may die tomorrow. If that happens, how long will your dependents need financial assistance? I personally feel that you should always consider the worst possibility, even though everyone may be on their feet and off and running within a few years. In the following section, the table entitled "How

Much Life Insurance Do You Need?" should be of some assistance in determining how much insurance is appropriate for you and/or your dependents.

HOW MUCH LIFE INSURANCE DO YOU NEED?

In the table below, you will notice, under the columns headed 25 years, 35 years, etc., that there are two percentage numbers—75% and 60%. These are your replacement goals and they refer to the actual percentage of current earnings that you would like to have available to your spouse if you were to die. In using the table, multiply this factor by your current gross earnings. The result will tell you approximately how much life insurance you need. If earnings and/or age of spouse fall between the indicated figures, you can determine your multiple by averaging the difference between the age span and the earnings. The replacement percentages refer to the percentage of income that is represented by your spouse. If, however, you make more than your spouse, he should carry the amount of coverage on you that the loss of your earnings would represent. For example, let's assume that you make $30,000 a year and your spouse makes $22,500 a year. $22,500 is 75% of $30,000. Let's also assume that your spouse is 35 years of age. If you were to die tomorrow and your objective was to leave him with replacement dollars for your lost earnings, you would multiply 8 times $30,000 and arrive at $240,000. That would be the recommended amount of insurance coverage for you to carry on yourself.

MULTIPLES-OF-SALARY TABLE

	Present Age of Spouse							
Your Present	25 Years		35 Years		45 Years		55 Years	
Gross Earnings	75%	60%	75%	60%	75%	60%	75%	60%
$ 7,500	4.0	3.0	5.5	4.0	7.5	5.5	6.5	4.5
$ 9,000	4.0	3.0	5.5	4.0	7.5	5.5	6.5	4.5
$15,000	4.5	3.0	6.5	4.5	8.0	6.0	7.0	5.5
$23,500	6.5	4.5	8.0	5.5	8.5	6.5	7.5	5.5
$30,000	7.5	5.0	8.0	6.0	8.5	6.5	7.0	5.5
$40,000	7.5	5.0	8.0	6.0	8.0	6.0	7.0	5.5
$65,000	7.5	5.5	7.5	6.0	7.5	6.0	6.5	5.0

BANKS

In this life phase you will continue to build your credit, and as you do so you will not only get to know your banker better but will learn what his various programs are and how they can benefit you. You will recognize the value of having more than one banker. Why? Because money tightens and loosens and interest rates go up and down, you may find that the bank that offered "a great deal" yesterday may be offering far less today. It makes sense for you to at least check the Sunday business section of the major newspaper in your city. Often they will do a comparison of various financial institutions on such items as home loans, automobile loans, unsecured loans and what they are willing to pay on various types of savings programs. It is surprising how wide a variation there can be between one financial company and another.

STOCKS

In this life phase you may become more involved in the stock market. If you have an unpleasant experience and lose what in your opinion is a substantial amount of money, it may influence you for several years to come. Some people have become extremely successful in the stock market while others have been unsuccessful and never recover from the pain. My experience has shown that most clients have a love-or-hate relationship with the market. They either want to take part in it because they think there is a great potential there or they want nothing to do with it and would rather deal with something they can see and feel, such as real estate or collectibles.

If you elect to participate in the stock market, place your dollars with young companies that appear to have great growth potential. Keep in mind that the old rules of supply and demand will always apply. For example, in 1981 and 1982 there was a young company called Pizza Time Theatre. What this company offered was twofold. First, you could go in for a quick bite of an all-American favorite—pizza. Second, you could be entertained—although some might question the form—by computerized animals that sang and danced and told jokes and by various video-game machines. When I first visited Pizza Time Theatre I felt it offered an exciting opportunity to make money. Why? When I walked in, the place was packed. We had to wait for a table to open before we could sit down. Also, it was an establishment catering to young families with children ranging in age from four to eleven. These kids were driving their parents nuts with their demand for quarters to play the games and were also clearly enjoying the antics of the various animals on stage. The pizza wasn't terrific, but the action was. Was there anything else like it? Not at that time. But I knew that if it worked as well as our initial encounter indicated it would, there would soon be several imitations. Sure enough, time has borne that out.

Now, how do you take advantage of what appears to be an opportunity? First of all, you want to find out whether the "opportunity" is a publicly owned company, as was the case with Pizza Time Theatre. If so, you can purchase stock directly. If, on the other hand, it is a subsidiary of a larger company, what portion of the parent company's earnings does this subsidiary represent? This, by the way, can be determined by obtaining research reports from brokerage firms and/or looking into the Value Line Survey or Standard & Poor's Stock Report. Both are available at intermediate and larger libraries around the country, as well as at independent brokerage firms. I have included here a copy of one of the Value Line reports. A quick look will give you an idea of the scope of information you can get on a given corporation—in this case, Advanced Micro Devices (AMD).

1. This chart illustrates that Advanced Micro Devices has fluctuated in price, beginning in 1972 with a low of 25 cents (a) per share and a high of $42 (b) per share. From the year 1972 through 1983 AMD has had several price swings, as the chart illustrates. In taking an aggressive or trading posture on a stock, stock-market price movements such as this offer numerous profit opportunities—also loss.
2. Note that there have been not only stock dividends (c) but also stock splits (d).
3. I ignore the projection figures for stock price—they are nice to have, but rarely are they gospel.

ADVANCED MICRO NYSE-AMD

RECENT PRICE	42	P/E RATIO	45.2 (Trailing: 53.8 Median: 17.0)	EARN'S YLD	2.2 %	DIV'D YLD	Nil	1037

	1972	1973	1974	1975	1976	1977	1978	1979	1980	1981	1982	1983
High	2.1	3.7	2.5	2.2	5.0	4.3	6.3	12.9	29.7	24.2	28.0	42.0
Low	1.5	0.9	0.2	0.3	1.3	2.5	2.5	4.1	8.9	9.3	10.4	24.3

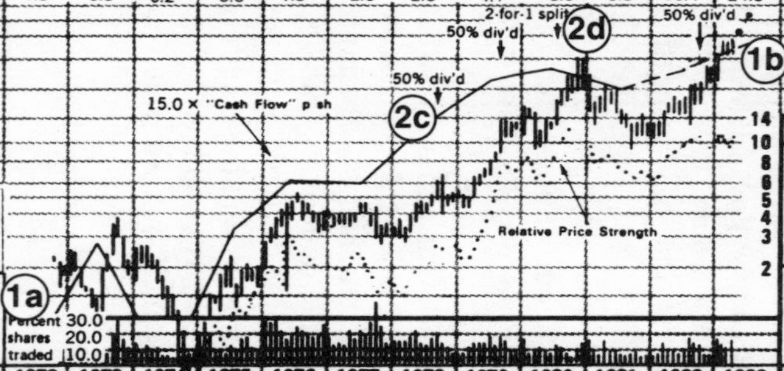

Insider Decisions 1982

	J	F	M	A	M	J	J	A	S	O	N	D	J	F	M
to Buy	0	0	0	0	1	0	0	0	0	0	0	1	0	0	0
to Sell	0	0	2	0	0	0	0	0	0	0	0	0	0	9	0

Institutional Decisions

	4Q'81	1Q'82	2Q'82	3Q'82	4Q'82
to Buy	18	20	24	31	32
to Sell	12	14	18	24	22
Hldg's(000)	8563	8317	9235	11500	12597

May 13, 1983 Value Line

TIMELINESS (Relative Price Performance Next 12 Mos.) **2** Above Average

SAFETY (Scale: 1 Highest to 5 Lowest) **4** Below Average

BETA 1.60 (1.00 = Market)

1985-87 PROJECTIONS

	Price	Gain	Ann'l Total Return
High	85	(+100%)	19%
Low	55	(+ 30%(	8%

③

1966	1967	1968	1969	1970	1971	1972	1973	1974	1975	1976	1977	1978	1979	1980	1981	1982	1983	© Value Line, Inc.	85-87E
--	--	--	--	--	--	.69	1.61	1.57	2.10	3.72	4.47	6.99	10.05	13.39	11.77	12.55	15.85	Sales per sh (A)	30.65
--	--	--	--	--	--	.05	.19	.04	.22	.41	.40	.81	1.49	1.78	1.32	1.80	2.60	"Cash Flow" per sh	4.85
--	--	--	--	--	--	.05	.15	d.06	.08	.24	.26	.51	.98	1.03	.37	.78	1.25	Earnings per sh (B)	2.60
--	--	--	--	--	--	--	--	--	--	--	--	--	--	--	--	--	Nil	Div'ds Decl'd per sh	Nil
--	--	--	--	--	--	.09	.44	.25	.04	.40	.36	1.10	1.96	2.17	2.53	2.45	3.60	Cap'l Spending per sh	3.90
--	--	--	--	--	--	.61	.76	.61	.71	1.01	2.18	2.71	3.90	5.13	5.52	6.45	7.75	Book Value per sh	15.65
--	--	--	--	--	--	16.33	16.37	16.41	16.35	16.71	20.64	21.22	22.44	23.11	23.92	28.50	29.00	Common Shs Outst'g (C)	31.00
--	--	--	--	--	--	37.1	13.8	--	23.3	15.6	12.8	8.6	8.8	16.5	37.5	29.6		Avg Ann'l P/E Ratio	27.0
--	--	--	--	--	--	2.7%	7.3%	--	4.3%	6.4%	7.8%	11.6%	11.4%	6.1%	2.7%	3.4%		Avg Ann'l Earn's Yield	3.7%
--	--	--	--	--	--	--	--	--	--	--	--	--	--	--	--	--		Avg Ann'l Div'd Yield	Nil

④

1972	1973	1974	1975	1976	1977	1978	1979	1980	1981	1982	1983		85-87E
11.2	26.4	25.8	34.4	62.1	92.3	148.3	225.6	309.4	281.6	358.3	460	Sales ($mill) (A)	950
13.0%	18.8%	3.7%	14.3%	17.6%	13.5%	17.5%	21.1%	17.7%	9.8%	13.5%	19.0%	Operating Margin	21.0%
.1	.7	1.7	2.1	2.3	3.2	5.8	10.1	16.4	22.5	30.0	40.0	Depreciation ($mill)	70.0
.7	2.4	d1.0	1.4	4.5	5.0	11.3	23.3	24.7	9.0	21.0	35.0	Net Profit ($mill)	80.0
52.0%	47.7%	--	35.9%	45.4%	41.9%	44.5%	37.5%	32.5%	--	--	20.0%	Income Tax Rate	35.0%
6.6%	9.2%	NMF	4.2%	7.2%	5.5%	7.6%	10.3%	8.0%	3.2%	5.9%	7.6%	Net Profit Margin	8.4%
8.4	4.5	6.6	6.9	11.5	30.8	25.5	34.1	56.2	32.6	39.7	55.0	Working Cap'l ($mill)	145
--	.2	7.1	4.2	8.6	6.8	6.4	14.5	29.0	36.8	37.3	75.0	Long-Term Debt ($mill)	70.0
10.0	12.5	10.0	11.6	16.9	45.0	57.5	87.5	118.6	132.0	183.4	225	Net Worth ($mill)	485
7.4%	19.2%	NMF	10.8%	18.5%	10.1%	18.0%	23.1%	17.5%	6.2%	10.0%	12.5%	% Earned Total Cap'l	15.0%
7.4%	19.5%	NMF	12.3%	26.4%	11.2%	19.6%	26.6%	20.8%	6.8%	11.5%	15.5%	% Earned Net Worth	16.5%
7.4%	19.5%	NMF	12.3%	26.4%	11.2%	19.6%	26.6%	20.8%	6.8%	11.5%	15.5%	% Retained to Comm Eq	16.5%
--	--	--	--	--	--	--	--	--	--	--	Nil	% All Div'ds to Net Prof	Nil

CAPITAL STRUCTURE as of 3/27/83

Total Debt $46.3 mill. **Due in 5 Yrs** $19.7 mill.
LT Debt $37.3 mill. **LT Interest** $3.8 mill.
(LT interest earned: 12.1x; total interest coverage: 9.9x) (17% of Cap'l)

Leases, Uncapitalized Annual rentals $4.5 mill.

Pension Liability None in '81 vs. None in '80

Pfd Stock None

Common Stock 26,348,000 shs. (83% of Cap'l) as of 12/26/82

(7)

CURRENT POSITION ($mill.)	1980	1981	3/27/83
Cash Assets	12.6	9.1	28.9
Receivables	62.3	48.9	60.4
Inventory (FIFO)	29.3	31.7	31.1
Other	12.1	7.1	1.7
Current Assets	116.3	96.8	122.1
Accts Payable	22.2	27.1	32.7
Debt Due	6.4	8.3	9.0
Other	31.5	28.8	40.7
Current Liab.	60.1	64.2	82.4

ANNUAL RATES of change (per sh)	Past 10 Yrs	Past 5 Yrs	Est '79-'81 to '85-'87
Sales	—	36.5%	*17.5%*
"Cash Flow"	—	47.0%	*21.0%*
Earnings	—	55.5%	*22.0%*
Dividends	—	—	*Nil*
Book Value	—	44.0%	*21.5%*

(8)

Fiscal Year Begins	QUARTERLY SALES ($ mill.) June 30	Sept. 30	Dec. 31	Mar. 31	(A) Full Fiscal Year
1979	50.5	55.7	57.1	62.3	225.6
1980	70.6	77.1	81.4	80.3	309.4
1981	70.9	65.0	70.4	75.3	281.6
1982	83.0	86.4	91.6	97.3	358.3
1983	***105***	***110***	***115***	***130***	***460***

Fiscal Year Begins	EARNINGS PER SHARE June 30	Sept. 30	Dec. 31	Mar. 31	(A)(B) Full Fiscal Year
1979	.20	.24	.26	.28	.98
1980	.29	.29	.23	.22	1.03
1981	.07	.04	.13	.13	.37
1982	.15	.15	.24	.24	.78
1983	***.20***	***.25***	***.30***	***.50***	***1.25***

Calendar	QUARTERLY DIVIDENDS PAID Mar. 31	June 30	Sept. 30	Dec. 31	Full Year
1979	NO CASH DIVIDENDS BEING PAID				
1980					
1981					
1982					
1983					

(5)

BUSINESS: Advanced Micro Devices, Inc. manufactures microprocessors, memories, and their associated peripheral and linear circuits using MOS (metal-oxide-semiconductor) and bipolar technologies. Sales breakdown: MOS, 42%; linear and bipolar, 55%; microcomputer, 3%. Major markets: computers, communications equipment, defense and instruments. R&D about 19% of sales. '81 deprec. rate: 10.8%. Est'd plant age: 2.5 yrs. Has 10,500 employees; 5,505 shareholders. Siemens AG owns 19.9% of stk.; insiders 2.9%. Chrmn., C.E.O. & Pres.: W.J. Sanders, III. Inc.: Del. Address: 901 Thompson Place, Sunnyvale, CA 94086.

(6)

AMD is currently the fastest-growing of the major semiconductor companies. While declining prices restrained the growth of the industry as a whole, AMD's sales advanced some 27% in the fiscal year ended March 31st. In the latest quarter, sales were up 29% over the year-earlier level. Orders and backlog are also reaching record levels, suggesting that sales growth in coming quarters will continue at a healthy post-recession pace.

The increased demand is broad-based, with small-computer makers and domestic distributors in the vanguard. Even the Europeans are biting: Sales to them are up 30%, though admittedly over a depressed year-earlier level. Only the video game ROM (read only memory) market is soft; but that makes the overall advance all the more impressive, because this market had become a significant one for AMD. The broadness of the demand and confirming signs of a general economic recovery suggest that this time—unlike last spring—the upturn is for real. Moreover, the military sector, normally a steady 20%-25% of AMD's sales, has not yet participated; as prime and subcontractors start volume production later this year on contracts initiated under the Reagan defense budgets, military business could catch up. Already set for a good year, too, are AMD's new telecommunications-related products.

Operating margins could climb quite rapidly as volume expands. . . thanks to a new state-of-the-art facility in San Antonio, which could be on-line by the second fiscal quarter, and increased capacity utilization. R&D (19.4% of sales last year) and other operating expenses will be hard pressed to grow at the same rapid clip we expect for sales. Margin improvement could be evident in the second half.

. . . but nonoperating factors may slow net margin growth. With capital spending likely to exceed "cash flow" again this year, AMD will probably have to assume more debt—and interest expense will rise accordingly. The tax man will want his bite, too, after giving AMD 9¢ a share in credits in each of the last two quarters. On balance, however, upcoming comparisons should be favorable.

The stock is timely, though with its low price stability, not for the nervous investor. Long-term prospects are about average.

O.S.C./K.C.B.

(A) Fiscal year ends last Sunday in March of following calendar year.
(B) Next earnings report due mid-July. Primary earnings. Est'd current-cost egs./sh.: '82, 35¢.
(C) In mill., adjusted for stock splits & div'ds.

Company's Financial Strength	B
Stock's Price Stability	15
Price Growth Persistence	85
Earnings Predictability	40

4. The actual financial reports are important. Note the increased sales per share, earnings per share, book value per share, capital spending (desirable in an expanding company), average annual P/E (price/earnings ratio), and net profit margin.
5. This section tells what the company does, who its chief officers are, its location and various products.
6. What's happening in its current environment.
7. Current financial position regarding both assets and liabilities.
8. Current financial data on earnings per share, as well as dividends paid, if any, and quarterly sales for the preceding three years. Projections for the next year are also included.

Value Line charts give a great deal of information on one page. Learn how to use this readily available information and you will discover that you know more about stocks than 90 percent of the brokers!

In early 1982 I had a speaking engagement in Hawaii. In the area adjacent to the bar were several video games, among them one called Pac-Man. As I passed through the lobby, I noted that this game was always surrounded by teenagers and young adults. They were obviously having a good time and, clearly, someone was making money from the participants' obsessive feeding of quarters into the coin slot. I must confess I became increasingly curious. I had heard about Pac-Man, but I had never had the experience of playing.

As I am an early riser, and Hawaii's time is three hours earlier than the West Coast's, I found myself up at dawn and went downstairs to have a cup of coffee. Lo and behold, there was no one around the Pac-Man game. I stuck a quarter into the coin slot, and the instructions popped onto the screen. I read, found the appropriate lever, pushed the start button and quickly bombed out. Obviously the kids I had been observing were aces. The game clearly required skill, as well as many, many quarters to master it. An opportunity? You bet! After all, who cares about quarters when there are dollars to be made?

And there were two ways to participate in the Pac-Man craze. First, the equipment was produced by a company called Bally Manufacturing. You may be unfamiliar with Bally, but you are surely familiar with something called the slot machine. Bally is one of the country's largest manufacturers of "one-armed bandits." In addition, the parent company which had leased all the rights to manufacture and produce Pac-Man for a fee was called Atari. Atari had been bought by Warner Communications a few years ago. So I had the opportunity of purchasing stock in either Warner Communications or Bally Manufacturing in order to realize what I saw as a substantial potential for appreciation via Pac-Man. In order to determine which company to invest in, I needed to decide which stock would benefit most from the increased sales and publicity of Pac-Man. I would therefore seek out sources, such as Value Line and Standard & Poor's and would also pay attention to what was being written up in the newspapers.

Once you buy into a rapidly moving stock like Pac-Man or Pizza Time Theatre, you should also determine at what price you are going to sell. One of the mistakes I see stock-market investors make time after time is to purchase a stock, put it in a drawer and then forget about it. A stock that makes significant advances might eventually lose some of its glamour and begin to retrench or decline. Timing is important. You should consider selling Pizza Time Theatre the day you go into one of them and find that there is not only an open table but also empty space around many of the games. The same holds true for Pac-Man. When the quarters stop flowing, it's time to exit. When announcements were made to the press that Christmas sales in 1982 had not reached the original projections for computer games, the stock value of Warner Communications plummeted.

Large companies like Warner Communications have many subsidiaries that contribute to revenues and, hopefully, profits. In our example, if you had purchased the company solely because of its relationship to Atari/Pac-Man, it made sense to cut your losses and get out when the news turned negative. On the other hand, if you had purchased Warner Communications because of the variety of subsidiary companies that still report consistent profits and if, in your opinion, the problems that Atari is experiencing are minimal in comparison to the overall value of the company, it may make sense to hang in there. Keep in mind, though, that stocks often trade in an emotional environment and when a particular segment of a parent company receives headline coverage on its problems, there is, as a rule, a significant negative effect on the stock, and its value declines on the open market.

By purchasing stocks in young aggressive companies, you have time to sit and wait out management growth plans as well as the stock market's response to them. Often, stocks take awhile —anywhere from several months to several years—before they achieve their potential. You may, though, become too impatient and want the reward overnight. If that is the case, stock options might be the investment instrument for you.

OPTIONS

Investors who are in a hurry often move into an area that has been highly touted in the last decade—the option market. The option market can be exciting. You may make a lot of money quickly—or lose a lot, just as quickly. The unpredictable nature of this market means that options should be viewed as highly speculative. The only funds you should commit, if you do commit to option trading, are those you could lose without looking back. I refer to these as "kiss-off funds." They are not funds with which you pay your mortgage or food bills or save for the down payment on the new car you need. They are funds whose loss would not adversely affect your life style. The amount that can be identified as disposable will vary from person to person. You may have none or you may have an extraordinary net worth which allows you to place 10 percent of your overall assets into high-risk situations. And option trading is indeed risky. No matter where you are financially, I would highly recommend that you not place more than 10 percent of your assets into any investments or combination of investments that would be described as high risk.

Just what is an option? Basically, an option gives a holder (the owner) the right to purchase 100 shares of a specific stock at a specific price (also known as the exercise price) within a specific period of time. This period is no more than nine months if the option is traded on one of the listed option exchanges. The most common options are the "calls" and "puts." A call is the right to *purchase* 100 shares of a stock at a stated price and within a defined period of time. A put, on the other hand, is an option to *sell* 100 shares of stock, at a stated price, and within a defined period of time. The majority of options are traded on the Chicago Board of Options, also known as CBOE. There are other exchanges for trading in options, such as the American Exchange, the Philadelphia Exchange and the Pacific Coast Exchange. Bear in mind that each option you purchase or sell will always be for 100 shares of the particular stock it covers. Ten options, then, represents 1,000 shares of stock.

An analogy to the option market would be the leasing of a house with a lease-option provision. In a lease-option provision or clause, the lessee and the homeowner agree on a specific sum of money (known as a "lease-option payment" or "premium") that will secure the lessee's right to purchase the home within a specified period of time at a specified purchase price. If the real estate around the lease-option property appreciated substantially during the term of the lease, the lessee's option would have a real value.

Let's say you had leased a home for $600 per month. Let's also say that for a lease-option payment of $2,000, you could secure the right to purchase that home within a year's time for $75,000. Let's also assume that substantially similar houses on both sides of you had sold during that period for $90,000. It is reasonable to assume your house would also be worth approximately $90,000. But, because you had placed a $2,000 premium to the owners to purchase the house at $75,000, you would be able to buy it at that price. Therefore, that $2,000 premium you paid has actually increased in value to $15,000 ($90,000 minus $75,000 = $15,000).

The option market has some similarities to this aspect of the real-estate market. There is a specific period of time and a specific price for the stock and a premium payment that you make up front. It is not a down payment and should not be confused with one payment. Let us say that you hear someone at work talking about a cosmetic company that has had a great deal of press coverage. Your co-worker invites you to her home and introduces you to a friend of hers who sells Mary Kay Cosmetics. You are intrigued and decide that the product seems to be good and reasonably priced. You are also intrigued by the company's growth as indicated by the sales representative, and you decide to do some homework. You check with the Value Line Survey to assist you in stock selection—this survey can be viewed at almost any brokerage firm or public library—and you write for copies of the company's annual report. In reviewing the Value Line report, you observe that the stock appears to be highly ranked and recommended for continued growth. The problem is that Mary Kay is selling for $65 a share and you don't have $6,500 to buy 100 shares. Your research indicates that this company could appreciate in price in a fairly short time. This could be the chance of a lifetime—or your Waterloo.

The following is a reprint of "Listed Options Quotations" from the March 2, 1983 issue of *The Wall Street Journal*.

CHICAGO BOARD

Option &	Strike	Calls—Last			Puts—Last		
NY Close	Price	Mar	Jun	Sep	Mar	Jun	Sep
Mary K	40	r	26	s	1–16	r	s
65⅛	45	19	r	r	1–16	r	r
65⅛	50	15¾	15	r	r	r	r
65⅛	55	10½	12¼	r	1–16	1¼	3½
65⅛	60	5½	9¼	r	9–16	3	r
65⅛	65	s	6	8½	s	5⅛	r
65⅛	70	s	3½	5⅝	s	r	r

You will note that under the company name there are several 65⅛ references. This merely means that Mary Kay stock closed at 65⅛ on the preceding day. The next column is headed "Strike Price." Strike price is the specific or certain price for which you can purchase the stock via the options market. In this illustration, Mary Kay has strike prices at $40, $45, $50 and on up to $70 a share. In the case of calls, when the strike price is below the price of the underlying stock (a strike price of $40 is 25⅛ points below the 65⅛ market price of Mary Kay), the call has a real value. Real value means that if you exercised your call at $40 a share and immediately sold it on the open market at $65⅛ a share, you have a gain of $25⅛. When the strike price is in excess of the underlying stock, it has an intangible value, also referred to as "total premium."

The next three columns relate to the call market, and you will note that the calls will expire in March, June and September. You will also see that there are both numbers and letters in the columns. The numbers represent the actual amount you will have to pay to purchase this specific call. For example, if you desire to purchase a Mary Kay March 60 call, and today's date is March 1, you would pay $5.50 per share or $550 for the entire call. Your purchase would reserve the right for you to purchase the stock at $60 a share, between now and the third Friday in March (options can be exercised through the third Friday of the trading month in which they expire (cease to exist). You will note that if you add 5½ (the strike price for this call) to 60 you will get 65½, which is ⅜ of a point higher than the current market price of the stock. That ⅜ of a point is known as a premium.

Now, if Mary Kay increases in value from March 1 through the third Friday of that month, the value of the options, and possibly the premium itself, will appreciate almost point for point with the stock. On the other hand, if you look at the next column, June, you will see an option price of 9¼. Adding the 9¼ to 60 and subtracting the underlying value of the stock, you will get a difference of 4⅛ (9¼ + 60 − 65⅛ = 4⅛). Therefore, 4⅛ is an excess premium that you will pay for an option to purchase Mary Kay at $60 a share, between now and the third Friday in June. Again, if the stock does well in a fairly short period of time, it is highly probable that the 9¼, or $925 for 100 shares, will increase in value. For the option to have a real value at the price of $925 or 9¼, the stock must advance to a minimum of 69¼ (60 + 9¼ = 69¼).

Let us say that you are excited about Mary Kay but you feel that three months from the June option is too short-term and you would like to own an option that extends to September. You will note that there is a letter "r"—the "r" means that no options have been traded for the month of September, at the specific strike price—60. On the other hand, if you look at the line below, which represents the strike price of 65, you will note that there is an "s" in the March column; "s" means that there is no option offered or available to trade for the March 65 option. Again, a numerical relationship usually exists between the strike price and the amount that you pay for your options. As a rule, the higher the strike price above the current market price of the stock that you select in the case of calls, the less you will be likely to pay in premiums.

In the case of puts, when the strike price is below the current market value price, and dependent upon how far below it is, you will pay less for the option premium. Call options that are above the current market price of a stock and put options that are below the current market price of the stock are also identified in the trade as "out of the money." Call options with strike prices below the underlying market value of the stock and put options that are above the underlying market price of the stock are known as "in the money." When an option is out of the money, there is minimal real value; when it is in the money, there is real or true value to it.

Again, let me caution that when you trade in the option market you should only buy puts and calls with "kiss-off" money. If the stock doesn't perform as you hope it will, you will never see this money again. At best, it will merely give you a tax deduction.

Let's say, then, that you have identified $600 as "kiss-off" money that you are willing to risk in hopes of reaping a substantial return in a fairly short time. Looking at the tables, you notice that Mary Kay has a call available at $70 a share that matures or will expire in September for 5⅝ or $562.50. This, of course, does not include any commission. You instruct your broker to purchase one Mary Kay September 70 call at 5⅝. Remember, in this case, each call entitles you to purchase 100 shares of stock at $70 a share between the time you purchase it and the third Friday in September when the option will expire. You now begin to watch the price of Mary Kay stock on a daily basis (and believe me, when you trade options, you must watch daily!). If the price goes up, it is highly probable that this will affect the value of the option you just purchased. For example, let us assume that there is some very exciting news about the company that causes the underlying stock to increase from 65⅛ to $72 a share, within a three-week period. Does that mean that your option goes up too? One factor affecting the value of the option is the amount of movement of the underlying stock. If you have a stock that moves several points within a few weeks and the option has six months before it expires, it is likely the option will reflect that movement. Instead of being up just two points over the $70-a-share real value of the stock option, it is probable that the option value will have increased to 10 or even 12. This would mean your option could increase in value from 5⅝, or $562.50, to $1,000 or $1,200—a handsome return in a very short time. When a stock has a substantial move in price within a short period of time, there is normally a large premium in the option value. This explains why so many people have been attracted to the option market.

On the other hand, what if Mary Kay Cosmetics does not appreciate in price? How does that affect the option? As time progresses, the premium or value over the actual value of the stock will decrease until, at expiration day, it will be trading at basically no value. This means that if you had not sold prior to expiration date, you would have lost all your money. But, because you were using "kiss-off" money, the loss shouldn't sting too badly and you will write it off on your taxes. In addition, you have another financial lesson to chalk up to experience. Participating in the options market forces you to make decisions. Procrastination is taboo!

Conversely, perhaps you feel that Mary Kay Cosmetics will actually decline in price, and that the current price of 65⅛ is too high, in your opinion, for the value of the stock. You can purchase a put, which is your way of stating your belief that the stock will decline. In looking at the table, notice that there is a June 65 put. This means that with the March 1 date, you have approximately three and a half months for your strategy to pan out.

Now, remember that puts are the opposite of calls—you *want* the stock to decline. In the example, the put in June is valued at 5⅛ or $512.50. For it to have a real value, the stock must decline below 65 and, on a dollar-to-dollar basis, should drop to 59⅞ for it to be worth what you had to pay for your premium of 5⅛ (65 − 5⅛ = 59⅞). If the stock actually declined to $50 a share, it would indicate an approximately 15-point drop. How does that affect the put? Substantially! Of course, one factor here will be dependent upon how quickly the underlying stock declines during the life of the option. If it does decline within a very short period of time, for example, a few weeks, then there will be more premium attached to the option. If there is a gradual decline up to the expiration date, then the put, at some point in time, will begin to increase in value almost on a point-for-point basis. If, for example, you own the June 65 put for the declining Mary Kay stock and the *value* of the underlying stock drops to $50 a share, the put would have a true value of 15, or $1,500 (65 − 50 = 15). Whoever sold the put to you for the original amount of 5⅛ must now purchase it back for 15 or be prepared to buy the actual stock for $65 a share. You can literally *put* it to the original seller. (Actually you will never know who sells and buys these options —the transaction is completed on the option trading floor and cleared in the computer.)

You may be wondering why anyone would want to buy stock for 65 a share when it can be purchased all day long at 50 a share. That is a good question. Keep in mind, though, that when you originally entered into this contract, the stock was trading at 65⅛ and the put premium was 5⅛. This means that whoever sold the put to you wasn't really at risk until the stock actually declined below $60 a share. (65⅛ − 5⅛ = 60). The seller of the put bet that the stock would not drop any lower than the premium you originally paid, 5⅛. In our example, the seller called it wrong and lost $987.50 (15 − 5⅛ = 9⅞).

Does it sound a little bit crazy? Some people think so; others think it's the best craps game in town.

Options can be fun and exciting, and they can wipe you out. *Set a limit to the funds you are willing to commit to this form of investing*. One client of mine set a limitation of $1,500 to commit to high-risk aggressive trading; whatever he made or lost he would reinvest. I was away on vacation and came back to find that the size of his portfolio had increased fivefold. My initial thought was that he had hit something big. In probing further, I discovered that during my absence he had sold one of the options in which he had made a reasonable profit and was so excited about the possibility of bigger profits with larger amounts of money that he infused more dollars into the account. To make a long story short, my client thought he had found his pot of gold. When the underlying stocks actually began to decline, he began to hope. He did not want to sell the options and cut his losses as they began to decline in value. He lost approximately 90 percent of the funds he started with, as well as the additional funds. The extra funds were not the "kiss-off" funds he had originally started with.

If you have any interest in participating in the options market, there are several brochures that are available, free of charge, from the Chicago Board of Options. The major brokerage firms carry them and they are available merely by phoning and asking for a copy. There are brochures on understanding puts and calls as well as various strategies in the option market.

In any trading-type market such as the option market, there seems to be a proliferation of investment advisory letters telling you what to buy and what to sell. None of them will be 100 percent right all of the time; some of them have a higher probability of being 100 percent wrong. Advertisements for these letters are often found in *The Wall Street Journal* and the Sunday business sections of your local newspapers. In addition, advertisements are carried in many financial publications found on your local newsstand.

MUTUAL FUNDS

If you think there is growth potential in stocks but do not have the time to follow or select them individually, then you should participate in one of the mutual funds that specializes in progressive growth. There are several such funds that have attractive track records. Remember that in a mutual fund you are not buying an individual stock or issue. You are purchasing a large portfolio of stocks and/or bonds. A mutual fund should always be purchased via a prospectus, which will not only state what the fund's objectives are but will also include a breakdown of what it has invested in. Unfortunately, such a prospectus is only published every 13 months and will not give you a totally accurate fix on where the moneys are at any given time.

If you participate in a mutual fund that charges a commission, or load, you should consider your investment to be on a long-term basis. If you invest less than $10,000, your commission is going to run a minimum of 8 to 8½%. Of course, when you liquidate, or sell, there is no commission going out. If you participate in a no-load fund (one that does not charge a commission), you will find that its trading value will fluctuate very much like that of a regular stock.

And finally, if you are involved in the stock market and aggressively turn your money over two or three times a year, you will find that you are paying a significant amount in commissions, probably in excess of 9 percent of your initial investment. If the stocks you trade do not show appreciation, or, if you simply select the wrong ones, then you should consider one of the mutual funds, where you will incur lower costs and enjoy long-term capital-gains treatment. In your purchase of individual stocks, remember that their tax consequences will be based on the length of time you hold them. Remember that long-term capital gains, which carry a tax advantage, are calculated when you sell a stock one year and one day after you initially purchased it. This, of course, assumes that you have a profit. Any selling that is done prior to that time will be considered a short-term capital gain, or loss, as the case may be.

I might also add here that there are times to be in the stock market and times not to be. You do not have to be "in" the market 100 percent of the time. There is nothing wrong with selling stocks, then taking the proceeds and keeping them in a money market fund or other form of investment for a period of time.

PURCHASE OF A HOME

Because taxes appear to be taking a greater bite of your revenues each year, you may begin to wonder if you are going to be able to purchase a home in today's real estate market. The first thing to decide is how much you can really afford to spend on housing on a monthly basis. In calculating that amount, you will need to consider what your current tax bracket is, how much you are paying in taxes in addition to your withholding, and the amount of rent you are currently paying. In order to determine your current tax bracket, refer to the tables located in the beginning of the Tax Fax section. For example, let's assume that you are single and making $30,000. You have no itemized deductions with the exception of a $2,000 contribution to an IRA account. Your taxable income will be reduced to $27,000 ($2,000 contribution, $1,000 personal exemption) leaving you with a Federal tax obligation of $5,469. If you are required to pay state taxes, then your gross taxes will be greater.

TAXES BEFORE BUYING A HOME

Before	
Gross Income	$30,000
IRA	-2,000
Personal Exemption	-1,000
Taxable Income	$27,000
Federal Tax (1983)	$ 5,469

Let's also assume you are currently paying rent at the rate of $400 a month for a total of $4,800 a year. This, of course, is not tax deductible, although some states do allow a renter's credit. Let's say that you find a condominium or small house that has a current market value of approximately $70,000. Let's also assume that you have been able to acquire a 20 percent down payment, or $14,000, from various sources and that you are able to obtain a $56,000 mortgage at 14 percent.

This may be done through a combination of assuming an underlying note and the owner carrying back financing for five to seven years, if available. In this case, "underlying note" means an already existing mortgage. For example, let's say you purchased a house, needed to finance $56,000, and are able to assume an existing $45,000 first mortgage on it. The owner is willing to lend you the additional $11,000 secured now by a second deed of trust, or trust deed, for five years. The two mortgages, or two deeds of trust, of $45,000 and $11,000 will total $56,000. Real estate taxes are estimated to be $700 annually. In addition, interest payments are approximately $7,900 for a combined annual cost of $8,600. (During the first few years of any payment involving a loan, the percentage of principal being repaid is at a minimum, so for illustration's sake we will assume that the great majority of your payment will be interest.) You would then divide the $8,600 by 12—resulting in a monthly payment of approximately $717.

Buy House	$70,000
Interest Payments	7,900
Real Estate Taxes	700
	$ 8,600 ÷ 12 =
Monthly Payment including taxes	$ 717

You may think there is no way you can afford to pay $717 per month. But there may be. Since you are currently spending $400 per month for rent, you may indeed be able to purchase a home. The key here is to consider the various tax benefits you will obtain by doing so. Under current tax laws your mortgage interest, as well as real estate taxes, are fully deductible. Often when individuals begin to itemize deductions, they will discover that numerous contributions, accounting fees, general sales, state and/or personal taxes, excess medical deductions, and miscellaneous professional obligations begin to add up to a tidy sum. And by the time they total up all these areas they find that they often have reached or exceeded $2,000. Keep in mind that as a single taxpayer you must have deductions greater than $2,300 to pass your zero bracket amount ($3,400 for married filing jointly). The IRS has ruled that taxpayers (single, married or head of household) must have gross deductions in excess of a certain amount before they can begin to use the itemized tax forms. That "certain amount" marks your zero bracket.

Now let's assume you have done a detailed analysis and have found that from interest on your various charge cards, medical payments in excess of 5 percent of your adjusted gross income, contributions, professional obligations, investment and accounting advice and state personal tax withholdings, you indeed do have $2,000 in deductions. (These and other tax deductions are further explained in Tax Fax.) If you include that amount with your real estate taxes (approximately $700) and add that to your interest payments, you will have a gross deduction of approximately $10,600. You would then deduct the $2,300 disallowance and arrive at an excess-deduction total of $8,300.

With Other Deductions	
Excess medical, misc., interest from charge accounts, states taxes, contributions, professional dues, accounting, etc.	$ 2,000
Interest	7,900
Real Estate Taxes	700
	$10,600
Zero Bracket Adjustment	−2,300
Excess Deductions	$ 8,300

Taking your gross income of $30,000 and adjusting for the $2,000 contribution for your IRA, the $8,300 for your excess deduction and $1,000 for your personal exemption, you will arrive at your taxable-income base of $18,700, or a Federal tax obligation of $3005. Before purchasing the residence, your Federal tax obligation was $5,469.

TAXES AFTER BUYING A HOME

After	
Gross Income	$30,000
IRA	−2,000
Personal	−1,000
Excess Deduction	−8,300
Taxable Income	$18,700
(Federal Tax = $3,005)	

With the purchase, Federal taxes have been reduced to $3,005 for an overall savings of $2,464.

Federal Taxes	
Before Purchase of House	$5,469
After Purchase of House	−3,005
Tax Savings	$2,464

Dividing that number by 12, your monthly tax withholding is reduced by a minimum of $205. When you add that amount to the rent that you had previous paid ($400), you have a total of $605.

Monthly Rental Payments	$400
Monthly Tax Savings	+205
($2,464 ÷ 12 = $205)	$605
Funds Available for Housing	

Originally, in calculating the cost of the residence plus taxes, we found that the cost averaged $717 a month. Of course this does not take into consideration any repairs or maintenance or additions to the house that you may incur. Taking the $605 and deducting it from $717, the overall monthly difference is $112.

Monthly Mortgage Interest and Taxes	$717
Rent and Tax Savings	-605
Monthly Difference or Shortfall	$112

You must then evaluate: Can you afford to expend $112 more per month on housing costs, can you save, or can you reduce other areas in which you are spending money by that amount to compensate for the difference? If you can't, then the purchase of a residence may be beyond your means at this time. But you should reevaluate it as income increases or expenses decrease.

Before purchasing a home, you should believe that housing values will continue to appreciate. A home today is no longer just a shelter. It has become an investment, as well as a tax reduction. There are still opportunities across the country in real estate. If you don't have the time, get the help of a professional to look for real estate in areas you may be able to afford. After considering tax savings, you may find you can afford more than you originally thought.

You may feel, however, that you need a home even if prices are not increasing; in fact, they may actually have declined. Again, you need to sharpen your pencil and get your calculator out. Take into consideration the various tax benefits that you would receive through home ownership. Determine the amount that your taxes would be reduced by these deductions and compare them with the amount that you would currently owe without home ownership. Divide the difference by 12 to determine the monthly tax savings. Add the monthly tax savings to your current rent and compare the total with the amount of the proposed monthly mortgage, insurance and real estate taxes. If the difference is one that you do not feel you can financially handle, then you should probably continue to rent. But if the difference turns out to be minor—and if the thrill, pride and emotional satisfaction of owning a home could offset a flat real estate market—if this is the case, then strongly consider buying.

What if you were fortunate enough to purchase a home that had appreciated substantially in value? This increased value is referred to as equity buildup, and is arrived at by calculating the appreciated value of your property less the balance of your mortgage. In the previous example, you purchased a home that cost $70,000 and you had made a down payment of $14,000. Suppose then, because of the law of supply and demand and possibly even a moratorium in your community on new building, its value increased to $125,000. Since the mortgage in our example is $56,000 you would deduct that amount from the $125,000 and your current equity value would be $69,000—which could represent a substantial portion of your net worth.

Original Purchase Price	$ 70,000
Down Payment	– 14,000
Mortgaged	$ 56,000
Increased Market Value	$125,000
Mortgage	– 56,000
Equity	$ 69,000

It may be possible at some time to refinance or incur a second mortgage on your current property. If so, what factors should you consider before you do? First, your personal tax situation; second, current interest rates; and third, your ability to "sleep with it." Let's assume that your earnings increased to $36,000 a year and your property had an equity value of the stated $69,000. You had incurred no additional deductions, and with the increase of $6,000 in revenues your tax obligation had increased to $4,733 annually. If you deducted your prior Federal tax obligation of $3,005, your net tax increase with the additional $6,000 would be $1,728, or $144 a month.

Income	$36,000	Federal Taxes on $36,000	
(Before Deductions)		After Deductions	$4,733
Equity	$69,000	Previous Federal Taxes on $30,000 Income After Deductions	−3,005
		Net Tax Increase	$1,728 ÷ 12 =
		Monthly Tax Increase	$ 144

If you decide to borrow $20,000 in the form of a second mortgage on the residence and have an average interest obligation of 15 percent, you will be paying roughly $3,000 a year or $250 a month in additional interest payments.

Borrow Additional Funds	$20,000@ 15% interest
Annual Interest	$ 3,000 ÷ 12 =
Monthly Interest	$ 250

Of course, even though you had a $6,000 increase in salary, the $3,000 in new interest payments could be deductable, adjusting your taxable income back down to $21,700 (after deducting $1,000 personal exemption and $2,000 IRA contribution, $8300 excess deductions) with a Federal obligation of $3,845 annually, or $320 a month.

Adjusted Federal Taxes	
Previous Taxable Income	$18,700
Income Increase	6,000
Interest Deduction	(3,000)
Present Taxable Income	$21,700
Annual Federal Tax	$ 3,845 ÷ 12
Monthly Federal Tax	320
Previous Taxes	4,733
New Taxes	−3,845
	$ 888
Annual Tax Savings From Additional Borrowings	$ 888 ÷ 12
Monthly Savings	74
New Payment	$ 250
Tax Savings	74
Shortfall	$ 176

With the increased debt and additional tax deductions, taxes would be reduced only $888 or roughly $74 a month. Since the payment for the $20,000 will be approximately $250 a month, or a difference of roughly $176 from the tax savings, it is essential for you to earn a minimum of 10.6 percent annually on the $20,000 ($20,000 × 10.6% = $2,120; $2,120 ÷ 12 = $177).

You need to look closely at whether you can afford the negative cash flow and/or what you will do with the $20,000 you have obtained as a loan. Even if those funds are placed in a money market fund or a savings account with a high yield of 10.6 percent, they should more than offset your monthly cost. If you place it in another vehicle that yields additional tax benefits, your overall tax savings could be even greater. If you choose the latter method, it is important to place your funds so as to make a profit via growth and appreciation.

With the new tax law, the tax rates have been reduced substantially. Taxable income of $34,000 just a few years ago would have thrown you as a single person into a 50% tax bracket. This is no longer the case. If interest rates decline substantially and if we are ever fortunate enough to see the 10 percent mortgage again, it may make sense for you to pull some of your equity dollars out in the form of a second mortgage. This could allow you to make investments in other areas or even begin to build up a cash nest egg that could lead to liquidity as well as security.

MS. MISC.

As you begin to build savings, you should make use of the available money market funds. These were discussed at length in Phase 1.

You may be tempted to invest funds in the many tax shelters offered by various brokerage firms, as well as private syndicators. Unless you have a substantial income and the opportunity to build your net worth in the other recommended areas, I would advise you to stay clear of tax shelters at this time. Most individuals aggressively pursue tax shelters when their income reaches the 45 percent tax bracket. This will most probably not happen in your present life phase. It is in the next three phases that earnings and revenues are often at their highest.

WINDFALL!

The company you work for has announced banner earnings and you are one of their best sales reps. They are giving you a bonus of 25 percent of your yearly salary. Your earnings came in at $30,000, so your bonus will be $7,500. Your company also has a credit union from which you can borrow up to $3,000 unsecured. With your recent 10 percent pay increase, you are comfortable in borrowing $2,500 to add to your $7,500.

In this particular life phase, there are two recommended investments for your $10,000. If you haven't already purchased a home, this might be your chance to do so. The person who makes $30,000 a year will be able to afford approximately $1,000 a month in mortgage payments. If you already own your own home, consider purchasing a rental property. Remember that when you buy rental property, you need not buy Tiffany style. You want a piece of property that is basically easy to manage and attractive enough to lure a purchaser at a later date, hopefully at an increased price. Another strategy in the real estate market is to find the real ugly duckling, turn it into a swan, and then immediately sell it. There are many millionaires who have used this strategy to build assets.

If real estate is not your cup of tea, or if you already own your home and do not wish to be a landlady, consider placing your funds in the stock market, primarily into high-technology stocks. Invest your dollars in the young emerging companies. Although older established companies such as IBM, Xerox and Hewlett-Packard are strong financially, they do not attract the same public interest as some of the newer companies. Consider purchasing stock in a company approximately six months after it first hits the public market. By that time, the price may have settled down, the speculators have made their quick profit or loss, and a fair assessment of the company can be made.

In a monthly newsletter I wrote in 1982, I included a survey of the technology stocks and their high risk/high reward. Over a six-month period, the best appreciation of an individual stock was 209 percent, the worst was 27 percent. Now there is certainly nothing wrong with a 27 percent increase over six months; but you must admit, 209 percent is much more attractive. If an individual had invested equally in the twelve stocks mentioned in the article, her portfolio would have increased by 88 percent. Again, not too bad, but that 209 percent is still awfully attractive! The companies that did the best were the young companies such as Apple Computer, Tandem Computer, Ask Computer; the ones at the bottom of the list were Xerox and IBM. For further reading I would recommend two recent books that focus on high technology investment: *High Tech: How to Find and Profit from Today's New Superstocks* by Albert Toney and Thomas Tilling (Simon and Schuster, 1983) and *High Tech Investing* by Roger W. Bridwell (Times Books, 1983).

I also recommend that you look for companies that have a history of splitting their shares. If you had 100 shares of a stock in a company that announced a three-for-one split, you would now have 300 shares. If the original value of your stock was $30 a share, your shares would have had a $3,000 market value. After the three-for-one split, your stocks would still have a $3,000 market value, but the value of each share would be reduced to $10. Statistically, however, a stock with a history of splitting has a 2½ times greater probability for overall increase in value than stocks that do not split. (Stock splits are discussed in further detail in Life Phase 3.)

N.B. If you had invested $2,000 every year from the age of 18 in an IRA account earning 12 percent per year, you would by the end of this life phase have accumulated $109,499.40.

LIFE PHASE 3: 35–40

> *"So what if Christopher Columbus discovered America? Queen Isabella gave him the money."*

If you are between 35 and 40, you probably feel you have many years of experience behind you. You have undoubtedly made mistakes, but possibly have been able to turn them to your advantage. You most likely are stable, know what you want, and may be ready to branch out. Perhaps that's why a second or side business often evolves during this period. I have often heard women in this phase, myself included, say they really feel that they have reached adulthood. Often you consult an attorney for the first time in reference to estate planning.

This particular phase is the shortest of all the cycles. Because it builds on the experiences of the two earlier phases, it is one in which there are fewer problem areas. Therefore, you should take advantage of what you have already learned and enter confidently into this one. It is the time to prepare for the next life phase which, in my opinion, is the time when the real living is done.

ADD VENTURE

During this phase you should become more aware of venture-capital opportunities. If you live in a community in which new ideas and opportunities are continually arising, this may enable you not only to make a killing in the investment area, but possibly also to pull off a major coup in your own career. Companies that are starting up, expanding or spinning off from other successful companies can offer you more than one method of capitalizing on their success. The first method would be to participate with a few thousand dollars in the initial capital formation of a company. But it could be many years before you ever see a return on your investment—and you also might lose all your money. Any time you invest in a start-up company, which is a venture-capital investment, you should more than likely be dealing with "kiss-off" money. The success ratio of such enterprises is not extremely high, but when they do succeed, they can be very profitable.

One of the key areas to investigate when analyzing a venture-capital investment is management and its experience. If you do not know the pros and cons and realistic potential of a particular company, at least make sure that the people who are running it are knowledgeable and sophisticated in business. Make sure also that they have the financial background to carry themselves if they cannot withdraw salary or expenses during the company's aggressive growth phase. You don't want to lose top management. You want to make sure there are sufficient dollars there. In addition, before placing your funds into any venture-capital business opportunity, make sure you consult either a Certified Public Accountant knowledgeable in the workings of this area, or a professional in the industry who can give you a black-and-white analysis of the prospects of such a venture.

STOCK UP

Another method of participating in the growth of new companies is through stock options. As companies are put together, officers, middle management and workers are hired. Often a company will offer these employees stock options. These stock options differ entirely from the ones discussed in previous sections under puts and calls. These options only relate to the stock of the company an employee works for. They are used as an inducement or a sweetener to attract talented people. Any time a company is putting a deal together or trying to entice new people to become part of its team, it helps to hang carrots out there. If the company is successful, it will sell stock in the public market and the options could have significant value. If, on the other hand, the company is not successful, or if it never goes to the public market, the options have little value.

Basically a stock option allows you to acquire the stock of the company at below market rates. If you join the company at the very beginning, the cost of the stocks could be as low as a few cents each. On the other hand, if you're working for a company that has been around for several years and has had stock traded on the open market, you may find that the options granted at employment may actually be in excess of the current market value of the stock. How does this happen? It really means that the stock has fluctuated. Your option may state that you can acquire shares at $20 each. At the time the option was granted the stock might have been selling for $30. But what goes up can also come down, and during a bad market or bad reporting period for your industry or company, the stock can decline below your option price. If this should happen, it is highly improbable that you would exercise the option and guarantee yourself a loss. After all, why pay more for something when you can buy it on the open market for fewer dollars?

A client of mine started a training school for chefs as a business, and later sold to a major corporation. Part of the package included her participation with the new corporation in the development and expansion of other schools, as well as stock options in the acquiring company. When the sale of her company was completed, the options she received really did not have any value. At the time they were granted, the open market price of the stock was actually below the option price, and to top this, the options had strings attached. They could not be exercised for at least a year. So to her, at that time, they were really worthless, but as the year wore on, the stock market started behaving quite well, and, in fact, the stock of the corporation appreciated significantly so that its open-market value was in excess of her exercise price. This meant that, if the stock maintained its value, after a year she could have the company deliver the shares of stock to her and she, in turn, would pay the stated option, or exercise, price. She would have the choice at that time either to sell the stocks on the open market or to hold them. And, even though the market price was in excess of her exercise price on the option, she did not have to exercise it after the year was up. She could wait several years before doing so. According to her contract, it was really up to her, after the initial holding period was up, to choose when to take the stock and do with it what she wished.

Options such as the ones described above are also known as incentive stock options, or ISOp. When an employee is initially granted stock options, there are no tax consequences until he or she actually exercises the options to acquire the stock. As a rule, exercising an ISOp will result in taxation at long-term capital-gain rates whereby 40 percent of the stock's increased value is taxable when the stock is sold. There is, however, an exception, an item called the alternative minimum tax. This particular tax is based on what is called alternative minimum taxable income. Alternative minimum taxable income is a taxpayer's gross income for the year, reduced by total deductions for the year including those exemptions and itemized deductions *not* reduced by the zero bracket amount ($2,300 filing single, $3,400 filing joint return). If the taxpayer does not itemize, then exemptions and the zero bracket amount are used in the calculation. If you receive incentive stock options, make sure you are working with a competent tax adviser. The rules are complicated and unclear in many areas. The alternative minimum tax could very well place you in the 50 percent tax bracket (or higher) because some of the deductions normally allowed under regular tax reporting requirements may actually be disallowed when the alternative minimum tax is taken into consideration. Before you exercise any option, make sure you talk to your tax adviser and learn the overall consequences.

In the Santa Clara Valley in Northern California, also known as Silicon Valley, there are a great number of new and existing technology companies. These companies employ many people who make $35,000-plus a year and who had the foresight to join the company and acquire the stocks early on. Some of this stock has made them millionaires overnight. If you find yourself in this situation, it may make a great deal of practical and financial sense to sell a portion of your shares, even though you will incur a tax consequence. Why? As in the example of an option stock that was obtained at the time the stock was high but declined because of varying market factors, your stock could also decline. You might, for example, work for a company whose cash is tied up in expansion, research and development. The company might, therefore, give you dividends in the form of more stock, rather than cash. In Silicon Valley the practice of giving dividends in the company's stock versus cash dividends is common in young companies. And if you were to look at the fluctuations of their stock prices over the last decade, you would see that some of these stocks had had one or more splits. If you had 1,000 shares of a company that elected to have a four-to-one split, it would mean that for every share you had, you would now have four. When a stock splits four for one it doesn't mean that you automatically have four times the value at the time of the split. For example, let's say that we have 1,000 shares of stock and the stock has appreciated to $50 a share, for a total value of $50,000. Management might meet and decide they will give a four-to-one split. This means that instead of having 1,000 shares, you now have 4,000, but the individual value per share is $12.50 versus the previous $50. Your overall market values are still the same but you now have more shares.

Why would a company do this? Well, often it is psychological. Many people can't afford to buy 100 shares of stock for $50 a share, or the total purchase price of $5,000 plus commission. But they may be able to buy 100 shares at $12.50 a share or a total price of $1,250 plus commission. As more and more people can afford to purchase the stock, and there is a general thrust toward buying and accumulating, it will probably move up in value. I have repeatedly seen people who bought 1,000 shares of a stock at $1 a share several years ago accumulate as many as 20,000 shares from various stock dividends and/or splits. And I am never surprised when these shares continue to appreciate to as high a per share level as they had enjoyed in previous years. If you had 20,000 shares of a $50 stock, they would have a market value of $1,000,000. If the company splits the stock again, you will still have a million dollars in stock, but you will also have many more shares.

The two negatives here are: (1) you have all your eggs in one basket, which is never a good position to be in; and (2) you now hold such a sizable portion that, if you elected to sell 5,000 or 10,000 shares at one time, you could actually, because of the size of your sale, force the price down. It is probably not a good idea to have many shares in a company that has only a few thousand shareholders. Your selling could cause a decline and, if you decide to purchase, could actually force the price up a little bit. Be careful here. When you win, it is absolutely wonderful; but when you lose it is not so terrific.

DO YOUR OWN THING?

I often find that, during this phase, the stability and your accumulated experience encourage you to think about starting your own venture. If this is the case, it is absolutely essential to begin to build up cash. My experience has also shown that when someone has written up a business plan for a company and estimated the amount of capital needed to start, it is wise to double it at least. Until you are actually "at the helm" of a business, you will probably not realize what the overall costs are. Often, as much as 40 to 50 percent can be hidden in items and expenses that you are not aware of and do not realize are essential to the ongoing operation of a small business. Before you contemplate starting your own business, it's advisable to have a few years experience in your chosen field. Many women I consult within my financial-planning practice say that they would like to go into business. Often, however, I find that they haven't really identified which business they want to go into, and do not have the necessary experience to support their new venture. Owning your own company can be great, but there are always dues that must be paid in advance.

Often, these can be enough to discourage you from ever wanting to become an entrepreneur. On the other hand, they could be just the incentive to make you actually take that step. And you will have to pay your dues. When I refer to "paying your dues," I literally mean having the experience that only the school of hard knocks brings. Behind every successful person there are failures—some spoken about, some unspoken. Paying your dues can be anything from negotiating lines of credit, hiring and firing, getting rid of too much supply (or inventory) when the demand no longer exists, to having to postpone paying your monthly obligations because you must meet your payroll. Besides paying your dues in the respective industry you want to enter, you ought also to get some basic background information. One of the sources is in your own backyard (i.e., your community college). Most community colleges offer classes and programs for the person who wants to begin a business or expand a hobby into a profitable business. The instructors are often professionals who have themselves become entrepreneurs. They can share with you the nightmares as well as the joys. They can often refer you to accountants and attorneys who specialize in small businesses. After all, the needs of a very small business are often quite different from those of IBM. When the senior management of IBM walks into a banker's office, they get the bank's attention immediately. Without preexisting banking relationships, if you walked into a banker's office to discuss your business venture, you might be met with a yawn.

It is also a good idea to get some experience in simple bookkeeping and/or accounting methods. I have seen some real snafus over the years, where women have started small businesses now grown into interesting moneymakers, but have not thought to separate their business accounts from their family accounts. If you are going to start your own business, it is important to run it that way. Segregate everything: have separate checking accounts, a separate business account, a separate name—or at least one that can be designated as a business name, as distinct from the one you use daily. If you sustain any losses or expenses in the first two years, no matter the size, you more than likely have a legitimate tax deduction. If you intend to take these deductions as write-offs on your tax return, it is essential to have the appropriate records. The IRS recognizes that start-up companies—incorporated or not—incur expenses and losses before realizing a profit. Not every business is able to show profits immediately. I should caution you, though, that the IRS's patience will last only so long when you take these deductions. They have clearly defined rules about hobby-related businesses. If your business continues to show a loss or your expenses exceed your revenues after three years, you should consider closing it down and moving in another direction. The IRS would like to see a business turn a profit for at least two out of five years.

If you should elect to incorporate your company, keep in mind that there are pros and cons. One of the pros is the possibility of fringe benefits. For example, you could increase payments to a pension fund and actually control such increases. Also, a corporation may retain a reasonable amount of earnings which eventually can be taken out in the form of capital gain when the corporation is sold. Generally, corporations are taxed at a lower level than individuals. In addition, many expenses are considered normal corporate obligations, and learning about these will permit you to expense these items against the corporation. The corporation can pay for the majority of your travel and entertainment expenses, automobile expenses, dues and subscriptions, to mention just a few areas. A corporation with as little as $25,000 in earnings will be taxed at 15 percent. Compare this with your taxes as a single person with the same $25,000 taxable income—you would be in a 32 percent tax bracket.

A corporation can also act as a shield against lawsuits. If you are sued as an officer of the corporation or as a representative of the corporation, the corporation will more than likely incur the necessary expenses in defending the litigation. If you decide at some point to sell your company and the corporation has already issued stock (assuming you have annually completed income and expense statements), as well as balance sheets, a price for the corporation can be determined. A corporation's balance sheet is similar to your net worth statement and its income and expense statement will be similar to your cash flow statement.

There are also disadvantages in incorporating. One is that when you, as an individual and employee, contribute to social security, and the corporation contributes an equal amount on your behalf, the IRS can, if it wants to become sticky, question the amount paid to the owner/employee. If it determines compensation is excessive, it could reclassify some of the income as dividends. Keep in mind that dividends are not deductible for a corporation. Therefore, the corporation is taxed on the dividend and you will also be taxed on the same dividend. Another disadvantage is that the fringe-benefit program, such as medical insurance the company pays for, must be nondiscriminatory. This means that the goodies you enjoy must be shared by all. Of course, if you are the only person in the corporation, this doesn't create a problem. And if you dislike paperwork, remember that there are state and local income taxes, franchise and other taxes on corporations that require a regular filing of returns, reports and other documents. If doing paperwork is one of your weak points, make sure to hire someone competent to take care of those needs.

Normally the paperwork for a corporation is done through a qualified attorney. There are also several do-it-yourself books available at your local bookstore. But this is one area in which it is better to be safe than sorry. Get a professional to help with the process.

Incorporation, as a rule, is an accounting decision. Make sure to confer with your tax adviser or CPA. The IRS is looking increasingly closely at potential abuses in the corporation area, and it certainly makes sense to avoid any pitfalls.

My firm had a client who "did her own thing." She loved animals—all kinds of animals. When she first came to us for advice on financial planning, she had a significant amount of cash. She invested $10,000 of her funds in a partnership involving the restoration of historical buildings. The remainder she wanted to allocate to the development of her business, which involved the training and care of unusual animals. We continued to touch base with her and keep track of her business. She always said things were great and she loved being able to work in an environment that gave her so much pleasure. During this time she brought in a business partner, and the two of them bought an elephant. The objective was, of course, to take care of the elephant; but they also intended to rent him out for parties and parades. Everything seemed to go well, but then the partners had a falling-out and the partner wanted to retrieve her money. Well, the court settled it and gave our client custody of the elephant. Now, for those of you who have never raised an elephant, I assure you its upkeep is not cheap. This particular elephant's room and board ran to $1,500 a month. Also, when he was transported to his various engagements, his trailer only got about two miles to the gallon. After all, an elephant is no lightweight, and a truck to haul him wasn't cheap. But my client loved the elephant and wanted to do all she could to make sure he was well fed and cared for.

She approached us about selling her interest in the restoration partnership because she needed additional funds. We knew she had had some problems because we had followed the recent custody settlement in the newspapers. I told her I had mixed emotions. I could certainly understand why she wanted to take care of the elephant and why she needed the funds and I wanted to do everything that I could to help her. My more practical side said it was a mistake, because I suspected that the $10,000 she would receive from the restoration business would quickly disappear into elephant maintenance, and it was her only source of investment and/or cash at this point. My humane instincts prevailed and we were able to replace her in the restoration partnership and get her money back. Needless to say, she ultimately had to sell her elephant friend anyway because she couldn't meet her bills.

Any bottom lines here? Well, it is not good business sense to become emotionally involved with your investments or your businesses. You are often so up to your ears in a day-to-day operation that you can't see what's happening. If you are going to start your own business, do it on a sound basis. If you are doing it as a humanitarian contribution, make sure you recognize it as such and that the amount of time and money and/or asset contribution is at least deductible on your taxes. Remember, your time is not.

A SHELTER FOR A SHELTER

Tax shelters begin to rear their heads during this phase and through the next. Investments and contributions to an IRA are one form of tax shelter. Another is the purchase of a home, a second home, or a piece of rental property.

If you haven't bought a house yet, this is a good time to do so—particularly from a tax standpoint. If you are anticipating purchasing a home as a sole investment and your intent is to rent it out, then it is important to analyze the tax situation.

I discussed the tax benefits and costs of owning your own personal residence in the preceding life phase. Now let's say you have done some scouting around and have found a piece of real estate for investment purposes in the $100,000 price range. Perhaps you have been able to save a few dollars and have developed what is called an unsecured line of credit at your financial institution. An unsecured line of credit is one in which you borrow money without putting up any collateral. In order to qualify for a line of credit, it is important for you to know what your credit rating is, to have a history of paying your bills on time, to demonstrate that you have a sufficient income in case you ever elect to withdraw any funds that have been granted on the line of credit, and that you have a steady job. When applying for a credit line, it really makes sense for you to know who your banker is and for him or her already to be aware of your creditworthiness. This, then, will enable you to pull down or withdraw funds merely by making a phone call, or in some cases, writing a check. Or you may have a partner or partners who will each put up the necessary funds and supply a reserve in case of negative cash flow so that you can go ahead and secure this as an investment. Whatever the case may be, it is essential to be aware of all the tax ramifications.

Let's assume you have placed $20,000 down and now have a mortgage in the amount of $80,000 at an interest rate of 14 percent. For illustration purposes, I am going to assume that you are married, that you have a gross income of $45,000 and, because of other allowable deductions, have combined excess deductions of $8,000, personal exemptions of $3,000, and an IRA contribution of $4,000, reducing your taxable income as a married individual to $30,000, or an overall tax obligation of $5,064 in 1983.

The cost of the rental property will be substantial, but a great deal of it will be offset by income. For example, interest on your $80,000 loan at 14 percent will be a minimum of $11,200 a year. For illustration purposes, I will assume $11,200 for interest payments, $1,500 for real estate taxes and insurance, $300 in management costs and $700 in miscellaneous expenses, totalling gross expenses of $13,700. In addition, the tax act of 1981 allowed for residential-property depreciation to be taken over a 15-year period versus the more traditional 30-year term. Of course there are ways to accelerate that amount, but I will use the straight 15-year write-off on a value of 75 percent of our original cost, or $75,000. What this means is that you will be allowed to take an additional deduction for depreciation purposes of $5,000 a year. Traditionally, 75 percent of a property's original value is attributable to the building, 25 percent to land.

Of course you certainly hope that the property you just purchased will not depreciate but appreciate. Depreciation is merely an accounting tool that is tied into what the IRS allows as a useful life. As you may be aware, there are several very sturdy houses across the country that are hundreds of years old.

With expenses and depreciation included, you now have total expenses, both "hard" and "soft", of $18,700 (13,700 + 5,000 = 18,700). Hard expenses are those in which you actually pay real dollars—interest payments, repairs and maintenance, taxes, insurance and other related costs. Soft expenses are those for which the IRS allows you a tax deduction but for which you do not incur any real dollars expended. Since depreciation is an accounting adjustment (you really do not want your property to depreciate), it is identified as a soft expense. You will now subtract your revenues, assuming that you are able to rent out the house for $700 a month, or a total of $8,400 a year. This leaves you with $10,300 (18,700 − 8,400 = 10,300) to be deducted from your gross income. With an original income of $45,000 and various adjustments, your taxable income became $30,000. With the additional $10,300 in deductions, you would now have a taxable income of $19,700. In checking the tax tables you will find not only that your taxes have been reduced substantially, but that you are now in a 19 percent tax bracket, which is really fairly low. Your overall tax obligation will be $2,549, or a savings of $2,515 ($209 per month) over your tax obligation prior to the purchase of the house.

Because our example was not in a substantial tax bracket, the overall tax savings are not really impressive considering the negative cash flow necessary for this particular piece of property. Recall that you had a depreciation figure of $5,000 and a write-off after revenues of $10,300. Your actual hard cost on this particular investment was $5,300 a year, or $441 a month. Taking into consideration your $209-a-month tax savings, your out-of-pocket expenses will be $232 per month, or $2,784 per year. Your primary question should be "Will this house or investment appreciate at least $2,800 on an annual basis?" If you do not believe it will appreciate at that level, then you have no business participating in something that will create such a negative cash flow.

By this stage it is possible for a married couple to be earning $60,000 and a single person $41,500. Of course, if your earnings do fall short of these amounts, don't despair—you still have many productive years ahead of you. This level of taxable income will bring you very close to the 50 percent tax bracket, which is usually a requirement for participation in tax shelters that have a high degree of risk (this is discussed in the next section). If you check the tax tables, you will note that these figures are somewhat below the 50 percent level, but because so many states have a form of income tax, I have assumed that the majority of married couples who both work will fall into this area. Also note that I have used mortgage rates that are considered high. If you are able to obtain an interest rate lower than my 14 percent example, then the negative cash flow will be reduced.

GRAB A PARTNER!

In addition to personal ownership of rental property, there are other investment forms that offer tax shelter. I refer to the "limited partnership."

The most common limited partnerships are in the areas of real estate, oil and gas, and research and development. Limited partnerships are also available in almost any investment vehicle you can imagine, but if you participate in one, it will more than likely be one of the three mentioned above.

Probably the most common real estate limited partnership involves either a commercial building, an apartment house, a shopping center or a combination of these properties. And it could require anywhere from a few hundred thousand dollars capital to megamillions. In any case, tax benefits will flow through the venture to the limited partners. A real estate limited partnership will offer tax write-offs of anywhere from 15 percent up to 25 percent per year the first few years, and as a rule will involve much less risk than a research and development or oil and gas investment.

The term "tax write-off" is one that is often thrown at a first-time investor. Tax write-offs are similar to tax deductions and they come in all shapes and sizes. You may recall that we talked about depreciation in purchasing a rental property. Well, depreciation is a major write-off when you invest in areas such as real estate and equipment. The IRS allows special deductions to take into consideration the wear and tear on property or equipment. Additional tax write-offs are generated from ongoing expenses and the cost of management.

If someone tells you that $5,000 placed in a particular investment will generate a 20 percent write-off, this means that you will have a $1,000 loss to report against your taxable income at year's end. These write-offs will be passed through to the individual partner's files when the partnership files its tax return, which, by the way, is not due until an individual's tax return is due on April 15 of the following year. This leads to frustration because often the person who is managing a particular partnership does not complete the returns until March or even early April. If you have not received the appropriate form, which is called a K-1, prior to April 1, the filing of your taxes may be delayed. If you are using a tax preparer who in turn uses computers, it is highly probable that he will request an extension from the IRS for the filing of your taxes. (The computer-service companies that assist in producing completed returns usually have cutoff deadlines in early April.) On the other hand, if your returns are being done by hand and not with the assistance of the computers *and* you have completed and totaled other sections of the tax return, you should be able to wait up to the last day for filing. At this point, completing the return is merely a matter of addition and subtraction to obtain your taxable income, and finding the total tax due. In some cases that may be all right with you, but in others it becomes frustrating—especially when you are entitled to a refund.

In a limited partnership, all losses and gains are passed through to each of the limited partners on a pro rata basis proportionate to the size of their investment; therefore the partnership as a whole does not pay taxes on any income that is earned, nor does it take advantage of any losses incurred. Those will be passed along to each of the partners.

Real estate is often attractive to those of you who are conservative in your investment profile or risk-taking ability, but even conservative investments may provide a handsome bonus via a profit on sale. After the initial excitement wears off, however, you may come to realize that you have substantial taxes due as a result. You may decide to take a portion of that bonus and place it into an oil-and-gas-drilling partnership in order to obtain tax deductions to offset part of the gain. The write-offs you will receive will be greatest in the first year, as much as 80 percent of your original investment. For example, oil and gas demands that equipment be placed and serviced. Not only will you get depreciation on the equipment, but you will also get an investment tax credit. (Tax credits actually reduce the amount of tax you owe and are explained in "Tax Fax.") In addition, if the venture is successful, part of the cash flow that you will eventually receive could be tax sheltered. This is due to the depletion allowance. The depletion allowance is an annual tax deduction that the IRS allows an owner of a mineral property for the actual, or even theoretical, decline in value of the property due to the actual extraction of the mineral.

If you elect to participate in an oil-and-gas program, be it exploration or development, there can be drawbacks. For example, before you start to count your profits, be aware that oil and gas can be elusive. While there are proponents of the oil-shortage theory, there are others who believe no shortage exists. Regardless of your position on the issue, oil in general has increased in cost, thus yielding a higher price per barrel. However, the odds of striking a potentially exploitable reserve or find are not terrific. And if the venture is totally unsuccessful in finding oil or gas, you will lose your investment and will have to be satisfied with the mere tax savings through the write-off of losses. You may finally decide that the risk is worthwhile because a substantial portion of the amount you invested would have gone to the government in the form of taxes.

If you wish to have the deductions that oil and gas can offer you but not as risky a situation as an exploratory program, you can participate in a developmental or developmental-and-exploratory program. In a developmental program, the operator leases already proven fields. Therefore, you will not be engaging in exploratory or "wildcat" drilling. A developmental program often yields an ongoing annual income of anywhere from 10 percent to 15 percent, which as a rule is covered by the depletion allowance and is, therefore, exempt from taxation and will be tax sheltered. You will also receive write-offs that could be as high as 80 percent of your initial investment. On the other hand, if you are a greater risk-taker, you can invest in wildcatting. As I mentioned, the risk is substantially higher. You may be totally unsuccessful and end up with only a tax write-off. On the other hand, if the venture is successful and actually locates a major reserve, you could make a bundle.

Research-and-development projects will increasingly be offered by the major brokerage houses. Research and development can involve many things, from solar energy to a totally new technology. Often, when people talk research and development, they are referring to the new technology companies that continue to sprout. These new technologies include research-and-development opportunities in such areas as gene splicing, robotics, artificial intelligence, and medical advances like new X-ray and diagnostic techniques. Believe it or not, research and development actually entails a higher risk than oil and gas, and, as a rule, the first year you will end up writing off the entire amount of your investment. For example, if you invest $5,000 in a research-and-development program, you will more than likely receive a $5,000 write-off. If you are in a 50 percent bracket, that means your actual tax savings will be $2,500 and therefore your real "at risk" will also be $2,500. If you pay state taxes, then your actual "at risk" amount will be reduced even further due to the reduction in your state tax obligation.

Another common tax shelter area is equipment leasing. Equipment leasing is attractive not only because of the depreciation on the equipment itself, but also because of the substantial investment tax credit involved. This particular credit is one of the primary reasons most investors enter into an equipment-leasing program. Because of the various combinations of deductions, depreciation and credits, you may often get a write-off that is, in hard dollars, in excess of the amount you put in.

One phenomenon you want to be aware of is "phantom income." It is an interesting term and graphically descriptive. In this case, it means income that you actually generated, but because of other obligations, didn't receive. You may think that does not pose a problem. But, in actuality it does because, as mentioned earlier, all income earned by a partnership is declared to limited partners, just as all expenses incurred are declared to the limited partners.

Phantom income consists of revenues from a particular venture that produces taxable income in excess of the cash generated to each of the investors. For example, let's say that you are one of several partners in an oil well and as a group are able to obtain a bank loan that would allow you to complete the well and begin pumping. Let's also say that the terms of the loan agreement require regular monthly interest payments as well as quarterly payments on the principal. Let's also assume that your well is producing revenues that meet the partnership obligations. You have enough money to pay the interest payments and you are going to have enough money to pay down your contractual obligation on the principal. The year comes to a close, the partnership completes its return, and it forwards to you a copy of your K-1. On it, to your surprise, is taxable income. You may be wondering how this happened when you actually received no checks from your partnership. Well, it is not too complicated. Indeed, you did have revenues, and you did have expenses. But the funds the partnership paid on the principal amount of the loan were nondeductible. And the revenues that went toward the reduction of the loan, in fact, became taxable income to you even though you did not receive them. Hence, the term "phantom income."

There are innumerable other tax shelters—coal and other energy-related investments, movies, records, art, books, farming, cattle and timber, to mention just a few. If you can think of something that has value, there is probably an investment or tax shelter out there that encompasses it. You will probably do yourself a favor if you stick to the first four I mentioned: real estate, research and development, equipment leasing and oil and gas. You have a higher probability of making money here than in the other areas unless you have a great deal of knowledge about the project and industry in question.

One of the most improbable tax-shelter investments in the past few years involved the recovery of treasure from two Spanish ships sunk off the coast of Florida in the year 1622. A partnership was formed to salvage this treasure and was actually successful. When the divers began bringing up bags of gold and silver, both the state of Florida and the Federal Government attempted to claim it all. The managers of the salvation operation fought a long legal battle which eventually led to the Supreme Court. The court, in 1982, stated that it was a finders-keepers situation. In that particular instance the good guys won, which means the limited partners. They all received a significant return that exceeded their original investment.

Unusual tax shelters (also known as exotic tax shelters) do not always work out to an investor's benefit, however. In the same year that the treasure find was being heralded in the financial communities on the East Coast, the West Coast was also grabbing headlines. At that time there was a senatorial election. During political elections, the various candidates' financial positions are openly reported, as well as their tax liabilities. One particular candidate paid minimum taxes, primarily due to his investment in a tax shelter whose major purpose was to develop an alternative fuel. The source of the fuel? Why, cow manure. And, in fact, the headlines in the newspapers stated that the mayor (he had not been elected senator as yet) eliminated taxes by investing in cow dung. Apparently he didn't make any money, although he publically stood by the validity of and rationale behind his "investment."

How can you go wrong with a tax shelter? First of all, you

might jump into one knowing absolutely nothing about the subject and being totally unqualified to evalute the offering competently. If you find yourself in this category, and you haven't received a professional evaluation as to the feasibility of the deal, the odds are against you from day one. You might also become blinded by the promise of spectacular tax deductions and at the same time ignore the economic considerations of the proposed investment. Finally, you might invest in a business that is absolutely alien to you and/or put your money into the hands of people you know very little about. These are common mistakes that could cause you either to miss out on a good opportunity or to get badly burned.

It is important to get adequate and professional financial-planning counsel when you are looking at tax shelters and limited partnerships. I live in an area dominated by high-tech firms. Most people who work in these companies earn impressive salaries and are very bright. Fortunately they are sane most of the year, but something happens to them in November and December and their minds turn to mush when they think about the taxes they have had withheld and/or are going to have to pay within the next few months. As a result, they get involved in the most unusual and absurd deals.

One of my clients thought the traditional shelters too boring. I mean, after all, they have been around for years and years. He decided he wanted to acquire something a bit more jazzy. During preceding years, he had invested in a plane, a locomotive, solar energy, windmills, records of a top country singer, and a Treasury bill future. Well, the locomotive didn't work, and the jury is still out on the plane; the windmills appear to be having blade problems, although the utility company said it would buy whatever energy was produced; the tax credits he was to receive for his investment in the solar energy project turned out to be a total scam, as the promotors of the project had sold the same component over and over again but to different people, thus disallowing tax credits for all participants. The Treasury bill futures had been disallowed by the IRS in previous years, as a sham method of deferring income. (Interesting to note that when this person went into the Treasury futures, the IRS position was already known to most of the financial community.)

What happened to my client? Well, the railroad project generated a good deal of the phantom income I just discussed, and he had to declare a handsome income, even though he didn't receive any revenues. This was an extremely hard concept for him to grasp but, unfortunately, it was not thoroughly explained when he originally entered into the transaction. He won't make any money from the windmill; the Treasury straddles will all be declared as ordinary income, and the tax write-offs and investment tax credits thought to be valid in the solar deal will be totally disallowed and the IRS will assess penalties at a substantial rate for the prior years. I asked him how he had heard about some of these so-called "investment opportunities" and he said that he had seen ads in the November issues of various newspapers.

The moral of the story is to read the ads and be aware of what the new gimmicks are—but don't call the phone numbers listed. Stick with people who have been in the investment- and financial-counseling businesses for at least five years. An individual will not be able to offer tax shelters year after year and survive unless those shelters are also investments, make their clients money, and meet IRS standards. And remember, even the pros can be wrong. The economies of 1981 and 1982 turned many a valid and reasonable investment/tax shelter to mush.

If you anticipate participating in any of the areas we have just discussed during this life phase, make sure you adjust all your withholding to reflect your total projected tax obligation for the year. If you plan on investing in a specific amount at some time in the year, go ahead and adjust your withholding now to reflect your tax savings.

One last word on participating in tax shelters: *Always look at the worst case—if you lose your money, how does it affect you financially and emotionally?*

WHERE THERE'S A WILL, THERE'S A WAY

I came across this column several years ago, saved it, and now pass it on to you for what it's worth. It has been repeated numerous times in Ann Landers' syndicated column:

> DEAR READERS: If you want to do something nice for your family, get your affairs in order.

I came across this gem in *The Survivors,* a splendid magazine for widowed people. I obtained permission from the author, Judge Sam Harrod III, of Eureka, Illinois, to reprint it.

IF YOU DON'T HAVE A WILL
YOUR STATE HAS ONE FOR YOU

The Statutory "Will" of John Doe.

I, John Doe, make this my "will," by failing to have a will of my own choice prepared by my attorney.

1. I give one-half of all my property, both personal and real estate, to my CHILDREN, and the remaining one-half to my WIFE.
2. I appoint my WIFE as Guardian of my CHILDREN, if she survives me; but as a safeguard, I require that:
   a. my WIFE make written account every year to Probate Court, explaining how and why she spent money necessary for proper care of our CHILDREN;
   b. my WIFE file a performance BOND, with sureties, to be approved by Probate Court, to guarantee she will properly handle our children's money;
   c. when our CHILDREN become adults, my WIFE must file a complete, itemized, written account of everything she has done with our children's money;
   d. when our SON and DAUGHTER become age 18, they can do whatever they please with their share of my estate;
   e. no one, including my WIFE, shall have the right to question how our CHILDREN spend their shares.
3. If my WIFE does not survive me, or dies while any of our CHILDREN are minors, I do not nominate a Guardian of our CHILDREN, but hope relatives and friends may mutually agree on the one, and if they cannot agree, the Probate Court can appoint any Guardian it likes, including a stranger.
4. I do not appoint an Executor of my estate, and hope the Probate Court appoints someone I would approve.
5. If my WIFE remarries, the next husband:
   a. shall receive one-third of all my WIFE'S property;
   b. need not spend any of his share on our CHILDREN, even if they need support; and
   c. can give his share to anyone he chooses, without giving a penny to our CHILDREN.
6. I do not care to learn whether there are ways to lower my death

> taxes, and know as much as possible will go to the Government, instead of my WIFE and our CHILDREN.
>
> In witness whereof, I have completely failed to make a different will of my own choice with the advice of my attorney, because I really did not care to go to all that bother, and I adopt this, by default, as my "will."
>
> (no signature required)

As this stage progresses, and assets build up, you must begin to consider that you are mortal. Rarely do I see people under 40 with a will that is properly put together, and I do believe that wills should be written as soon as you begin to acquire any assets.

The average woman who works spends over 10,000 days making money. It seems shortsighted not to spend one day making a determination of where our assets should go when we die. Unfortunately, over 80 percent of those who will die today leave no will. When you leave no will, the state in which you reside will step in and assist you in determining exactly where the assets will go.

One of my clients was in her late 30s when her husband died of a heart attack. He was only in his early 40s. It was just one of those things that happen without warning. They had three children. Because there was no will, the courts decreed that she was to get one third of his estate and the children two thirds. And because the children were all minors, she would have to get approval from a judge in order to sell some of the assets of which the children were part owners, such as the second car. She had actually to prove to the judge that the selling of a car would not reduce the amount of the children's estate. In addition, there was a significant amount of cash from life-insurance proceeds, as well as a pension from his employer. The kids actually came out with more money than she did. Is this what you want for your spouse? Probably not. But most of us don't think about it until it is too late.

Wills are important and they should be written now. If you don't have an attorney, or you are shopping around for one, by all means sit down and make a holographic will until you can get a formal document drawn up. A holographic will is merely one which is handwritten by you. In that will, you will recite who you are, your permanent address (and, if applicable, any secondary addresses), your place of birth and your marital status. Your spouse should do the same. If there are any previous marriages, make sure that information is included, and include the names and addresses of your immediate family, which would include your sons, daughters and parents. If you have ever created a trust, make sure you indicate the appropriate title for that. If you are entitled to any pensions, profit sharing or other things, include that information. If you have any insurance policies, make sure you include the numbers, the beneficiaries—both primary and secondary—and, if you are covered under any group policies, have a complete list of all your assets, as well as current market value. If they were made out under a name different from your present one, make sure that it is specified. If you have any safe deposit boxes, state where they are located. You should indicate the name and address of an executor or executrix of your estate, as well as a guardian if you have children under the age of 18, and a trustee if that is appropriate for the management of your assets until your beneficiaries reach the age in which the actual distribution will be granted. If you have any stocks, bonds, limited partnerships, IRA accounts, passbooks, time deposits or any other marketable assets, make sure they are included, as well as the location of your previous tax returns for the last three years. Finally, make sure that you spell out exactly what your plans are for your beneficiaries. Then sign it.

This document acts only as a temporary instrument. It is much preferred that you have an attorney who specializes in estates look it over and make whatever changes are necessary. If you have already gone over the location of your various assets and listed them, this should reduce your bill substantially. Remember, changes can be made as the circumstances warrant, and an addendum, or codicil, can be added to your will. If you have made any previous wills, state in your new one that it revokes any previous testaments. In addition, to be safe, destroy all copies of any old wills. If you have out-of-state assets, make sure you deal with them accordingly. Some states will demand that you go through a separate probate in their respective state. Liquidate your assets and bring them into the current state in which you reside and/or set up a separate will that covers that respective state's laws.

If you have any personal belongings of sentimental value, do yourself a favor and attach to the will a letter of intent that states exactly who gets which belongings. If the majority of your property is divided by percentage, the items covered in your letter of intent will be excluded from a distribution of the primary estate.

You are probably wondering, if you have done all this, why you would need an attorney. For two reasons: First, the tax laws that deal with estate and trusts keep changing. Unless you are in the legal profession, it is highly unlikely that you are going to be up-to-date on the current laws. Second, there are often inaccuracies in your wording, which could actually change your intent.

When should you update your will? One time to do so is when you move from one state to another. It is important to check whether the probate laws are comparable in your new state. If you have moved, play it safe and have a local attorney check your will. Another reason to update your will would be that the executor you have selected is no longer acceptable or has died; in this case you should name a new one. (It is often a good idea to choose an executor or executrix who is younger than you are.) In addition, if the number of children you have has increased or decreased, that should be noted in your will, and if your family size had increased with grandchildren and in-laws, you may desire to include them.

If the value of your estate has risen or substantially declined, it may make sense to look over once more the distribution you have previously stated. Or if you have disposed of any real property listed in your previous wills, you should readjust the document accordingly. I recommend an overhaul of your will approximately every three years. With the way our laws keep changing, as well as our own personal objectives, it makes sense. If you have a few changes, it is not necessary to have the whole will rewritten. It can be handled with a codicil. A codicil is merely an afterthought and is added on to the will and then initialed or signed separately.

You probably feel that assembling all those bits and pieces is a tedious and time-consuming chore. But you can be assured that it will be time well spent, should the unforeseeable occur. Do yourself a favor, as well as your heirs, and make sure you have this base covered.

MS. MISC.

During this phase you should continue contributing to the IRA, and, as in the two previous life phases, your choices for investment placement will more than likely be in the stock, mutual fund or limited partnership area. You still have many years before what is considered the normal retirement age, and therefore your investment objectives will probably be overall growth.

During this phase you should begin to build more and more liquidity. Your funds, as in prior phases, should be placed in instruments that are not only accessible but also offer you a reasonable and current market rate of return. With the recent changes in the tax law, remember that the maximum tax bracket any of us will reach at this time is 50 percent. Of course, there is no guarantee that Congress will not reverse previous laws.

At this time your relationship with a bank or several banks should be excellent. You should definitely be on a first-name basis with your banker, and, if you have been presenting him or her with an annual statement of your income and expenses and net worth, he or she should be able to respond very quickly when you have need for banking services.

WINDFALL!

Two years ago you were employed by a young start-up company which had an incentive stock option. The company's management philosophy was that even entry-level receptionists and stock clerks could participate if the company succeeded. When you went to work for the company, you were granted 300 shares that could be purchased at $4 a share after one year of employment. Your year has passed, and lo and behold, the company stock is trading on the market for $40 a share, giving your option a current market value of $12,000. You tell the company you are going to exercise your option and you need $1,200, which you don't have, to pay for the stock. In such a case, the company will probably lend you the money through its credit union. (If you don't have a credit union, most banks will lend you the necessary funds to exercise your option.) If your purpose is to sell within the year, the company may also withhold a percentage of the market value of the stock at the time you exercise your options for withholding tax purposes. Let us assume that you exercise your option, 20 percent of market value price, or $2,400, is withheld for tax purposes, sell the stock, and you immediately pay back the credit union for lending you the funds to purchase the original stock. After all this is sorted out, you have $8,400 to invest.

Stock Sale	$12,000
Tax Withheld	× .20
	−$2,400
Pay Back Credit Union	−$1,200
Net Proceeds	$ 8,400

This opens up a number of choices for placement of your funds. If you have not already purchased a home, this may be the time to do it. If you have a home and don't own other stock, consider purchasing those issues that are considered aggressive growths.

Technology stocks and/or discount bonds should be on top of your list. When you purchase bonds you are a creditor. This is the opposite of purchasing stock, which designates ownership. When bonds first come to the public market, they are originally offered in $1,000 denominations. This does not mean they will always trade or be valued at $1,000. To guarantee receiving the $1,000, you could wait until the bond matures. Normal bonds, such as those offered by a corporation, have a maturity range of anywhere from ten to 30 years.

The primary factor affecting a bond's price is the interest it pays. For example, if current interest rates are around 10 percent (I am referring to the prime rate), then that is the rate the issuing corporation would have to pay. Why would a corporation come to the general public market to borrow funds instead of going to the usual financial institutions? The answer is fairly simple. First of all, once the offering is made, the general public does not require the ongoing financial statements a banker would require of a customer. Second, the corporation is able to borrow funds for a much longer period of time than a bank would be willing to lend. Third, and most important, corporations are generally able to borrow from the public at rates lower than those charged by a bank.

When a bond trades at its original offering price, or matures, it is also known as trading "at par." There are two other methods in which it can trade, either at a discount or at a premium. When a bond trades at a premium, it means that the whole bond's value is actually in excess of what it will be when it matures, and what it was when it was initially offered. On the other hand, a discount bond is the opposite, trading for less than it was when originally offered, and less than it will be worth at maturity.

There are different forms of discount bonds—some are slightly discounted, others are deeply discounted. A slight discount would be merely below the par value. How can this happen? One important variable would be the interest market. For example, let's assume a bond was first sold to the public and carried an interest rate of 7 percent; current obtainable rates are in the area of 13 percent or 14 percent. The old bond would reflect the increased interest rate or yield by a reduction in its overall market value. As a rule, the general public is only willing to buy a bond that offers a return or yield comparable to other bonds that are currently available. The bond market merely reflects that philosophy.

There are, of course, exceptions. Some bonds are known as junk bonds. Junk bonds are also discounted bonds, but they have a special stigma attached. Junk bonds are notorious for being affiliated with companies that are having trouble. There is a possibility that the company will declare bankruptcy. If a bond can no longer make its semiannual interest payment (which is normally the rule in interest payments for bonds) then the issuing company holding the bond will declare bankruptcy. Bankruptcy is also known as Chapter 11. The fact that a company has filed for bankruptcy does not necessarily mean that its bonds are worthless and, in fact, some significant gains can be made in such situations.

Several years ago I can remember making a recommendation to a client of mine to purchase bonds in a company in California called Memorex Corporation. There was a general feeling throughout the financial community that Memorex would be filing for bankruptcy and that its major banker would not continue to loan funds to the company. In talking to a few of my clients, I discovered that the company not only paid its bills on time (in fact, better than some of the huge corporations that were certainly much healthier financially), but that its lead banker had been lending them money on a monthly basis. The next interest payment, which amounted to a few million dollars, was due in a few weeks. In talking with my colleagues and clients, it was difficult for me to imagine the bank's backing away at this time when they had so many dollars tied up in Memorex. Some of my clients were interested in more speculative investments. I recommended that they purchase the bonds, which at this time were selling at almost a tenth of what they normally would sell for if they paid the bonds off in full. I also recommended limiting the amount of funds for the purchase due to the extremely high-risk situation. After all, the bank might have said "no more" and let the company go under.

I was able to purchase the bonds for $90 to $160 per bond. Not only did the company pay its interest payment, but it turned itself around, was relisted on the New York Stock Exchange, and eventually was sold to Burroughs Corporation. The clients who were able to risk the dollars made a significant return on their funds, since the bonds traded as high as seven times what they paid for them. On top of that, they received interest of approximately 5¼ percent for each bond. Again, remember that bonds are normally valued at $1,000. An investor who was able to buy a $1,000 bond for $100 then received $55.25 annually for every bond he held. Not bad. However, those investors were also aware that if the company did go bankrupt, it was highly unlikely that they would receive their original funds back. Bear in mind, *anything* that has such a high possibility of failure is an extreme risk, and this is another instance in which it is appropriate to deal only with "kiss-off" funds.

How do you read a bond quotation? Below, we exerpted a portion of a chart from *The Wall Street Journal* that identifies American Telephone and Telegraph bonds. Note that there are several issues. The first example, AT&T 3¼ s84, means that Ma Bell is paying 3¼ percent on each $1,000 bond on this particular day and that it promises to give you back your money by the year 1984. The next column, under "Current Yield," states 3.5 percent. Note that 3.5 percent is slightly higher than the stated interest rate (or coupon, as it is also known in the trade) of 3¼ percent. Because the current yield is greater than the stated coupon of the bond, you know that this bond is selling at a discount. Again, discount means that the bond is selling for less than it will be worth when it matures.

Continuing along, the Volume column indicates that 35 bonds traded ($35,000 worth). The high, low and close indicate that the bond traded as high as 93⅜ (which was also its low and closing price). Ninety-three and three-eighths actually means $933.75 (93.⅜ = 93.375% × $1000.00 = $933.75). The final column, Net Change, indicates a −⅞. This means that the bond is down $8.75 (⅞ = .875% × $1000.00 = $8.75) from the day before. If you were to purchase this bond and hold it until it matured in 1984, you would receive $1,000. Therefore, for each bond you originally purchased at $933.75, you would have a $66.25 gain. The gain would be taxed as long-term gain if it was held for more than one year and as a short-term gain if held for less than one year.

NEW YORK EXCHANGE BONDS, APRIL 18, 1983

Bonds	Cur Yld	Vol	High	Low	Close	Net Chg.
ATT 3¼ s84	3.5	35	93⅜	93⅜	93⅜	−⅞
ATT 4⅜ s85	4.7	7	92½	92½	92½	....
ATT 4⅜ s85r	4.7	10	92½	92½	92½	....
ATT 2⅝ s86	3.1	11	85⅝	85½	85⅝	+⅛
ATT 2⅞ s87	3.4	55	84	83¾	84	....
ATT 3⅞ s90	5.2	11	74⅝	74⅜	74⅝	+⅞
ATT 3⅞ 90r	5.3	10	73¼	73¼	73¼	....
ATT 8¾ 00	10.	205	84¼	83⅝	83⅞	+¼
ATT 7 s01	9.9	138	71½	70½	71	+⅛
ATT 7⅛ s03	10.	129	70½	70	70⅛	+⅛
ATT 8.80 s05	11.	170	83¼	82¾	82¾	....
ATT 8⅝ s07	11.	89	81⅜	81⅛	81⅜	+¼
ATT 10⅜ 90	10.	213	100⅜	100	100⅜	+¼
ATT 13¼ 91	12.	60	108¾	108½	108⅝	+⅛

Now look at another bond—the AT&T 13¼ due in 1991. Note that the current yield is 12%. Since the 12% is less than the stated 13¼ interest, or coupon, that is designated on the original bond, you can tell that this bond is trading for a premium. This means that it is actually selling for more than it was really worth when it was first sold to the public, or for what it will mature for. In the next column, Volume, you note the number 60, which means 60 bonds or $60,000 in maturing value traded on this particular day; the High column tells you that the high was 108¾, the Low, 108½; and the bond closed at 108⅝, up ⅛ for the day. Translated into dollars, this means that this bond, at its high, could have been purchased for as much as $1,087.50, $1,085 at the low and at the close of the day's trading, $1,086.25. A rise of ⅛ of a point means that it is up $1.25 from the preceding day. The reason the bond is trading for more than the price at which it was originally brought to market is that interest rates declined and market values for bonds will adjust to reflect what the current going interest rates are.

A word of caution here: If interest rates continue to decline, this bond would actually appreciate in value. For someone who owns a bond in a situation like this, it is important to determine whether or not your bond has a callable feature. A callable feature means that the parent company can actually call in the bonds and redeem them at a predetermined value. Your gain could suddenly disappear. The way to avoid this is to make sure you fully understand the terms and conditions whenever you purchase any investment, be it stocks, bonds, or even a partnership unit. When a company, as in our illustration, calls in an outstanding issue per the initial features of the bond, you have no choice but to surrender the bond and some of its gain. It is really unfortunate, but I have seen many people lose significant profits because of a call feature that they were not aware of. Discount bonds carry some risks, but they give you an opportunity for significant capital gains.

Another investment you might consider is companies that are in trouble. Many companies having stocks traded on the public market are in bankruptcy proceedings. But just because a company files a Chapter 11 petition does not necessarily mean that it is going under. When Chrysler Corporation stock was trading for

DIVORCE COURSE

If you are involved in a divorce, you may have received a settlement. A settlement can take the form of various properties which have been accumulated over the life of the marriage. You may also have received stock, cash or other valuable items. If so, it is important for you to assess fully your objectives, as well as your current situation. A windfall in any form requires a specific financial strategy and demands that you follow some basic steps. The first is to place your funds in a fairly liquid environment, such as a money market fund or the newer checking accounts that allow you day-to-day liquidity and high interest earnings. Most of the "new rich" want to jump in immediately and invest funds in various areas. Friends and family are quick to make recommendations. This, though, is the time to shop around for sound financial advice. You should already have developed a financial team —a tax attorney, a CPA, a stockbroker, a financial planner— even insurance brokers can be important. As always, it is essential to set up both short- and long-term goals and investments. You will find that the individuals on your financial team will have different recommendations and may even contradict each other. This is normal; they should all have one basic goal, however— that your cash be preserved and that you realize growth from it. You would also like to have some tax benefits, if possible. Anyone who has received a substantial sum of money from a bonus or windfall such as a lottery or stock should be aware of income-averaging techniques.

THROW ME A LINE!

If you have not already secured a line of credit, by all means get it set up at this point. Most banks offer lines of credit which will be dependent upon your ability to repay. Some even offer you checkbooks that allow you to write a check to yourself or to whatever entity you desire, and the corresponding bank will fund your loan when it is in receipt of your check. Of course, interest does not accrue during the time that funds are not used. As a rule, these unsecured lines of credit will be tied into what is called the prime interest rate. You may be questioning the need to obtain a line of credit, but believe me, it makes sense. There will be rough times—and other times when it appears that you can do no wrong. If a financial opportunity arises, but you cannot come up with the cash necessary to take advantage of it, a line of credit could suffice. Always have it in readiness before any need arises. Rarely is there a charge to you until it is actually drawn on.

DON'T COUNT ON IT!

If you or, if married, you and your spouse have not planned for retirement in your earlier years, you must learn what you have accumulated from private programs and your IRA account. Since there is strong speculation that the government will increase the age at which you may begin to collect social security, as well as reduce the amount of benefits paid to recipients, it does make sense to find out exactly what you are entitled to from that program—and *when*. Social security was never intended to be a retiree's sole support. It does, though, offer supplementary income that is beneficial to a retired person.

During this time you would be wise to check with the Social Security Administration and inquire as to the status of your earnings and whether they have been reported accurately. Mistakes do happen. Someone may put the wrong digit down on your social security number or someone may be using your social security number in error and you may not be accumulating the credits you should have. Any local social security office can be contacted for a Form OAR-7004, an official administration form that requests a statement of your earnings. All you need do is give your name and address, your social security number and your date of birth. They will respond to you in writing with a complete record of your earnings since you began contributing to the fund. If there has been any error, make sure to contact the office directly. If you have changed jobs every two or three years, it is particularly important to make sure your earnings have been properly recorded. There are times, believe it or not, when your social security contribution hasn't been paid even though it has been deducted from the paycheck.

Another name for your social security number is TIN (Taxpayer's Identification Number). Both will probably be used on an interchangeable basis.

A TAXING BUSINESS

If you have a successful business and are anticipating selling or expanding it, it is important for you to look clearly at the tax ramifications. If you sell a company and make a substantial profit, more than likely you will incur a capital gains tax. If you are just now beginning to acquire an estate, you may contemplate making some gifts. It often happens that someone who is very successful enjoys sharing that success with family and friends. Whatever the case, I recommend that prior to selling your company, you make some transfers to family members. When the company is finally sold, the recipients, as individuals, will incur their respective capital gains taxes on the portion that they hold.

This has two benefits to you. Although we have a maximum tax of 20 percent of long-term capital gains at this time, there are also gift taxes to be considered. If you have already successfully transferred a portion of the assets to others—hopefully below the rates that would incur gift taxes at that time—you will save yourself money, first, by not having to pay the total capital gains tax and second, by not having to pay gift taxes. Transfers of $10,000 per person on an annual basis can be made without gift taxes. The gift tax is imposed on all transfers of money or property by an individual in excess of this exclusion. Any taxes that are imposed must be paid by the donor, the individual making the gift, not the recipient. In my financial-planning practice, I have seen several people actually claim gift funds as taxable income on their tax returns. This, of course, is inappropriate and an absolutely unnecessary burden—certainly a windfall for Uncle Sam!

The donor is required to file the appropriate information on a gift-tax return. If you are contemplating making a gift in excess of the annual exclusion of $10,000, it would make sense to contact your tax adviser regarding the necessary forms. In addition, the IRS has issued Publication 904 which illustrates how to determine the tax on a particular gift situation. It is also recommended that before you make a substantial gift, you determine what the tax is and retain the necessary cash at the time you make the gift, so that you can pay the gift tax when due.

I had a close friend who had a successful business; in fact, it was so successful that he sold it and realized substantial profits, which led him to a major problem—taxes! The tax year was fairly new and he decided to reinvest his funds in another venture that would produce significant tax losses and tax credits. These, in turn, would offset a great deal of his tax liability from the sale of his first business.

He invested the funds in a small airline. This airline flew to an island which was a few miles from the coastline. Initially, the game plan worked; he received a substantial tax benefit from the depreciation on the equipment (airplanes), as well as various tax credits on the airplanes themselves. What he didn't take into consideration was some of the risk that was involved with his ownership. One afternoon after a flight, the pilot "parked" the plane in its water berth. Unfortunately, there was a bridge overhead, from which a despondent individual jumped. The person landed on the airplane wing, actually broke through it and died. My friend felt horrible. There were rumblings that if the plane had not been there, the individual who had jumped might have landed in the water and lived. In addition, the plane was damaged, and required substantial repair. Needless to say, my friend is no longer enamored of small commuter airlines. The lesson here is to expect the unexpected and never enter into anything just for tax purposes.

CASH IN YOUR CHIPS

Cash becomes more interesting during this phase and aggressive accumulations in the various money market instruments should be of some benefit. In addition, some of the bond markets may be attractive. The bond market will reflect any change in interest rates. For example, when interest rates are very high, and the prime rate ranges anywhere from 15 percent to 18 percent, ongoing yields or returns on bonds will be in the 14 percent to 16 percent area; and when the prime rate is at or below 10 percent, interest rates on bonds will be in the 8 percent to 10 percent area. The type of bond I recommend is one that is selling at a discount. A discount means that it is selling well below the price at which it was originally brought to the market. As a rule, bonds are treated in $1,000 units. Their principal will vary depending upon interest rates. When the current prime rate is 15 percent, a bond that was brought to the market at 8 percent will more than likely sell at half of its original price of $1,000. This can benefit you in two ways. First, you get an ongoing, comparable and reasonable rate of return; and second, you get the opportunity for a capital gain through either a decline in interest rates and appreciation in value of the holding of the bond until it matures at full value at its normal maturity date. This, of course, could mean several years. For a complete explanation of discount bonds, see pages 136–140 of the previous phase.

AVOID THE TAX BITE

This phase is usually the most productive in earnings revenues. As a rule, tax obligations are at their greatest. This doesn't mean you should throw funds indiscriminately into various ventures simply to avoid paying taxes. What it does mean is that you should take a careful look at your spending and should place accumulated assets into tax-sheltered, tax-deferred or tax-exempt environments.

In this phase, the short-term market is attractive, and, if you are purchasing items in the bond area, maturity dates of ten years or less should be sought. Municipal bonds are tax exempt. The interest that is paid to the holder of such a bond is nontaxable, and, if you participate in a fund that allows for the reinvestment of interest into additional units, the overall value can actually grow. Of course, if you purchase any of the bonds at a discount, then you have the opportunity not only for tax-exempt income, but also for a long-term capital gain.

But suppose you purchased a bond when it was at a higher price and interest rates then went up and forced the value of the bond down? This is the time, especially when you are looking at your tax situation, to consider what is called a bond swap. In swapping a bond, you merely sell it, and the broker with whom you made the transaction will find you a comparable bond in rating and/or interest—but not with the same company. This new bond will be selling close to the price at which you sold your original bond, maintaining your income, but allowing now for a gain on principal if interest rates decline or the bond matures, and finally, giving you a tax deduction from the loss you took when you sold the first bond. The reason you do not repurchase an issue with the same company upon selling at a loss is that the loss would be disallowed if the repurchase was completed within 31 days. A transaction that involves that repurchase of a stock or bond that was sold at a loss within the 31-day period is also known as a "wash sale." If you wait more than 31 days for repurchase, then the loss will be allowed.

LESS IS MORE

This is the time when your assets are growing and your net worth is becoming more and more substantial. It is also the time to make appointments with an estate-planning attorney to consider the feasibility of various trusts and their applicability to your own situation. Often individuals consider purchasing larger homes during this particular phase. This may be because their children are growing noisier and take up more space in the house. Believe me, it doesn't last long, and you may later wish that you had kept your small house. You may even consider purchasing a smaller one now.

If you have bought a home in any of your prior phases, you have probably accumulated considerable equity by the time you enter this one. If so, explore the possibility of withdrawing your equity and actually purchasing that smaller house now. Such a purchase could reduce some outgoing expenses as you enter the next phase. Also, if you sell your residence after the age of 55, which is our next life phase, you can enjoy the lifetime tax-free capital gain of $125,000 (See section on Tax Fax). The house you then purchased could also be used as a rental unit, yielding tax benefits and other monetary advantages during the rental period.

How? By leveraging. Let's say the sale of your current residence yields $120,000. Using the leverage concept, you would buy two houses each costing $120,000, put $30,000 down on each one and negotiate two $90,000 mortgages at 13 percent interest. You would then put the remaining $60,000 into a cash money fund averaging 10 percent interest over a four-year period.

	House #1	House #2
Down payment	$ 30,000	$ 30,000
Mortgage	90,000	90,000
Total cost	$120,000	$120,000
Reserve account	$ 60,000 earning 10%	

During that time you must continue to pay mortgage costs, real estate taxes, depreciation and miscellaneous costs. Our calculations show that for both houses, these total expenses add up to $169,440 in four years.

Expenses:

90,000 × .13 =	$11,700	mortgage
	1,500	real estate taxes (estimated)
	1,980	maintenance & insurance (estimated)
× 4 years × 2 houses =	$121,440	

Depreciation:

75% of original price 120,000 =	$ 90,000
÷ 15 years =	6,000
× 4 years × 2 houses =	48,000

$121,440 expenses
+ 48,000 depreciation
$169,440 total expenses

But, assuming you can rent each house for $650 per month, $62,400 in rental revenue will be received during that same four-year period.

Rental income

$650 × 12 months	= $ 7,800
× 4 years	= 31,200
× 2 houses	= 62,400

This will result in total expenses, including depreciation calculations of $107,040, or $26,760 per year. Without depreciation, your real expense (hard dollars) or negative cash flow would be $14,760 per year for both houses.

4 year
Estimated Gross Expenses:
$121,440—Expenses
48,000—Depreciation
$169,440
−62,400—Revenues (rent)
$107,040 (gross expenses)
÷ 4 (years) = $26,760 (annual expense for both houses)

The $60,000 in a money fund plus its 10 percent interest will offset that negative cash flow during its four-year duration.

Funds needed from reserve account:
$121,440 − 62,400 = 59,040 ÷ 48 months = $1,230 per month
Adjustment of interest earned on reserve account minus monthly withdrawals

	Interest Earned	Withdrawals	Balance
1st year	$5,640	$14,760	$50,880
2nd year	$4,704	$14,760	$40,824
3rd year	$3,876	$14,760	$29,940
4th year	$2,412	$14,760	$17,592

With the negative cash flow and the depreciation, tax write-offs to the investor will be approximately $26,760, minus interest earned for the year.

Write-off per year before interest
$107,040 ÷ 4 = $26,760

After four years, assuming that both houses are liquidated, and they have appreciated annually at 8 percent, the liquidation price will be $326,516. That amount, less the mortgages, leaves $146,516. Since you set aside $60,000 in cash reserves in a money fund, which have been used to offset expenses you must subtract that amount, leaving a final net gain of $86,516.

Sales Price for Both Houses	$326,516
Mortgages	− 180,000
	$146,516
Cash Reserve	− 60,000
gain	$ 86,516

This represents an approximate return of 72 percent on your original investment of $120,000. Not taken into consideration are any of the tax benefits taken over the previous four years of ownership.

In the above example, the depreciation deduction has been taken as a straight line and not accelerated, eliminating the possibility of an unpleasant phenomenon known as "recapture." When you own real estate as an investment, there are various methods for depreciating the building. The method used in our example, straight-line depreciation, means that you take the number of years that the IRS allocates as "useful lifespan" and divide the actual cost of the building and any improvements by that figure. In the case of real estate, straight-line depreciation occurs over a 15-year period of time. A single-family residence, for example, valued at $100,000 may have a land valuation of $25,000. The remaining $75,000, the value of the house itself, would be divided by 15, yielding a $5,000 depreciation expense per annum.

Individuals who use straight-line depreciation will reduce the original cost of the property by the amount of depreciation that is declared each year. For example, in the above illustration, you hold the residential property for four years and then sell it. Each year, you have taken a deduction of $5,000 in depreciation expenses for a total of $20,000. Your cost basis at time of sale would be reduced from the original $100,000 cost to $80,000 (100,000 − 20,000 = 80,000). Remember, however, at the time of sale, this adjustment will be considered part of the long-term capital gain. This means that if you sell the house for $120,000 your taxable gain on the sale will not simply be the increase over original purchase price ($120,000 − $100,000 = $20,000 long-term capital gain), but the amount of profit in excess of the depreciated value ($120,000 − $80,000 = $40,000 taxable gain).

There are other methods of depreciation. For example, you could accelerate it and actually declare the depreciation expenses in half the time allowed under straight-line depreciation guidelines. This may look terrific for the first few years when you get substantial tax benefits via the accelerated depreciation expense. But there is a catch. At the time of sale, when accelerated depreciation has been used, the proceeds from the sale will be declared as ordinary income. This is where "recapture" comes in. Keep in mind that ordinary income is taxed at your regular income tax bracket level, perhaps as much as 50 percent, and long-term capital gain is taxed at a maximum rate of 20 percent of the gain. This, of course, is subject to change of the whim of Congress.

In conclusion, if you choose to use straight-line depreciation, the only consideration to keep in mind is that you will increase your original purchase price by the amount that is depreciated. The entire capital gain of the property that is sold is then calculated from that new adjusted basis.

Today, however, interest rates have reached such extraordinary highs that it is difficult to implement this plan. With interest rates in the two-figure category, anyone who purchases property for investment purposes usually needs extra available cash—more than can be covered by interest from a money market fund—in order to supplement the monthly payment. In addition, the example above assumes that the investor has been able to negotiate $90,000 in loans at 13 percent. In view of this, it might be appropriate to examine some possible sources for such money.

SOME GROWTH, MORE YIELD

Stocks that allow for some growth opportunity as well as a reasonable dividend should be considered during this phase, and especially as you enter the next phase. Stocks such as IBM are considered classic blue chips. They offer some growth, a respectable dividend and peace of mind. Again, familiarize yourself with advising tools such as the Value Line Survey. The following Value Line Survey chart indicates some of the areas to note on IBM.

1. This chart illustrates that International Business Machines (IBM), has fluctuated in price beginning in 1967 with a trading range as low as the mid-30s to a high of 118. As you can see, the stock has had some price swings, but not as wide-ranging as that of Advanced Micro Devices (see pages 90–91). In taking a conservative or medium-risk posture on a stock, market price movements such as the ones demonstrated in the IBM trading history offer a less anxiety-making position while you hold the stock. This means that since there was minimal movement (i.e., during 1976 and 1977) there is only a few points' variance on the actual stock movement. In 1978 and 1979, there was more trading movement when the stock went up into the $80-per-share range and began to climb, and then in 1980 dropped down into the 50s, to recover later in the year and then again begin to drop somewhat in 1981, and to pick up again in the latter part of 1982. IBM is a stock that has been traditionally selected by banks that are trustees of individual and corporation accounts, due to the overall strength and basic stability of the stock's price.
2. Note that IBM has split its shares three different times over the last 15 years.
3. Take projections with a grain of salt.
4. In a stock such as IBM, there has been a consistent increase in the dividends paid out on each share. In 1983 they estimate the total dividend will be $3.95 for each share. Therefore, if you held 100 shares, you would receive $395 per annum. Keep in mind that the dividends can be increased or decreased depending upon the company's profitability.
5. The actual financial reports are important. Note the increased sales per share, earnings per share, book value for share, capital spending (if a company is planning on any growth at all, there should be some funds allocated toward capital spending), average annual P/E (price/earnings) ratio, and net profit margin.
6. This section tells what the company does, where it is located, who the chief executive officer is, and what its product line is.
7. What is happening in its environment and any new developments for the company within the next year.

INT'L BUS. MACH. NYSE-IBM

RECENT PRICE **117** | P/E RATIO **14.2** (Trailing: 15.2 Median: 14.0) | EARN'S YLD **7.0%** | DIV'D YLD **3.4%** | **1101**

	1966	1967	1968	1969	1970	1971	1972	1973	1974	1975	1976	1977	1978	1979	1980	1981	1982	1983
High	64.8	75.0	73.8	77.4	73.2	85.3	91.3	63.5	56.8	72.1	71.5	77.8	80.5	72.8	71.5	98.0	118.0	
Low	35.4	56.0	58.3	43.7	56.6	66.3	58.8	37.6	39.3	55.8	61.1	58.7	61.1	50.4	48.4	55.6	92.3	

18.0 × "Cash Flow" p sh

2-for-1 split

5-for-4 split

4-for-1 split

Relative Price Strength

Options Trade On CBO

(2)

(1)

Target Price Range

1984 | 1985 | 1986 | 1987

Insider Decisions 1982

	J	F	M	A	M	J	J	A	S	O	N	D	J	F	M
to Buy	0	0	0	1	1	1	0	0	0	1	11	13	13	14	12
to Sell	0	0	1	0	2	0	0	1	1	1	2	1	2	1	0

Institutional Decisions

	4Q'81	1Q'82	2Q'82	3Q'82	4Q'82
to Buy	188	197	198	239	201
to Sell	167	188	186	156	162
Hldg's(000)	285663	286247	290756	301463	300803

Percent shares traded 6.0 4.0 2.0

May 13, 1983 Value Line

TIMELINESS (Relative Price Performance Next 12 Mos.) **1** Highest

SAFETY (Scale: 1 Highest to 5 Lowest) **1** Highest

BETA 1.00 (1.00 = Market)

1985-87 PROJECTIONS

	Price	Gain	Ann'l Total Return
High	250	(+115%)	24%
Low	205	(+ 75%)	18%

(3)

© Value Line, Inc.

1966	1967	1968	1969	1970	1971	1972	1973	1974	1975	1976	1977	1978	1979	1980	1981	1982	1983		85-87E
7.61	9.53	12.20	12.66	13.10	14.32	16.38	18.73	21.37	24.09	27.05	30.74	36.14	39.18	44.90	49.08	57.04	**64.70**	Revenues per sh	**90.65**
2.10	2.71	3.27	3.42	3.64	3.84	4.43	5.17	5.75	6.12	6.83	7.67	8.88	9.14	10.83	11.21	13.23	**14.80**	"Cash Flow" per sh	**20.70**
.94	1.16	1.54	1.64	1.78	1.88	2.21	2.70	3.12	3.34	3.99	4.58	5.32	5.16	6.10	5.63	7.39	**8.80**	Earnings per sh (A)	**13.60**
.42	.44	.52	.72	.96	1.04	1.08	1.12	1.39	1.63	2.00	2.50	2.88	3.44	3.44	3.44	3.44	**3.71**	Div'd Decl'd per sh ■ (B)	**6.75**
2.71	2.47	1.92	2.76	3.59	3.06	2.76	3.51	4.69	3.83	3.94	5.43	6.51	9.66	10.61	11.56	11.10	**10.75**	Cap'l Spending per sh	**13.50**
5.94	6.83	8.09	9.28	10.38	11.50	13.00	15.02	17.05	19.05	21.15	21.39	23.14	25.64	28.18	30.66	33.13	**37.75**	Book Value per sh	**56.25**
558.09	561.14	564.84	568.59	572.93	577.67	581.99	586.85	593.04	599.38	602.78	589.88	583.24	583.59	583.81	592.29	602.41	**612.00**	Common Shs Outst'g	**640.00**
35.8	43.5	42.3	40.4	33.0	34.4	35.4	28.5	16.5	15.3	16.6	14.5	12.7	13.9	10.4	10.3	9.4		Avg Ann'l P/E Ratio	**17.0**
2.8%	2.3%	2.4%	2.5%	3.0%	2.9%	2.8%	3.5%	6.1%	6.5%	6.0%	6.9%	7.9%	7.2%	9.6%	9.7%	10.6%		Avg Ann'l Earn's Yield	**5.9%**
1.2%	.9%	.8%	1.1%	1.6%	1.6%	1.4%	1.5%	2.7%	3.2%	3.0%	3.8%	4.3%	4.8%	5.4%	5.9%	5.0%		Avg Ann'l Div'd Yield	**2.9%**

(5) (4)

1972	1973	1974	1975	1976	1977	1978	1979	1980	1981	1982	1983		85-87E
9532.6	10993	12675	14437	16304	18133	21076	22863	26213	29070	34364	**39600**	Revenues ($mill)	**58000**
37.9%	38.5%	37.4%	35.4%	35.5%	35.6%	35.6%	33.1%	32.4%	32.2%	33.8%	**35.0%**	Operating Margin	**35.5%**
1296.6	1460.8	1575.0	1680.0	1717.0	1806.0	2071.0	2321.3	2759.0	3329.0	3562.0	**3725**	Depreciation ($mill) (D)	**4600**
1279.3	1575.5	1837.6	1989.9	2398.1	2719.4	3110.6	3011.3	3562.0	3308.0	4409.0	**5340**	Net Profit ($mill)	**8650**
47.3%	46.5%	46.5%	46.5%	46.9%	46.6%	46.4%	45.8%	39.6%	44.8%	44.4%	**44.5%**	Income Tax Rate	**45.0%**
13.4%	14.3%	14.5%	13.8%	14.7%	15.0%	14.8%	13.2%	13.6%	11.4%	12.8%	**13.5%**	Net Profit Margin	**14.9%**
2562.5	3274.9	3800.1	4751.8	5838.1	4864.1	4510.8	4405.8	3399.0	2983.0	4805.0	**5800**	Working Cap'l ($mill)	**8500**
772.9	652.2	335.8	295.1	275.1	255.8	285.5	1589.4	2099.0	2669.0	2851.0	**2900**	Long-Term Debt ($mill)	**5300**
7565.9	8812.0	10110	11416	12749	12618	13494	14961	16453	18161	19960	**23100**	Net Worth ($mill)	**36000**
15.7%	16.9%	17.7%	17.1%	18.5%	21.2%	22.7%	18.6%	19.8%	16.5%	20.0%	**21.0%**	% Earned Total Cap'l	**21.5%**
16.9%	17.9%	18.2%	17.4%	18.8%	21.6%	23.1%	20.1%	21.7%	18.2%	22.1%	**23.0%**	% Earned Net Worth	**24.0%**
8.6%	10.5%	10.1%	8.9%	9.4%	9.8%	10.6%	6.7%	9.5%	7.1%	11.8%	**13.5%**	% Retained to Comm Eq	**12.0%**
49%	42%	45%	49%	50%	55%	54%	67%	56%	61%	47%	**42%**	% All Div'ds to Net Prof	**50%**

CAPITAL STRUCTURE as of 12/31/82

Total Debt $3380.0 mill. **Due in 5 Yrs** $2369.0 mill.
LT Debt $2851.0 mill. **LT Interest** $295.0 mill.
(LT interest earned: 27.9x; total interest coverage: 18.5x) (13% of Cap'l)

Leases, Uncapitalized Annual rentals $417 mill.

Pension Liability None vs. None in 1981

Pfd Stock None

Common Stock 602,406,006 shs. (87% of Cap'l)

(8)

CURRENT POSITION ($mill.)	1980	1981	12/31/82
Cash Assets	2112.0	2029.0	3300.0
Receivables	4877.0	4792.0	5433.0
Inventory (Av. Cst)	2293.0	2805.0	3492.0
Other	643.0	677.0	789.0
Current Assets	9925.0	10303.0	13014.0
Accts Payable	721.0	872.0	983.0
Debt Due	591.0	773.0	529.0
Other	5214.0	5675.0	6697.0
Current Liab.	6526.0	7320.0	8209.0

ANNUAL RATES of change (per sh)	Past 10 Yrs	Past 5 Yrs	Est '80-'82 to '85-'87
Revenues	13.0%	13.0%	*12.5%*
"Cash Flow"	11.5%	11.5%	*12.0%*
Earnings	12.5%	10.0%	*16.5%*
Dividends	13.0%	11.0%	*14.5%*
Book Value	10.0%	8.5%	*13.0%*

(9)

Cal-endar	QUARTERLY REVENUES ($ mill.) Mar. 31	June 30	Sept. 30	Dec. 31	Full Year
1979	5295	5355	5384	6829	22863
1980	5748	6181	6478	7806	26213
1981	6461	6895	6721	8993	29070
1982	7066	8053	8171	11074	34364
1983	8287	***9200***	***9550***	***12563***	***39600***

Cal-endar	EARNINGS PER SHARE Mar. 31	June 30	Sept. 30	Dec. 31	(A) Full Year
1979	1.14	1.15	1.14	1.73	5.16
1980	1.17	1.31	1.51	2.11	6.10
1981	1.25	1.37	1.18	1.83	5.63
1982	1.33	(E)1.81	(E)1.75	(E)2.50	7.39
1983	1.62	***1.90***	***2.20***	***3.08***	***8.80***

Cal-endar	QUARTERLY DIVIDENDS PAID Mar. 31	June 30	Sept. 30	Dec. 31	(B) Full ■Year
1979	.86	.86	.86	.86	3.44
1980	.86	.86	.86	.86	3.44
1981	.86	.86	.86	.86	3.44
1982	.86	.86	.86	.86	3.44
1983	.86	.95			

BUSINESS: International Business Machines Corp. is the largest supplier of data processing equipment. Also makes typewriters, dictating machines, copiers. Owns Science Research Associates (education materials). Operates 89 IBM Product Centers selling office equipment, small computers and terminals. Foreign business accts. for 45% of revs., 41% of pretax earnings. R&D costs equal 6.0% of revs.; est'd payroll, 35%. '82 deprec. rate: 11.6%. Est'd plant age: 4 yrs. Has 364,800 empls., 725,745 shrhldrs. Insiders control .8% of stock. Chairman: J.R. Opel. President: J.F. Akers. Incorporated: New York. Address: Armonk, New York 10504.

(6)

Directors have voted a dividend increase—from 86¢ to 95¢ a share quarterly—the first one since 1979. (IBM has been conserving cash to help finance the massive capital spending programs of the past several years.) But the hike, effective with the June 10th payment, wasn't surprising . . .

Timing and execution of late have been excellent. Despite economic softness worldwide and adverse foreign exchange rates, the margin expansion and record profits that characterized IBM's 1982 continued in the March period just ended. Credit a revved-up new product cycle, a streamlined marketing force, state-of-the-art manufacturing facilities, and a big shift toward purchases in the sales-lease mix.

A full-year share earnings advance of 19% is within reach. Order trends indicate that 1982's star performers—the 308X processors, the 3380 disk files, and the hot-ticket personal computers—still have plenty of shine left. And although a dramatic retreat of the dollar isn't likely, currency comparisons should ease as 1983 unfolds.

Good gains are sustainable into 1984 and beyond. The 3081 and 3083 systems may be past their prime. But new entries from top to bottom in the product spectrum will more than pick up the slack. The high-end 3084 mainframe is due for initial shipment in the coming fourth quarter. (Other recent releases include enhancements for the Series/1 and System/38 lines, expanded capabilities for the 3270 display terminals, and a more powerful front-end processor.) Also auguring well for the future is MVS/XA, IBM's new extended architecture operating system, which will offer improved performance for the company's large computers.

Wall Street likes what it sees, and has bid these shares to a series of all-time highs of late. Price action will continue to be impressive, in our opinion, both in the year ahead and over the pull to 1985-87. Aggressive penetration of low-end high-growth markets and a leadership position in mainframes should generate earnings sufficient to produce wide capital gains for long-haul investors.

K.C.B./E.F.S.

(7)

Restated Sales (and Gross Profit Margins)* by Business Line

	1980	1981	1982	1983
Product Sales	10919.0(61.6%)	12901.0(58.8%)	18815.0(60.3%)	***21800(61.5%)***
Rentals	10869.0(65.3%)	10839.0(61.7%)	11121.0(64.4%)	***10100(65.0%)***
Services	4425.0(50.7%)	5330.0(52.3%)	6428.0(52.6%)	***7700(53.0%)***
Company Total	26213.0(61.3%)	29070.0(58.7%)	34364.0(60.2%)	***39600(60.7%)***

*After depreciation.

(A) Based on avg. shs. outstanding. Next earn'gs rep't due mid-July. Est'd constant-dollar egs./sh.: '82, $4.50.
(B) Next div'd meet'g about July 26. Goes ex about Aug. 4. Div'd payment dates: about Mar. 10, June 10, Sept. 10, Dec. 10. ■ Div'd reinvestment plan av'ble (no cost).
(C) In mill., adj. for stock splits & div'ds.
(D) Deprec. on accelerated basis.
(E) Restated to reflect accounting change.

Company's Financial Strength	A++
Stock's Price Stability	95
Price Growth Persistence	5
Earnings Predictability	90

(10)

Factual material is obtained from sources believed to be reliable but cannot be guaranteed.

8. The current financial position regarding both assets and liabilities.
9. Current financial data on earnings per share, as well as any dividends paid and quarterly sales for the preceding three years. Projections for the next year are also included in italics.
10. The rating of a company's financial strength is important. If you want to sleep at night, it makes sense to be with a company that has a financial strength of A or better. Companies that have financial strength, but with lower ratings, often have greater swing in their overall stock price.

TOO GOOD TO BE TRUE?

Another vehicle in which you might place funds (usually with a minimum participation of $5,000) is the tax-deferred annuity. Annuities are products of life insurance companies and have some attractive guarantees for women in this life phase. Your principal will not decline as it may in the case of a bond, which can go up and down depending upon the interest market and the success of the company behind it. Second, it should give you an ongoing rate of interest that is appropriate in today's economy. Third, it can often be used as collateral with banks, and even with the insurance company itself. Fourth, if you die it will bypass probate, thus saving your beneficiaries some money. Fifth, the interest is allowed to accumulate on a tax-deferred basis. This means you will not have to declare any of the interest on your taxes until you withdraw funds at a later date.

Annuities, like any other investment, come in all shapes and sizes and are offered by a number of companies. If you have a serious interest in annuities, I would recommend you contact a major brokerage firm or financial-planning organization. Make sure that the company has more than one product line to offer, so you should make some comparisons. One of the key questions to ask is what the penalties are if you change your mind and decide to withdraw your funds, either as cash or for transfer to another insurance company that may be offering a better interest rate. Before entering into an annuity contract, make sure you read the small print; understand the penalties as well as the benefits.

of attorney—written authorization for her to act on your behalf in all your financial affairs. Then, in your will, leave your assets to her.

WATCH THE UNDERDOGS!

Because of your experience with economic cycles, you should be able to recognize, evaluate, and even benefit from "undervalued" situations. Even companies that have gone bankrupt can offer interesting investment opportunities, if management is able to turn the situation around and again succeed in the business environment.

If you haven't consulted the Value Line Survey referred to under earlier life phases, this is the time to become well acquainted with it. Look into companies that are having serious financial difficulty and are publicly traded. The annual reports and the latest interim reports will be of great assistance. If you do not know where to obtain these reports, merely check with an intermediate-size library or brokerage firm and request them. Also check in the Standard & Poor's individual company reports, or the corporate records that Standard & Poor publishes. If you already have a broker, you should call him/her and ask for a copy of the latest report from both services. Otherwise, you can visit the firm and request a copy or go to the library and have a copy made. All of these items not only carry the corporate office and address of the firm you are interested in, but also identify the chief executive officers.

CORPORATE REPORT CARDS

Annual reports are interesting instruments. The amount of money invested on glossy pictures and presentation is phenomenal. An annual report provides a lot of information, and in order to evaluate it you need to learn where to concentrate your energies. First of all, you want to make sure the report conforms to generally accepted accounting principles. This means that a Certified Public Accountant will verify the numbers, balance them out, and state that in their opinion, the company conforms. If you don't see the words "generally accepted accounting principles'' on the back of the report, then you should be very cautious, as that company is asking you to accept their figures on faith. Their accountants have not been able to validate or verify the exactness of the numbers that have been produced.

Prior to studying the balance sheet and income-and-expense statement, look at the footnotes. Footnotes will tell you if the company has incurred any additional debt and at what cost and maturity level. It will also let you know whether or not they have had any accounting changes, as well as any once-in-a-lifetime increase in revenues. Sometimes accounting changes can be very positive.

For example, the company could change from FIFO accounting to LIFO accounting. This means that prior to the current year their inventory value was based on ''first in, first out'' versus ''last in, first out.'' In LIFO accounting, the inventory could be carried at current inflated levels. This is actually a more conservative way to state the position of a company. LIFO accounting gives a truer picture of current market reaction and, when the bottom line is brought about by year end, does not show an extraordinary jump or gain in earnings. In FIFO accounting the overall cost is reflected at a substantially lower value. It is true that if you had purchased inventory several months or years prior, before prices increased, and it is actually being moved off the shelf at this time at higher prices, the company will show a greater percentage increase in earnings when the quarter or year-end finishes. The problem with FIFO is that this method of accounting often produces a nonrecurring gain. For example, a company reports extraordinary gains because they are on FIFO accounting. The following year, they replace new inventory at current market prices. Because of the replacement at higher cost, they could actually show a decrease in profit, which could be reflected negatively in the market place via a decline in its stock price. Sometimes a company will restate its earnings by switching from one accounting method to another. This rattles the investment community. Sometimes it is viewed as positive, sometimes as negative. As a rule, if the company is on, or switches to, a LIFO method, it does have an overall calming effect both to stock analysts and investors.

Often companies sell divisions and subdivisions to other companies or individuals. If you have noticed a substantial increase in earnings per share, it makes sense to verify whether it is attributed to increased revenues via sales of a particular product or to the sale of a major division. If a company sells a major division, settles some extraordinary legal case, or even sells off some of its real estate, these revenues will be classified as nonrecurring gains or revenues on the balance sheet. Keep in mind that "nonrecurring" is exactly what it means—a one-time-only incident. If a company you currently own or are considering purchasing reports revenues derived from nonrecurring entities, be cautious. The sales or earnings per share that they report may be extraordinary and reflect a substantial increase over the prior year—but, if probing into the balance sheet you find that it is due to a nonrecurring source, their earnings may not be increasing, and could in fact be decreasing. *Make sure to read between the lines.*

Often, when companies begin to sell divisions, they are having major financial problems and, in fact, the most salable of their divisions would be their more profitable ones. In the long run, or even the short run, this could have a substantial negative effect on a company whose annual report you are reading.

If a company has sold additional shares to the general public or bought back shares on the open market, footnotes will also reflect that, and should in fact restate the total number of shares outstanding and if there has been an increase or decrease.

In the report will be a letter from the President and/or Chairman of the Board; he or she will give you an update on what has happened the preceding year as well as a projection of how the company is expected to fare during the coming year(s). If a company has had problems, it should say so in the letter and should also include information on what has been done to rectify them.

By this time you have been producing net worth statements for yourself on an annual basis. A company's net worth is reflected in its balance sheet. When examining a company's report, you will note that all its assets are laid out on the left side and are broken into areas such as "current" and "other" assets. On the right side of the page the liabilities are laid out. Again you will notice current liabilities and then liabilities that are due a year or more after the company's year end. Most annual reports not only set forth the current status of a company, but also that of its preceding four years. This will allow you to get a quick fix on whether or not the current assets, such as cash, are increasing or decreasing. It will also tell you the inventory position of the company. When you deduct current liabilities from current assets (assuming that the assets are greater than the liabilities) you will get what is called the "net working capital." *This is an essential figure to examine*. Most healthy companies have what is called a two-to-one ratio—for every dollar in current liabilities, there should be two dollars in current assets. If the company you are looking at carries inventory, subtract that figure from the current assets and then compare the result with current liability. This will give you what is called a "quick ratio," and it should be one to one—for every dollar of liability, there should be one dollar of assets. If you find the ratios to be lower than those I have cited, there could be a problem. For example, the company may not be able to meet any of the short-term debts that mature within the year, or it may have to reduce or eliminate a dividend that would normally have been paid.

Another term for "net worth" of a company is "stockholder's equity." It is also referred to as "shareholder's equity" and it is simply the difference between total assets and total liabilities. If stockholders' equity in a company is $500,000, for example, and there are 10,000 shares outstanding, you merely divide 10,000 into $500,000 to learn that each share would bring $50 upon liquidation. This is known as book value and has nothing to do with the company's current trading value. It is important for you to pay close attention to the liabilities side, and in particular to increased amounts allocated either to short-term or long-term debts. If a company is aggressively growing and doing well, as a rule there is no problem in acquiring debt, because that helps fuel the growth, which should bring in additional revenues and bottom-line profits. It may, however, spell disaster for a company that is having problems and continues to incur debt to help finance the operating expenses during times of declining revenues.

Recent examples of this are companies such as Braniff Airlines and World Airlines, both of which went into bankruptcy. Once a company is in a bankruptcy proceeding, which is also known as "Chapter 11" or "reorganization," there may be a significant opportunity for return to good health, if the respective creditors work together and allow the company to continue operation. It could actually pull itself out of its troubles. On the other hand, if you are a shareholder in a company that declares a "Chapter 7," I would suggest that you merely kiss your dollars goodbye. Chapter 7 is a form of bankruptcy in which the individual or company literally gives up and tells the creditors to come take whatever they can get from the proceeds—that's it, and no more.

The other item that is always included in an annual report is the income-and-expense statement. You will hear of companies that make so much per share. Earnings are up, down, or flat. This is a good reason for looking at the footnotes. Earnings per share can be increased artificially if a company has, for whatever reason, sold a portion of its assets to bring in revenues. It is important to deduct any nonrecurring revenues that are generated from one-time-only sales. This will give you a truer picture of the actual sales of the company. On the other hand, if the company has sold a division that was actually a drain on other profitable divisions, the profits may actually begin to increase significantly as a result. Again, read the footnotes.

In analyzing a company, it is important not only to look at its annual reports for the last few years but also to do a comparison study of what is going on in the industry. You can do this by subscribing to the Value Line Survey. It examines both industries and individual companies and provides you with a reading of what they are all doing, what kind of debts they are carrying, what kind of growth patterns they are showing, and what kind of stock activity or market prices have been enjoyed during good times and bad. The company that you are analyzing may be a true underdog and ready to take off. On the other hand, it could be at the height of its value and ready to plummet. Information from an annual report and supplemental reports such as the Value Line and Standard & Poor sheets are essential aspects of decision making on stock market investments. One final word here. Even though an annual report may indicate that a company is turning around, doing well, and/or comparing favorably with others in the industry, there is no guarantee that your stock will increase in value. If the economic environment is generally negative or if the company you are looking at is not enjoying a favorable press, it may make sense to step aside until things look better.

In these days of money market funds and other instruments that offer liquidity with a comparable rate of return, it is important to determine, prior to purchasing shares in a company, whether or not your expected return (via profits) or yield (via dividends) is comparable to the inflation rate. If you invest in the stock market, your objective should be to achieve a greater rate of return than money market funds would offer.

MOVING DOWN

At this time you may have realized a substantial increase in the equity of your home. If so, and if you are past the age of 55, you may want to sit down and closely evaluate selling your residence and taking advantage of the once-in-a-lifetime $125,000 gain allowed for those over 55 who have lived in the house for three years immediately prior to sale. As I mentioned before, this is a time when your changing circumstances will make it possible to move to a smaller, less expensive home. In addition, with the cash that you have received from the sale, you may be able to purchase a house with a minimal mortgage. As you approach retirement, this aim should become a strategic part of your overall planning. Remember, however, it is preferable to avoid becoming a banker upon the sale of your house. Any outstanding mortgages on your home should be assumed by the new owner.

In addition to the new buyer's assuming your loan or obtaining new financing, you may be required to "loan in" some funds to complete the transaction. Let us say you sold your home for $125,000 and, because you had owned the home for a long time, had an outstanding mortgage of $6,000 at 5 percent. The buyer of your home has a $30,000 down payment and is able to obtain a first mortgage for $85,000. He is then $10,000 short of the total purchase price of $125,000. Because he is short the $10,000, he has asked you to consider loaning him that amount in the form of a second deed of trust earning, for example, 10 percent. This means that after the new owner is able to obtain the first mortgage and it is recorded with a title company, he will record the second mortgage, also known as a deed of trust, so that there will be an official record of the outstanding loan from you. If he decides to sell the house in a few years, it is a normal procedure for a title company to search the records to see what loans are outstanding. This gives you some assurance as well as insurance in protecting the funds you have loaned to the new owner for this limited period of time. This is also known as "carry-back financing" or "carrying back paper." If you agree to the loan, he can pay you interest on it in a variety of ways, including a monthly payment, quarterly payment, an annual payment or even a deferral of all interest until the second trust deed matures. If you are ever in a position where you must take back paper, or carry a note for a new purchaser, make sure it is in the form of a deed of trust and has a reasonably short maturation date—no more than five years. If the new owner sells the property within that five-year period, your note should be paid off prior to the original due date. If the note you have taken back from the owner has an assumability clause in it and the house is subsequently resold prior to that due date, the second new owners can take over the note you offered and pay you when the date becomes due.

When you are loaning funds against a house you sell or, frankly, in any situation when you must act as a banker, it makes sense for you to do some of the things that a banker would do. For example, ask what the person's credit looks like. Contact your local credit bureau and obtain a copy of his/her credit report, if possible. If you can't, ask the person to obtain a copy for you. In addition, make sure you get a financial statement and verify that the borrower is working and that his/her source of payments is stable. Although time seems to pass quickly, five years is, in my opinion, more than ample time to carry anyone. This should give the purchaser of your home a reasonable period to negotiate another form of mortgage.

If, for some unforeseen reason, the buyer of your residence cannot pay, you have two options: at the time of the maturity of the note you could begin foreclosure proceedings and eventually take the house back, or you could possibly renegotiate the loan at a higher interest rate for a shorter period of time. This means you are willing to continue the loan but you are now demanding an increased interest rate on the amount due.

Our economy has oscillated so greatly over the last decade that it does not make economic sense to lock yourself in for 30 years. Such long-term mortgages were one of the primary reasons for the failure and poor earnings growth of many savings & loans in the early 1980s. It is interesting to note that in the spring of 1983 many financial institutions were offering 30-year mortgages. If inflation ever returns to the way it was in 1980 and 1981, the mortgage lenders may find themselves in the same fix.

DOUBLE YOUR MONEY

Tax-exempt bonds and annuities should become very attractive to you as you progress through this phase. If you are able to make a consistent 12 percent on your funds, your money will double approximately every six years. As you step back and enjoy life a little bit more, you should be planning to place your dollars in assets with continual growth but with the safety feature of preservation of capital. As retirement approaches, it is important for you to reevaluate what the tax ramifications are. In this particular phase, as I have stated earlier, you are often making a reasonable amount of money and, with your reduced debt, you may have fewer tax deductions. On the other hand, your expenses should also be reduced, thanks to the fact that your costs of raising a child or children have decreased or disappeared totally. Therefore you should be adding to your liquid net worth in cash assets.

HOME, SUITE HOME

From your preceding phases, you may have developed an interest in an avocation or business. Although loss of dependents and decreases in debt obligations have reduced your deductions, you may be able to pick up additional write-offs through home/office expenses and legitimate business deductions tied to business that is actually bringing in revenues. Keep in mind that the IRS keeps a close watch on what they define as hobby-related businesses. If you cannot turn a profit after three years in a particular entity, the IRS is going to question whether you had ever tried to realize anything but losses—certainly a method of tax planning, but not one that is recommended.

KEEP GROWING!

I think one of the worst things anyone can do in this particular phase is stop working completely. The work you have done in the preceding life phases may no longer interest you, or you may, because of your success, have the option of making a change. Even though you may be able to take early retirement, don't just stay at home. If you are married, you will probably end up driving your spouse nuts. What you *should* do, if you are in fairly good health, is divert yourself into other channels—either by helping others or reeducating yourself and focusing your energies on one of the hobbies you have kept on the back burner during other life phases. This is also a time to be checking in with various organizations, clubs or even community colleges where classes on preretirement and retirement planning are offered. These classes will often have up-to-date information regarding social security benefits, etc.

In addition, there may be new products in the financial market that are appropriate to your needs. For example, although annuities have been around for decades, they really didn't come into the public eye until recently. Ten years ago you would have been lucky to receive a 5 percent return on moneys placed in an annuity. In today's economy, because of interest rates and public awareness and pressure, these particular instruments are being updated constantly. For example, it would not have been difficult in the fall of 1982 to get a guarantee of 13½ percent for three years and a minimum of at least 10 percent for the next seven years. Of course, during that second phase, if interest rates are fairly high, it is improbable that the insurance company will offer you a lower rate when all the competition is offering higher rates.

The annuity concept receives the attention of the Tax Equity Fiscal Responsibility Act that was implemented in 1982. Prior to the summer of 1982, individuals could have had sums of varying amounts in an annuity contract. When they began to withdraw those funds they would be deemed as nontaxable until they had been withdrawn in excess of the funds originally invested. Under the new law that has changed. As soon as funds are withdrawn, a formula will be used to determine which are taxable and which are nontaxable. Because of your age, and particularly as you approach 65, the actuarial tables are used to determine what your "normal" life span should be. The shorter the number of years that the actuarial tables state, the greater the return declared as principal versus interest.

For example if you had placed $10,000 in a tax-deferred annuity in previous years and began to withdraw it when you were 60 years of age, the actuarial tables might state that your normal life span is 78 years. The amount that you wish to withdraw on a yearly basis would be considered, as well as the number of years left in your normal life span, and a portion of the withdrawal would be factored, so that your original principal would be returned to you over the 18-year period and anything over that amount would be considered as interest. If you withdraw funds prior to age 59½ the IRS will declare a penalty on it similar to that levied on IRA and Keogh accounts if withdrawn prematurely. Prior to the summer of 1982, annuities were far more attractive as investments, since a lump sum could be placed and interest could be earned on a compounded basis and deferred until you took out more than you originally started with.

The new laws still allowed the seven-day liquidity, the guarantee of principal, the ability to earn interest compounded and deferred until you take it out at a later date, and the pass-by of probate. The primary area of change was in the ability to withdraw funds construed as FIFO (remember, FIFO means "first in, first out"). Under the old rules, the IRS stated that when you withdrew funds from an annuity, the first dollars were representative of the initial moneys you began with. The new rule changed that and is more in line with LIFO accounting (last in, first out). Now the IRS says that the money you withdraw initially is the interest. It will not be 100 percent interest, but a portion will be, depending upon your age.

MS. MISC.

In the early part of this life phase, you might have placed funds in public limited partnerships such as real estate. Since these funds can take anywhere from seven to fifteen years to unwind totally, it doesn't make sense to make commitments to such investments during the latter part of this life phase. You should instead be taking profits and aggressively accumulating them in funds that will produce income, especially as you enter the next phase.

You may ask about the commitment sometimes needed to get the full benefits of an annuity. Keep in mind that the placement of funds in an annuity will allow you to change your mind and get your moneys back in seven days, thus satisfying your need for overall liquidity. There are, though, some strings attached, and there will be some penalties on the interest you have accumulated if you withdraw too soon. On the other hand, if you place your funds into a limited partnership, the probability of being involved as an investor for several years is great. Although some people think of an annuity as a long-term commitment, it need not be—you *can* get your money back. Limited partnerships, on the other hand, are very long-term commitments, and you should not anticipate that you can make a phone call and ask for your funds back on a week's notice.

Treasury obligations, tax-exempt bonds, corporate bonds and high-yielding time deposits are all reasonable alternatives for your liquid funds at this time.

Finally, if you have not taken a close look at your insurance needs, as well as the possibility of using trusts, this is the time to do so. Assuming you have fewer dependents now, your need for life insurance may be substantially reduced. If you are married and were to die unexpectedly, your assets could go to your spouse without incurring any taxes. Of course the question is: If your spouse dies, where will his accumulated assets go and what tax consequence will they carry with them prior to the next set of heirs receiving them? At this point, insurance is often carried to assist in the tax obligations that will be incurred at the time of death. Every time there is a new tax act, it appears to have some effect in the overall estate-planning area. If you have previously engaged an attorney to put together a trust, make sure you have it reassessed and/or revised each time a new tax act passes. Hopefully, our government will cease issuing a new tax act each year. One of the primary beneficiaries each time is the legal profession.

Trusts often involve emotional issues. If you are unwilling to pass the responsibility and power of handling your money to someone else, either for your own benefit or that of your heirs, then trusts may not be your cup of tea. I would recommend that you enter this phase with some flexibility so that you can make decisions and later change your mind if a decision proves inappropriate for you emotionally and/or physically.

WINDFALL!

A $10,000 windfall during this phase can affect people in a number of ways. If you haven't done any saving at all for your retirement and you recognize that it is not that far off, you may grasp the money and almost squeeze it to death. If this is your feeling, you should put it into preferred stocks, utility stocks, high-yield savings accounts, an annuity or discount bonds. Rarely will you go into a speculative endeavor. On the other hand, if you have been saving through the various life phases and a $10,000 windfall comes your way, you may look at it almost as a reward—something you can spend in order to have a good time. I have known many women who have taken a dream cruise or trip abroad, feeling that they would never have had the opportunity if Great-uncle Waldo hadn't left them the $10,000.

Another way of dealing with such a windfall is to place it, as you had in the previous life phases, in different investments such as the stock market, an art collection, or even to lend it to the kids for a first home. A word of caution here. I have always felt that if you choose to lend funds to family members, it is best to consider them a gift. But I definitely feel you should get a promissory note as you normally would with any loan you would make. Then if the money that you lend can't be paid back at the appropriate time, your mental note that it was a gift will reduce the anxiety and anger you may feel—otherwise you may end up terminating a relationship. I can remember lending some funds to a relative who could not pay me back. It became a sore point and he eventually no longer even wanted to call me or talk to me because he was embarrassed about his plight. I finally approached him and said I was going to call the loan. I was aware he couldn't pay it, and I was going to write it off on my taxes. I told him that if, at some point in time, things got truly better for him, then we could reexamine it, but I wanted to close the matter because it had become a barrier, and our friendship was really more important.

N.B. If you had put $2,000 per year from the age of 18 into an IRA earning 12 percent, your accumulated value at the end of this phase would be $3,821,179.60.

LIFE PHASE 6: 65+

> *"Mrs. Nancy McKeen, of West Stoneham, Maine, has the honor of having killed the largest bear ever captured in that region. The bear was chasing her sheep, when she attacked him with a club, and, after a hard-fought battle, succeeded in laying him out. Mrs. McKeen is eighty-three years of age, in good health, and says she is ready for another bear."*
>
> —Alice Stone Blackwell, ed., *The Woman's Column,* March 14, 1896

Obviously some incredible things can be achieved during this life phase. Because of the experience you have developed through each of the previous phases, you are now in a position to be considered a "master." Your depth of experience and common sense will guide you in the decisions you will make during the next few years. If you haven't already retired, you may be seriously considering it. You will hopefully live out your remaining years comfortably without worry, stress, or strain from money-related issues (or bears). This is a time to stay away from debt and to keep abreast of any tax changes. In this final life phase, liquidity should be the key to what is often referred to as the "golden years."

You are past the age of growth and capital appreciation and are now entering an era in which you will again become a consumer. As interest, dividends or other gains come to fruition during this period, you will more than likely spend these moneys on ongoing living expenses. You could, of course, have other supplemental income such as social security, private pensions and all the dollars you have been setting aside in your own retirement program such as the IRA. By the time you reach the age of 70½, you are required to begin withdrawing funds from your IRA or Keogh accounts. These funds have accumulated over the years if you were faithful and consistent in placing dollars there, and they should help enable you to enjoy this life phase.

If you haven't taken any classes on the needs of the retirement community, you should certainly enroll in one. Or, you might choose more active endeavors as did one of my over-65 clients, described below.

"WIN"COME DEDUCTIONS

Recently one of my clients brought her mother in for a tax workup and some minimal financial planning. After talking with her to determine where her income came from, she said she had a pension which she received each month, social security and some interest from moneys she had in a bank account. I asked her if there was any other income and she hesitated a moment and then said, "Well, there are my winnings." I said, "Winnings? What kind of winnings do you have?" She replied, "Well, I gamble!" As we talked further it was obvious that not only did she gamble but she was a serious gambler six days a week, almost all year round! In fact, not only did it give her pleasure, but she looked upon it as a job. In addition to her "normal" income statements, she had other statements of winnings from casinos in Las Vegas. Well, by now it was serious business because the winnings were going to place her into a higher tax bracket and she hadn't paid any quarterly withholdings to reflect the increased tax obligation. I asked her if she had any expenses—losses she had incurred until the winnings had come forward. She said she had actually kept track of that and that every time she went into a casino to play Bingo, she would cash a check and limit herself to spending that amount. She brought along the canceled checks, and after we examined them, we found that although she was certainly ahead in profits, she did have some allowable tax-deductible expenses incurred in the games. I am certainly not suggesting that you all rush out and play Bingo to supplement your income during this phase. What my client had done was find a pastime that was enjoyable and sociable and provided her with some extra funds. In fact, she told me she always came to the West Coast to visit her daughter for two weeks at Christmas and two weeks at Easter just to rest and get ready for the next round!

I know of many women who spend this phase rediscovering family, friends and fun. In the past they were too busy working to really let their hair down. They can now enjoy what they have been able to accumulate, spend their money, make gifts to family and friends, even be a philosopher.

At this point, taxes should not take up much time. They should be fairly simple. Income will come from retirement accounts—some taxable, some nontaxable—from interest and dividends and possibly even from an avocation or offshoot of your previous career.

Your nontaxable income will be in areas such as municipal bonds and social security. Other forms of income are partially taxable, such as a pension or profit-sharing account in which you actually contributed dollars that were taxed in previous years when you were employed with a particular company. Income from time deposits, passbook accounts and money market funds are taxable. If you are receiving funds on a monthly, quarterly or annual basis from an annuity, a portion of those will be taxable, a greater portion should be untaxable. You will remember from Phase 5 that taxes on annuities are a function of your predicted life expectancy and the amount of money you funded the annuity with.

If you have stocks—in particular, utility stocks—a portion of the dividend you receive may be nontaxable. The company you own stock in will inform you at the end of each year which portion of the dividend, if any, will be excluded from taxes. Also, you may wish to have the company reinvest your dividends in additional stock, thereby making them nontaxable until such time as the stocks are sold.

Bonds, as a rule, are fully taxable. Exceptions, of course, are municipal bonds, if you are a resident in the state of their origin. If you own a municipal bond that originates in another state, you should declare the interest you receive as income. You may be receiving cash flow from investments in real estate or oil and gas.

Because of the IRS's allowances for depletion and appreciation, that income may be nontaxable for you. If you are receiving income from retirement accounts such as an IRA or a Keogh, it is fully taxable, none of it being sheltered as you withdraw it. If you sell your residence during this phase, not all that income will be taxable. Remember that you have the opportunity to use the once-in-a-lifetime $125,000 exclusion for individuals over 55 years of age. Even if you bought a house several years ago for $25,000 and now sell it for $125,000, you will have no capital gains to declare.

I think it is a good idea to make a Taxation Chart with columns labeled TAXABLE, NONTAXABLE, and PARTIALLY TAXABLE. After listing your incomes under the appropriate columns, and totaling the columns, you will have an idea of your gross taxable income. You can then proceed to adjust for your personal deductions. For example, if you are over 65 years of age not only do you get a declaration for yourself, but also one for being 65; you know immediately that the minimum reduction from your gross taxable income will be $2,000. If you have any other areas that give you some tax benefits, such as interest payments or contributions, then follow the formulas under Tax Fax and determine your actual taxable income. It is important to do this because you no longer have regular withholding, unless you are still employed and receive a W-2 form at the end of the year. *The government now wants you to submit tax-liability estimates on a quarterly basis. This means you will be sending in Federal tax money every three months instead of having it withheld, as would happen with a normal paycheck.* If you continue to work and receive wages in addition to receiving funds from other sources, you will calculate the amount withheld from your paycheck as well as the amount you need to pay quarterly. It is not a lot of fun to do all these calculations, but it is essential.

The IRS has significant penalties, as well as interest charges, if you fail to have the appropriate funds on deposit with them. For those of you who still have a job that issues a W-2, you should have approximately 80 percent of the overall tax obligation in by December 31. For those of you who pay quarterly estimates, you should have forwarded the scheduled amount by January 15.

During this phase, your income may come from a variety of sources. Money market funds, short-term certificates of deposit, Treasury obligations, municipal bonds and short-term bonds are valuable in this particular phase. A word of caution here. I see a lot of women who have what we call their own "mutual fund." For example, let's say you have accumulated $100,000 in cash for investments exclusive of your IRA account and other retirement accounts. This $100,000 could be placed into municipal bonds, regular short-term corporate bonds, income funds, dividend-producing stocks, etc. If you have accumulated stocks over a period of time and haven't really updated them, you may find yourself holding as many as 30 individual issues. These are difficult to keep track of, and when you die they can become a headache for the executor or executrix of your estate and its respective heirs. Make life a little easier for yourself during this time and keep your portfolio down to ten or fewer issues. You will find it much easier to track the dividends and interest due you and keep updated on each of the companies.

If you have any real estate that is not returning a cash flow, you might consider selling it. If you have a substantial gain in some of your asset areas and are considering selling them, consider the capital gains tax. If you plan on leaving assets to heirs, it may make sense to make a gift prior to sale. For example, you have a parcel of land that has appreciated and reflected a gain of approximately $50,000. Your original cost was also $50,000, therefore it has an overall value of $100,000. Depending upon your overall estate situation, you may elect to gift a portion (perhaps 50 percent) to five beneficiaries and then encourage the sale of the land parcel. The result is that you are not responsible for the capital gain because you are retaining your original $50,000 contribution, and each of the beneficiaries or donees of your gift has received a $10,000 gift without declaring or owing any taxes. Remember also that when you make a gift, it is a gift and does not have any strings attached.

The old tax law stated that if any gifts were made three years prior to your death, they would be pulled back into the estate for tax purposes. The new law eliminates this possibility and allows that gifts made up to the day before your death will not be included in your estate.

If you are married it may not make sense to own everything in joint name. With the current tax law, if one of you dies, there is no limit on bequests and gifts that would go to the surviving spouse. Everything you decide to leave to your mate is considered tax-free under the new law. But, let's say that you had $30,000 in a joint savings account at your local bank. You also have jointly owned stock and bonds as well as other assets. If one of you were to die, everything that you owned jointly would be frozen pending probate. For those of you who have had the unfortunate experience of going through probate, you know that it can take months, even years to fully turn around. Unless the surviving spouse has personal assets to pay for ongoing living expenses, he or she may be in a fix, and for those of you who are the beneficiaries of life insurance, it could take several weeks or even months before it is finally paid out. You would probably have been better off to put the $30,000 in three different accounts, $10,000 of it jointly held, $10,000 of it in your spouse's name, and $10,000 in your own name. This way, while the probate paperwork is being done, you would have access to funds to take care of your living expenses.

If you are married and your spouse dies, be aware that the old $250,000 marital deduction has been revised with the Economic Recovery Tax Act of 1981, also known as ERTA. Under the old rules, one spouse could leave to the other $250,000 of her estate without incurring any Federal taxes. Under the new law, a person can leave a spouse unlimited assets without tax liability. A word of caution here, though. If you have a will that is dated prior to 1981 that specifically states that the marital deduction of $250,000 is in effect in the transfer of assets, you may have a problem. Your estate could be taxed from one spouse to another when assets exceed $250,000. To bypass this kind of change, provide in your will that if there is a marital deduction or transfer from one spouse to another, it should meet current law at the time of death. Because of ever-changing laws noted elsewhere in this book, it makes sense to have your will and estate planning reviewed every three years. Sometimes I think the only function of the tax-law changes is as an Equal Employment Act for the legal profession. Unfortunately, since lawyers are behind the majority of laws that are put into effect, we need them to help us interpret just exactly what they mean. And, of course, another complication here is that there is always more than one interpretation.

Not only did the Economic Recovery Tax Act reduce an individual's maximum tax bracket, it also reduced the rate of taxes on an estate—from 70 percent to 50 percent. The overall reduction will be phased in between the years 1982 and 1985. The top rate will be 60 percent for estates over $3.5 million in 1983, 55 percent for estates over $3 million in 1984, and in 1985 and thereafter a maximum tax of 50 percent will be levied on estates over $2½ million. This new maximum rate of 50 percent will apply to cumulative transfers of various gifts and estates. In this instance "cumulative" would meant gifts made to individuals during the giver's lifetime plus the value of her estate upon death.

Moreover, by the year 1987, estates that have assets of $600,000 or less will be excluded from Federal taxes. The tax consequence for the state you reside in at the time of your death could be another factor. Some states have no death taxes, others have minimal taxes, still others have levels in excess of the Federal. The $600,000 exclusion will take effect in stages. In 1983, $275,000 will be excluded, in 1984, $325,000, in 1985, $400,000, in 1986, $500,000 and finally, in 1987 the full $600,000.

All of this can be very complicated—which brings me to another issue that must be addressed: the choice of an estate administrator.

There are two schools of thought on who should serve as the administrator of an estate (the usual term is "executor" for males and "executrix" for females). A bank, attorney or accountant will charge a fee for this service. If you appoint someone close to you, such as a family member, he/she has the right to charge a fee, but it is probable that it will be waived. If you have your affairs in order and have spent time to make lists of where all the appropriate documents are, as well as an inventory of what assets you have, then a family member or a close friend could serve with relatively little trouble. But if your affairs are in disarray, it might make sense to bring in an outsider or professional. If things are a mess by the time your relatives achieve final dispersement of your estate, you may no longer be their favorite Aunt Martha.

Let's turn the tables and suppose that *you* are named as an executrix of a will. What does this job entail? Your basic charge is to gather together all the assets of the deceased, pay the appropriate taxes and debts of the estate and finally to distribute the remaining assets to the heirs. Well, you may be thinking, that doesn't sound too bad. Unfortunately, there is more to it than that. The following is a list of items you will need to cover:

Locate the last will.

If the decedent hasn't appointed an attorney, find one to act as counsel for the estate. (Use an attorney who has done this in the past and preferably specializes in estates.)

File the will for probate.

Obtain several copies of the certified death certificate. (You will need this over and over again for proof to banks, insurance companies, social security, stock transfers, etc., etc., etc.) If possible, also know the whereabouts of birth and marriage certificates.

File a claim with social security for the burial allowance.

If the deceased has any life insurance, make sure you contact each of the companies for the appropriate forms, fill them out and submit them with the policy. (This is often the largest amount of cash funds that you will receive during the probate process.)

If the deceased was a veteran, check into the possibility of veteran benefits.

If there are young heirs, it is important to file the appropriate forms with social security to get the available benefits for survivors.

If the deceased was working, verify whether or not there are any pension benefits forthcoming.

Make an inventory of all the decedent's assets, including contents of any safe deposit boxes.

Close bank and brokerage accounts and open a checking account for the receipt of proceeds of the estate during the administration process.

Make a list of all liabilities, as it is important to verify the validity of claims that are then presented for payment.

Maintain records of all income that is earned during the life of the estate.

Make sure you invest any surplus funds in short-term money market instruments, such as money market funds and money market checking accounts.

Determine the names and addresses of all heirs, next of kin, legatees and devisees.

If necessary, obtain court permission for allowance for support of the surviving family.

Determine the value of all assets as of the date of the decedent's death. If the amount of the assets has appreciated six months later, you will again determine their overall value. Estate taxes will be determined on the lower of these two assessments.

Pay all bills of the estate.

Arrange for any appraisals of real estate or personal property.

Collect any debts that are owed the decedent.

Publish a legal notice on claims against the estate in a newspaper that is acceptable by the court.

Set up appropriate bookkeeping records for the estate. Make sure there is an accurate record of all disbursements and receipts.

If required, sell assets to raise funds for the payment of any debts and taxes.

Notify all beneficiaries of their individual bequests.

If the decedent owned a business, obtain audits and appraisals of the books and records to determine the value of the business interest.

Provide an annual account. (This includes arranging for the preparation of Federal and state, if applicable, death tax returns and income tax returns.)

If the decedent owned any personal property that has tax obligations, pay these when they are due.

Determine the appropriate time to make distributions to the beneficiaries.

Obtain an estate-tax-closing letter from the IRS.

Prepare a detailed accounting to the court that is acceptable and final.

Obtain an order of distribution from the court.

Arrange for transfer and reregistration of securities, if any, with respective transfer agents.

Pay the Federal estate taxes within nine months of decedent's death, and state tax or inheritance tax, if any, when due.

Pay all bequests.
Petition the court for the discharge of the executor.

We have all heard horror stories about the widow who was notified shortly after the death of her spouse that an order had been placed for some specific item. Be aware, unfortunate as it is, that there are individuals who prey upon the sorrow and misfortune of others. They scan the death notices and then send out invoices for goods that were never ordered and probably never received. Don't let yourself be caught. It is your responsibility to oppose in court all incorrect or invalid claims against an estate.

Depending upon the complexity of the estate, there may be many more requirements. Needless to say, this is not something you want to take on as a lark. It's serious business and must be dealt with as such. When you are considering your estate, make sure that the person or persons you select to serve as the executor or executrix are able to do the job.

FEDERAL ESTATE TAXES

There are several taxes that may surface in the handling of an estate. The first is the Federal Estate Tax. This tax is levied on the current market value of any assets owed by an individual at her death. In making this calculation, the funds that have been spent on the estate administration, burial and final illness, debts, bequests to a spouse and any charitable contributions are deducted. If the final amount is less than $275,000 (for 1983), then no Federal estate tax is due.

STATE TAXES

State estate taxes are imposed by some states but not all. These will be based on the maximum Federal credit that is allowed for the state death taxes.

INHERITANCE TAXES

This, again, is imposed by some states, but not all, on bequests made by a decedent in her will. Depending upon the beneficiaries' relationship to the decedent, the tax will vary.

FEDERAL GIFT TAX

This tax is basically a tax on property that is transferred during an individual's lifetime. It is usually paid by the donor or the person who is making the gift.

STATE GIFT TAX

Here again, depending upon the state, the amount will vary according to the relationship of the recipient to the donor.

TRUSTS

You may be wondering after all this talk about taxes and estates, if there is any way to reduce the tax obligation if you exceed the Federal tax-free maximum. Through the use of trusts, part of the tax bite can be reduced. A trust is a legal agreement in which an individual, who is also known as the creator, settlor, or grantor of the trust, transfers ownership of her assets to a trustee (who may be an institution or another individual) who will then manage the assets for the benefit of one or more of the beneficiaries. The primary purpose of trusts is to control the distribution and use of the assets, as well as to minimize taxes. There are several kinds of trusts. One is a revocable trust, which merely means that you can change the basic provisions of the trust, or totally void it. An irrevocable trust is a trust that cannot be changed.

A trust can be established at any time. If in your will you state that you want to establish a trust, then it will be titled a "testamentary trust." A testamentary trust provides that a specific percentage of your overall estate will be set aside and managed for a particular individual. The person who manages the trust is called a trustee. This may be either an individual or an institution such as a bank. Some banks do an excellent job of managing trusts, others do not. Some individuals do an excellent job of managing trusts, others do not. Before you decide who is to be the trustee of your assets, make sure that you check them out thoroughly. Some of the biggest banks in the country have the worst track records.

There are two schools of thought on whether to have the individual or the institution, such as a bank, act as trustee. It is clear that a banking institution will have more experience. It is, *hopefully,* competent and, if there is any mismanagement or fraud, has the necessary bonding to make restitution. Individuals as a rule do not have that. But there is still the nagging fear that once you let an institution take over the management and responsibility, it is out of your control. How can you handle that? By making the bank or trust company serve as a "co-trustee" with a relative or a valued personal adviser of the grantor. A stipulation can be placed in a trust agreement stating that the individual trustee—for example, your spouse, or your primary beneficiary—has the right to remove the corporate trustee and name another in its place. Another method of dealing with that is setting up an *inter vivos* revocable trust. This will provide the opportunity to evaluate the trustee's competency during the grantor's lifetime.

INTER VIVOS TRUST

What are the most common kinds of trusts? The first, as mentioned above, is the *inter vivos* trust, also known as the living trust. This trust is created during an individual's lifetime and is revocable. This means that it can be terminated or changed during the grantor's lifetime. After the grantor dies, the trust then becomes irrevocable. However you set up the term of the trust instrument, it will be administered for the benefit of the various beneficiaries. Any assets that are placed in a revocable trust are considered part of the decedent's estate and therefore will be subject to Federal estate taxes. This is because the grantor can change her mind at any time and take back all of the assets by revoking the trust. If, on the other hand, the trust is irrevocable, the grantor would give up the right to change or terminate the trust and the assets would not be considered part of her estate. If an irrevocable trust is set up, the assets will be taxed as a gift at the time they are transferred to the trust.

TESTAMENTARY TRUST

A testamentary trust is also known as a "trust under will." The terms of this trust are stipulated in the will and are only activated upon the death of the creator.

IRREVOCABLE INSURANCE TRUST

An insurance trust which is funded by insurance policy proceeds is an irrevocable insurance trust. The appointed trustee administers the trust and pays policy premiums during the creator's lifetime. An insurance trust which is unfunded is the owner and beneficiary of any insurance on the life of the creator and is activated upon her death. The irrevocable insurance trust is used to exclude proceeds of insurance policies from the estate, as well as estate taxes. If the trust exceeds the maximum amount that is allowed for the tax-free passage to heirs, consider making tax-free gifts to as many people as feasible without depleting the trust below that amount. That way you can assure yourself that you will have the necessary funds for ongoing needs. Keep in mind that you can give $10,000 per year per individual without incurring any tax obligations to the donor or the donee.

By the time you have reached this life phase, you have probably received all four types of income. As you'll recall, taxable income includes the amount you received on your W-2 during your working years, and the majority of any interest income that you received from savings, bonds, and/or dividends. You were introduced to tax-deferred income when you initiated your IRA account. Annuities also bring you a form of tax deferral. Remember that tax deferral is merely a means of deferring your tax obligations until a later date. As a rule, tax-sheltered income is not a form of income that should come back to haunt you at a later date. Tax-sheltered income is normally received from investments that have a form of depreciation attached. They actually produce cash flow, but because of the depreciation loss, the IRS allows that cash to come to you without a tax obligation attached. The final type of income is tax exempt. This is the income that is received, for example, from municipal bonds for which you don't have to declare any state or Federal tax. There are other forms of partially exempt bonds, such as Treasury obligations. Treasury bills, bonds, and notes are taxable on your Federal return but tax exempt on your state return. Tax-sheltered and tax-exempt incomes are the best kind. These are what you should be working for.

You will find this to be an era of simplicity. The control and placement of your funds is the cornerstone of your personal money management success. It has little to do with the overall dollars you have accumulated over a lifetime in a bank or savings institution. By the time you reach this phase, you should be able to control your money as if it were a puppet and you the master puppeteer pulling the various strings.

MS. MISC.

Raw land can be one of the most expensive investments you have during this phase. As a rule it produces no income, so your money might have been better placed in other investments. This is the time, if you haven't already done so, to move away from illiquid and non-income-producing items such as land. Do not feel a real rush to unload anything, but be aware that when the economic cycles are right, this may be the time to list your property or sell it privately.

If you are thinking of investing in mutual funds, consider the following: Statistics have shown that commission funds do not exceed noncommission funds in overall appreciation. Since it takes several years to offset money paid to a broker, be sure to direct your moneys to a no-load fund since you don't want to spend this phase waiting for an investment to mature.

N.B. If you had started your IRA during Phase 1 and continued annual investments of $2,000, accumulating at the rate of 12 percent, sometime during Phase 6 you will have amassed over $3,821,179.60!

Part IV

TAX FAX

TAX FAX

"Anyone may so arrange his affairs that his taxes shall be as low as possible; he is not bound to choose that pattern which will best pay the Treasury; there is not even a patriotic duty to increase one's taxes."

—Judge Learned Hand
Senior Judge, U.S. Circuit Court of Appeals

In my financial-planning practice, there are several items I ask new clients to bring to the first appointment. One is the latest copy of their tax return. In addition, I request a copy of their payroll stubs, which show exactly how much money is being withheld in the various categories. This allows me to get a fix not only on what their overall current tax obligation is but also on how closely they are meeting it. Often I find that they are "overwithholding," which means they will be receiving a substantial refund the following year with no interest earned on those dollars. I also find that significant tax deductions may be overlooked because of ignorance of the current laws.

Most participants in classes and lectures I give throughout the country feel that they carry more than their fair share of the tax burden. In order to analyze what your fair share is, you must have a good idea of your current financial situation, what your risk-taking ability is, and what resources you have to further reduce taxes. At this writing, there is general talk about the possibility of a flat income-tax rate, with rates varying anywhere from 10 percent to 28 percent on overall income. Each of these various proposals has different strings attached. It is projected that if we move to an overall flat tax, it will not occur for another five years. Taking this into consideration, I will discuss the latest tax act and give specific recommendations that might provide overall tax benefits.

First of all it is necessary to acquaint yourself with the current tax schedule. The following tables cover married individuals filing jointly, married individuals filing separate returns, single individuals, and those filing as head of household. For those of you who are contemplating gifting or establishing a trust, I have also included an estate and trusts tax table that will indicate what your heirs will be taxed on if you choose to leave them any proceeds.

According to the accompanying table for single persons, an individual with a taxable income of $34,100 was in a 40 percent tax bracket in the year 1983. This meant that her obligation to the

1981 ECONOMIC RECOVERY TAX ACT
INCOME TAX TABLES

TABLE I—JOINT RETURN OR QUALIFIED SURVIVING SPOUSE

	Tax Rates for 1983		Tax Rates after 1983	
Taxable Income (Col. 1)	Tax on Col. 1	% on Excess	Tax on Col. 1	% on Excess
$ 3,400	$ 0	11	$ 0	11
5,500	231	13	231	12
7,600	504	15	483	14
11,900	1,149	17	1,085	16
16,000	1,846	19	1,741	18
20,200	2,644	23	2,497	22
24,600	3,656	26	3,465	25
29,900	5,034	30	4,790	28
35,200	6,624	35	6,274	33
45,800	10,334	40	9,772	38
60,000	16,014	44	15,168	42
85,600	27,278	48	25,920	45
109,400	38,702	50	36,630	49
162,400	65,202	50	62,600	50

TABLE II—HEAD OF HOUSEHOLD

	Tax Rates for 1983		Tax Rates after 1983	
Taxable Income (Col. 1)	Tax on Col. 1	% on Excess	Tax on Col. 1	% on Excess
$ 2,300	$ 0	11	$ 0	11
4,400	231	13	231	12
6,500	504	15	483	14
8,700	834	18	791	17
11,800	1,392	19	1,318	18
15,000	2,000	21	1,894	20
18,200	2,672	25	2,534	24
23,500	3,997	29	3,806	28
28,800	5,534	34	5,290	32
34,100	7,336	37	6,986	35
44,700	11,258	44	10,696	42
60,600	18,254	48	17,374	45
81,800	28,430	50	26,914	48
108,300	41,680	50	39,634	50

TABLE III—SINGLE PERSON (EXCEPT IF TABLES I OR II APPLY)

	Tax Rates for 1983		Tax Rates after 1983	
Taxable Income (Col. 1)	Tax on Col. 1	% on Excess	Tax on Col. 1	% on Excess
$,2,300	$ 0	11	$ 0	11
3,400	121	13	121	12
4,400	251	15	241	14
6,500	566	15	535	15
8,500	866	17	835	16
10,800	1,257	19	1,203	18
12,900	1,656	21	1,581	20
15,000	2,097	24	2,001	23
18,200	2,865	28	2,737	26
23,500	4,349	32	4,115	30
28,800	6,045	36	5,705	34
34,100	7,953	40	7,507	38
41,500	10,913	45	10,319	42
55,300	17,123	50	16,115	48
81,800	30,373	50	28,835	50

TABLE IV—MARRIED PERSONS—SEPARATE RETURNS

	Tax Rates for 1983		Tax Rates after 1983	
Taxable Income (Col. 1)	Tax on Col. 1	% on Excess	Tax on Col. 1	% on Excess
$ 1,700	$ 0	11	$ 0	11
2,750	115	13	115	12
3,800	252	15	241	14
5,950	574	17	542	16
8,000	923	19	870	18
10,100	1,322	23	1,248	22
12,300	1,828	26	1,732	25
14,950	2,517	30	2,395	28
17,600	3,312	35	3,137	33
22,900	5,167	40	4,886	38
30,000	8,007	44	7,584	42
42,800	13,639	48	12,960	45
54,700	19,351	50	18,315	49
81,200	32,601	50	31,300	50

TABLE V—ESTATES AND TRUSTS

	Tax Rates for 1983		Tax Rates after 1983	
Taxable Income (Col. 1)	Tax on Col. 1	% on Excess	Tax on Col. 1	% on Excess
up to $1,050	11%	—	11%	—
$ 1,050	$ 115	13	$ 115	12
2,100	252	15	241	14
4,250	574	17	542	16
6,300	923	19	870	18
8,400	1,322	23	1,248	22
10,600	1,828	26	1,732	25
13,250	2,517	30	2,395	28
15,900	3,312	35	3,137	33
21,200	5,167	40	4,887	38
28,300	8,007	44	7,584	42
41,100	13,639	48	12,960	45
53,000	19,351	50	18,315	49
79,500	32,601	50	31,300	50

Federal Government was $7,953. Because of the 1981 Tax Act, that same person in 1984 and after will be in a 38 percent tax bracket and will have a tax obligation of $7,507, for a total tax savings of $446. This, of course, assumes that there will be no additional tax-rate changes in 1984.

Let's return to the previous example of a hypothetical wage earner with a taxable income of $34,100. If in 1983 she elected to pay $2,000 to an IRA account, her taxable income would be reduced to $32,100 and her tax bracket would drop to 36 percent. The overall tax obligation would be $7,233, resulting in a total savings on her Federal tax of $720. How did I get this figure? Simple. By noting in the tax tables (page 191) that the taxable income of $32,100 falls between $28,800 (36% bracket) and $34,100 (40% bracket). I therefore deducted $28,800 from $32,100 for a difference of $3,300. Multiply $3,300 by 36% for $1,188. Adding $1,188 to $6,045 (tax already determined for income of $28,800) equals a $7,233 tax obligation. If you pay state taxes, it is important for you to determine whether or not your particular state has increased the deductions for an IRA contribution to match the Federal. Not all states have. In the above illustration, our sample wage earner has not expended the actual dollars for an IRA account but intends to do so by April 15 of the following year. She should therefore take that into consideration and adjust her withholding accordingly. This will allow her to take the approximately $720 tax savings and place it into a higher interest-bearing account.

For another example, let's suppose you are considering the purchase of a home. If that is your objective, and if you have completed that purchase within the calendar year, you will want to begin taking advantage of your specific tax benefits. For example, under current tax law, interest paid on your home mortgage is deductible, as are any real estate taxes you pay. In addition, there are often closing costs and a loan origination fee associated with the purchase. These are also deductible. Also, if you paid an accountant, financial planner, or real estate expert to advise you on the purchase of the home, those expenses are deductible. All these costs should be considered in determining your taxable income. If for some reason you don't purchase the house, or the purchase is deferred to the following year, you can immediately adjust your withholding to allow additional dollars to be withheld or you can pay the IRS an extra sum before the year ends.

As I have stated before, tax laws keep changing; but at this writing the IRS will give you no real trouble if you have withheld at least what you withheld the previous year, or if you have withheld 80 percent of what your overall tax consequence will be by year's end. If you determine that you are actually overwithholding taxes and that you will get a refund at the next tax-filing date, you can make an adjustment at this time to eliminate the refund or reduce it substantially. The adjustment will be the declaration of additional allowances on your W-4 form (a W-4 form is the form that you complete at the time of your employment that states whether or not you are single or married, and gives a numerical value of how many deductions, dependents, or credits that you are entitled to).

Let's say, for example, that it is the end of June and you find that if you continue to withhold at the rate you are withholding, you will receive a refund of approximately $600. Let's also assume that you get paid on a semimonthly basis and therefore have 12 additional pay periods. This means that you need to reduce your withholding by $50 per pay period to come out even at year's end. If you had noted that this was the case in January, you would have adjusted to a $25 reduction per pay period. This would have meant that in January you would have increased the number of your withholding allowances to reflect a $25 adjustment. Because you are halfway through the year, you must now play "catch up."

If you are someone who receives income from sources such as dividends, interest, trusts, self-employment, or investment property, you should consider making an adjustment, if appropriate, by the third quarterly payment. This adjustment would be reflected by a decreased amount of dollars paid, or in the case of significant underwithholding, an increased amount of dollars sent to Uncle Sam toward your overall tax obligation. If your state has a state income tax, it will be necessary to adjust either your withholding or your quarterly payments. Keep in mind that your state taxes are different from Federal taxes and the number of withholding allowances may be greater or less.

ADJUSTED GROSS INCOME

One term you will hear throughout your tax paying life is "adjusted gross income." That number is derived by taking into consideration all your taxable income from various sources and adjusting for a number of factors. Included in that adjustment would be any capital gains or losses that are declared; any pensions, partnerships or annuities that are taxable; moving expenses; business losses or gains; deductions for excessive business expenses; interest penalties for early withdrawal from your savings account; IRA or Keogh contributions; disability income exclusions; state or local income tax refund you received during the year; alimony that has been paid or received; royalties or distributions that are taxable from estates or trusts; farm income; and, of course, something that was added just a few years ago—unemployment compensation.

Once you have determined your adjusted gross income, the next step in calculating your taxable income is to subtract your excess deductions. If you are married, you deduct $3,400 from the overall itemized deductions to arrive at your excess deductions; if you are single or head of household you will deduct $2,300; and if you are married but file separately you will deduct $1,700. This adjustment to your itemized deductions is also referred to as the "zero bracket."

The next item that will reduce your overall income and bring you down to the bottom line, before any consideration for credits, is the number of exemptions. As of this writing, single women will get $1,000; married women who claim both exemptions will get $2,000; and if you have other valid dependents, you may take $1,000 for each dependent.

THE BOTTOM LINE

If you have no credits or other tax obligations such as self-employment or a minimum for social security taxes that hasn't been reported, you will consult the tax table and figure the exact amount you owe. If you are entitled to credits for such things as contributions to political candidates—with a maximum credit of $200 for married and $100 for single—elderly or child care expenses, investment tax credit, foreign tax credit, any work incentive or job credits and/or any residential energy credit, these amounts should be totaled and subtracted from your estimated overall tax obligation.

You should now know how to adjust your overall withholding. Also, if you discover more than $200 worth of deductions or credits that you have overlooked in previous years, you may want to file an amendment to get the appropriate refund.

KEEPING TRACK

It was Oliver Wendell Holmes who said, "Insanity is often the logic of an accurate mind overtaxed." If you are going to use any tax laws to your advantage, it is essential that you keep accurate records of your financial transactions. We all have different methods that are satisfactory and fit our own style. I have seen clients who are meticulous about tracking every dollar that goes out. They spend a great deal of time recording their expenses so that when income-tax times comes around, they merely total up the numbers at the bottom of their monthly ledgers and turn them over to their accountant. Other clients claim they don't have the time or energy for such record keeping. They simply compile all their receipts and backup data in a large shoebox or an empty drawer. They find that they can take one or two days out of the year, divide their receipts into various piles and then tally each individual pile. I must confess that I am one of those who stockpile everything and then sit down at tax time to do a final tally. Both my husband and I allocate one evening of the year to work side by side as we go through our various canceled checks, receipts, partnership returns and the like. Since neither one of us really loves to do this, we have found that if we open up one of our favorite bottles of wine or champagne and make an evening of it—since it usually lasts until the wee hours of the morning—it becomes an evening that may be long but not too painful.

If you also accumulate all your tax-related data in a central spot and then sit down once a year to organize it, do be aware that we are gradually moving into a "checkless" computerized society and that the day is fast approaching when we will not be able to use canceled checks as a substitute for a real record-keeping system. Whatever method you choose, the key is to do *something* and be consistent about it.

In keeping up-to-date on taxation, there are three areas which should be addressed—itemized deductions, tax credits, and changes in the tax law that are applicable to you.

DEDUCTIONS AND EXEMPTIONS

Charitable

Keep in mind that there are two contribution sections on your itemized statement. Part A is for listing those contributions for which you have canceled checks. Part B is for cash contributions or items donated to charitable causes such as the Salvation Army or Goodwill. In this particular area, I find that most individuals with whom I consult substantially understate their donations to charitable causes. The next table will give you some idea of what is considered a norm in each contribution area. If your contributions fall within the norm for your income it is highly unlikely that you will ring any bells in the IRS computer banks. These numbers act as a guideline. If you don't make any contributions, for heaven's sake don't put in the number for your income bracket just because you think it would be the appropriate thing to do or because you think you can get away with it. In addition, if your contributions for any other areas listed in the table are in excess of what is considered the average, you should definitely take them as a deduction. Just remember that no matter what you do, you should have appropriate backup data in case of an audit.

Adjusted Gross Income	Contri-butions	Medical & Dental	Taxes	Interest
$20,000–$25,000	$ 615	$ 664	$ 1,719	$ 2,782
$25,000–$30,000	$ 666	$ 604	$ 1,997	$ 3,004
$30,000–$50,000	$ 893	$ 549	$ 2,725	$ 3,510
$50,000–$100,000	$ 1,770	$ 730	$ 4,856	$ 5,532
$100,000–$200,000	$ 4,605	$1,167	$ 9,639	$ 9,844
Over $200,000	$23,919	$1,691	$27,777	$24,211

It used to be that if you hadn't itemized in the past, you were not allowed to take any deductions for charitable contributions. Under the new law, however, there has been a change. In 1983, even if you have not itemized on your return, you will be able to take a deduction of $25, in 1984 up to $75, in 1985 $150, and in 1986 up to $300. This provision will expire in 1987.

Medical

You will note that the table above contains a column headed "Medical & Dental." The numbers here represent an amount derived by deducting 5 percent of your adjusted gross income from the gross medical expenses you paid for the year. For example, if your adjusted gross income was $30,000 and your combined unreimbursed medical expenses were $3,000, your calculation would be as follows: 5 percent of $30,000 is $1,500. So $1,500 would be deducted from the gross amount you paid ($3,000), which would allow you an excess deduction of $1,500. You will note that in the column on medical deductions, the excess amount actually decreases where the individual has a greater adjusted gross income. This is due to the fact that you would need to have a substantial medical deduction to overcome the 5 percent excess to adjusted gross-income requirements. Thus, medical deductions as a rule are lower in the mid-income categories.

The "Taxes" heading on the table does not include any Federal taxes you have paid. This merely reflects general sales, property, state and any other local taxes you are obliged to pay. If you live in a state that has a general sales-tax table, it is highly recommended that you keep track of the items you have paid taxes on, which at this writing include almost everything. Time and time again I have seen individuals tally up these taxes to find that they far exceed the allocation that is granted on the general sales-tax table.

Interest

Deductible interest payments include those on a home mortgage, charge accounts and any outstanding bank or personal notes.

With today's high interest rates, you would do well to keep an accurate record of interest payments in order to enjoy the maximum tax deductions.

Keep in mind that in reference to interest income, there is no limit on the amount of personal interest that can be deducted, i.e., for charge accounts or mortgages. There is, though, a $10,000 limitation on investment interest. To determine whether or not you are safe, merely remember that each dollar of investment-related interest in excess of $10,000 must be offset from earned interest or dividends that may arise from stocks, any trust deeds, notes due you, any bond interest obligation or other investments that generate revenues.

Automobile

Another deduction area that should not be overlooked is automobile-related expenses. Remember that expenses incurred driving to and from work are not deductible. But if you need a vehicle to assist you in your business—for client calls, or attendance at various functions as a requirement of your particular occupation—you may have very valid automobile deductions which may end up being a tax shelter if you keep close track of them.

First of all, you must determine how much of your automobile usage is tied into actual business. For example, let's assume that you are anticipating purchasing a car within a year. You have been out shopping and the car you have selected has a price tag of $10,000. By keeping track of your mileage for the last few months, you have also been able to determine that 50 percent of your car usage is devoted to business. Normally, the IRS will allow you a business deduction of 20 cents a mile for the first 15,000 miles. With the shorter-term depreciation schedules effective in 1981, it makes sense to bypass the calculations for mileage and use the straight write-off numbers. For example, the car that cost $10,000 will yield several benefits. If you live in a state that has a sales tax, you will be able to take a deduction for that particular tax. In addition, using a $10,000 car cost, if you divide by 3, which is considered to be the useful life for depreciation purposes, you get $3,333. Multiplying that by 50 percent (the percentage of business use of your car) determines the correct usage figure and indicates that you would, over the next three years, be able to depreciate $1,667 per year. Of course, these numbers are rounded. In addition, you could deduct 50 percent of the maintenance and insurance costs, as well as all the finance charges incurred. You will also be allowed an investment tax credit of $300. The investment tax credit for three-year depreciation schedules is 6 percent. ($10,000 × 6% = 600 × 50% = $300). All in all, if you do use the car for your business, this could end up being one of your best tax shelters.

Business

As more and more women work, they find it essential to join various clubs and organizations relating to their careers. These organizations can be helpful in a number of ways. They allow you to stay up-to-date on your profession and sometimes even provide leads to a new job. A great majority of these organizations provide a bona fide tax deduction and will usually have an annual dues charge, as well as a separate fee for individual events. Make sure you pay by check, as this can be one of the best receipts you have. If you are in a business that requires entertaining clients, it is beneficial to have a separate charge card for that purpose. It will allow you to keep track, with good receipts and documentation, of various job-related costs.

When I was audited a few years ago all my business and entertainment expenses were questioned. I was able to verify them within a few hours because I had the receipts in the form of a general ledger. In this ledger I merely included columns for the date, the client, where we went and a few words about what was discussed. I presented this to the agent at the time of the audit and it was fully accepted because it was clear to him that all the deductions were relevant to my business. I can't stress enough how important it is for any of you who have business-related expenses to *keep accurate data* in case you are audited, since one of the primary areas the IRS looks at is business deductions.

Uniforms

If you are required to wear a specific uniform on your job, not only is the purchase cost deductible but also the cost of cleaning and caring for it. If you are a nurse and are required to have a particular kind of watch, then the cost of replacement and/or repair is also deductible.

Education

Another area the IRS likes to challenge is education deductions. If your career position demands that you take courses to keep you up-to-date on your profession and allow you to perform your job at a higher level of competency, then of course these are deductible. The IRS will often challenge them, however, so it is important for you to have the appropriate documentation and, if necessary, a letter from your supervisor stating that these were nonreimbursed expenses and that they were considered essential for your job. Make sure that these educational courses do not qualify you for a totally different job, in which case they will be challenged.

In the same audit I referred to previously, I was challenged for the educational cost of obtaining an MBA degree. The IRS's contention was that I was going to be shifting and moving into a management position. My accountant's and my contention was that I had had all the necessary licenses and requirements for the line of business I was in at that time and that the MBA was merely icing on the cake to allow me to better function as a manager in my current businesses. The IRS backed down on this one also.

Alimony

If you are required to pay alimony, that, of course, will be deductible. If you are the recipient of alimony, it is taxable income. Often in today's agreements between divorcing parties, spousal support and child support can be allocated to assist the one who needs the tax benefits. This could be a key point in a marriage settlement, as these payments can go on for several years.

Investment Counsel

Costs incurred for investment advice are deductible, as are various publications such as advisory letters, tax-shelter letters and business-oriented magazines and newspapers such as *Money* magazine, *Forbes, Fortune* and *The Wall Street Journal.* If you have funds in money markets or own any stocks, bonds or other investments, I would certainly include deductions for your daily newspaper, if you subscribe to one. It is important to keep up-to-date on economic events, and there might be a particular news item in the business section that could be crucial in determining whether to hold or buy a particular issue. Buying a television to watch Louis Rukeyser's "Wall Street Week" doesn't count as a deduction. Great idea, but it just won't fly with the IRS. If you incur any mileage costs associated with investment advice, it can be included at nine cents per mile.

Accounting fees are, of course, also deductible. Under the new tax laws however, the money you spend on an account or attorney for the purposes of evaluating an investment should be included in the overall cost of the investment. For example, say you are considering placing $5,000 in a limited partnership and you approach your attorney to analyze the documentation given to you by the promotor or syndicator. The accountant or attorney evaluates them and bills you for $500. According to the IRS, that $500 should be tacked onto the $5,000, and the real cost of your investment becomes $5,500. Under the old rules, you would merely have deducted that as investment expenses.

Medical Insurance

In the old days (pre-1983), you could deduct up to $150 of your health insurance premiums. The new tax laws state that this amount is to be included in arriving at excess medical deductions which must be more than 5 percent of your adjusted gross income. Also included in that calculation are prescription drugs and insulin. You should also be aware that transportation required to any doctors, dentists or hospitals should be added up and taken as a deduction at 9 cents a mile.

Home Office

If you legitimately use a portion of your home—owned or rented—as a primary or secondary business office, then you may take the appropriate deduction. It would be wise to measure out the square footage of the room you use and calculate its percentage against your overall living quarters. In addition, you may deduct a portion of your utility bills, and it is recommended that you have a separate telephone line to make a clear distinction between that business expense and the other normal living expenses. Previously, the IRS stated that if you were to claim a home-office deduction, it had to be your primary business as well as location. With the new tax law you can now legitimately claim a home-office deduction for business that provides a secondary or supplementary type of income. Do remember, though, that this room you claim should be used only for whatever business enterprise you are involved in, and of course the components of the room such as furniture, typewriters, calculator, personal computer, dictating equipment or any other items essential to your business will provide not only depreciation but also the possibility of investment tax credits.

Moving Expenses

If you take a new job and must relocate, you may have legitimate moving expenses. Do make sure that the new job location is in excess of 35 miles from your previous place of operation and that you keep all receipts for moving expenses, such as truck rental, moving-van charges, etc. In the case of cross-country moves, you may also be entitled to deduct hotel and food expenses.

If you fit into this category, it certainly makes sense for you to check with a competent CPA or financial planner to assist you in calculating total deductible amounts. The key here is to make sure you have the job before you move so that it is truly business-related.

Dependents

If you support any member of your family, including in-laws, grandparents and/or parents, you can claim them as dependents if you can verify that you actually pay for more than half of their care. If you share their care with others and the combined contribution of the contributing group is in excess of half the parents' support, then one of the contributors who gave in excess of 10 percent can claim the exemption if the others who also contributed will sign a multiple agreement to that effect. You might also note that if your contribution to their support is less than half the total and you pay their medical expenses, you can add those costs to your own medical bill when you are calculating the overall figure against your adjusted gross income.

Losses

If you have any business losses, these are deductible. And keep in mind that any losses from investments can be deducted and carried forward up to $3,000 a year. Larger losses can be spread over as many years as necessary in order to write them off fully.

A major change in the 1981 Tax Act was that the maximum capital-gain tax was reduced to 20 percent. This means that you would have to be in the 50 percent tax bracket to pay 20 percent of your gain out in taxes. A long-term capital gain is determined by the length of time you hold an investment. As of this writing, the long-term gain is in excess of one year from the time you purchase, and short term is anything less. Any short-term gains in excess of short term losses that are derived from the operation of a business or sale of an investment such as a stock are added to ordinary income. Short-term losses up to $3,000 are deducted from ordinary income. If you have short-term losses in excess of that amount, they will be carried forward until the next year. Unfortunately, once you begin to carry losses forward, you will need $2 of losses to offset every $1 of ordinary income. For example, if you have carry-forward losses of $10,000, $6,000 will be used the next year to offset $3,000 in ordinary income (two for one up to a net of $3,000) and the remaining $4,000 carry forward until the following year, giving you a net $2,000 offset to ordinary income.

Investments

If you have investment property, such as a second home that you rent out for vacation use, you will have various tax deductions.

The IRS will allow you to deduct the expense of a two-week visit to inspect the property on an annual basis. You, of course, can stay on the premises at this time as you do simple maintenance and repair work. Keep in mind that your travel to the particular rental unit will also be deductible.

If you have rental property, make sure to keep appropriate records. Also make sure you can verify and validate that you indeed have a property available for rent (i.e., newspaper advertisements, correspondence with prospective tenants, and/or actual records of expenses tied into the operation of the property). Too often, individuals are challenged by the IRS for write-offs attributed to rental units, especially if they are in attractive vacation areas.

LIMITATIONS ON DEDUCTIONS FOR CASUALTY LOSSES

According to the new tax laws, nonbusiness casualty and theft losses are deductible only to the extent that those losses exceed 10 percent of adjusted gross income for the year. Also, the first $100 on any single casualty is excluded from deductions.

According to present law, if a taxpayer has a disaster loss (attributable to a disaster determined by the President of the United States to warrant assistance determined as such under the Disaster Relief Act of 1974), she may deduct the loss for the taxable year prior to that during which the disaster occurred. If the taxpayer makes that choice, the prior year's adjusted gross income must be used to determine the extent to which the loss is deductible.

QUIZ

You have just been hired as a TV anchorwoman—you feel you need a new hairdo, manicure and tummy tuck. Can all these costs be taken as business expenses?

Answer: No. Only manicure and hairdo for a woman in the

public eye. A tummy tuck is not needed for her to be on camera, therefore it is not deductible.

TAX CREDITS

Many people are not aware that there is a difference between tax credits and tax deductions. While a deduction (such as interest expenses, contributions, real estate taxes) reduces your taxable income, a tax credit is actually taken off the bottom line of what you owe. For example, if you owe the Government a total of $4,000 and you have tax credits totaling $1,200, you deduct the $1,200 from the $4,000, making your net tax obligation $2,800.

The most common tax credits are political contributions, for which married couples can take a credit of up to $200 and a single person up to $100. Another tax-credit area is child care for working parents. The maximum child-care credit for one child has been raised to $720 and for two or more $1,440. Those of you who earn $10,000 a year or less will be allowed to take as much as 30 percent of child-care cost, up to $2,400, for one child or a maximum of $720 ($2,400 × 30% = $720). For two children the maximum allowed for child care cost is $4,800 or a credit of $1,440 ($4,800 × 30% = $1,440). This amount will be calculated on a sliding scale. For example, the percentage drops to 20 percent for those families who earn in excess of $28,000 a year. Therefore, someone who earns in excess of that amount will be limited to a maximum credit of $480 for one child ($2,400 × 20% = $480) and $960 for two or more children ($4,800 × 20% = $960). Even if you spend in excess of the $2,400 allowance for a single child or $4,800 for two or more children, you are not allowed to take those amounts into consideration when you calculate your percentages for the child-care credit. These ceilings may be changed as time goes on, but no changes are foreseen for the next few years. You should also note that the tax credit is not refundable. If your overall tax liability is less than the amount you are entitled to in child-care credit, then you are not allowed to take the difference. For example, if you are a head of a household and have taxable income of $10,000 and qualify for the maximum credit of $1,440, your Federal tax obligation would be approximately $813—far less than the credit you are entitled to.

Your taxes would only be reduced to zero. You would not be allowed to carry the additional amount forward or have it calculated against past obligations.

One particularly useful tax credit is the investment tax credit. With the 1981 tax act, the IRS has not only allowed a shorter life for capital equipment and depreciation, but it has also adjusted the investment tax credit to reflect that change. Under the old law, a company or an individual who bought eligible equipment, such as an automobile, was allowed to take an investment tax credit of 10 percent for anything that had a useful life of at least seven years. Under the new law much of the equipment most of us would consider purchasing now enjoys a useful life of three years and an investment tax credit of 6 percent. Let's use the example of an $11,000 purchase price, and assume that 60 percent of its use was for business. Under these circumstances you would be able to depreciate $2,200 a year as an expense ($11,000 ÷ 3 × 60%). In addition, you would be entitled to an investment tax credit of $396 ($11,000 × 6% = $666 × 60% = $396).

Another common credit many of us may receive is the energy credit. Although the amounts allocated on our Federal return are not substantial, many of the individual states encourage taxpayers to purchase solar-energy equipment and other related energy-conservation items. Some have, in fact, offered substantial tax benefits for these expenditures. Because of the variety of tax credits and the mistakes possible in calculating them, it makes sense for you to consult your accountant so that you can take advantage of the full tax benefit in every case in each state.

THE ECONOMIC RECOVERY TAX ACT OF 1981 AND THE TAX EQUITY AND FISCAL RESPONSIBILITY ACT OF 1982 AND THEIR EFFECT ON YOU

I have a theory on how our lawmakers name tax acts. I call it the "belly-up-to-the-bar" theory. First, "the boys in D.C." spend a few between-vacation hours devising the latest rules. Then they all go to the nearest tavern, belly up to the bar, and partake of all manner of spirits. When they are all so inebriated that they cannot remember Ron and Nancy's last name, they take a vote on what to call the latest tax act. Hence ERTA & TEFRA.

The passage of ERTA was welcomed across the United States. TEFRA, on the other hand, was viewed as a fiasco. It actually took away a great number of the tax benefits that ERTA initiated. Besides those mentioned in earlier sections of this book, there are others that may be beneficial to you.

MARRIED DEDUCTION

If you are married and both of you work, you may have suffered from the "married penalty tax." Well, help is on the way. The new tax act somewhat dulls the pain of being a married taxpayer. It now allows that the lower wage earner of any married couple can deduct 10 percent of his/her earnings up to $30,000. Therefore, if you earn $30,000 and your spouse earns $25,000, he would be entitled to a $2,500 deduction on your joint tax return.

INDEXING

Beginning in 1985, we will be introduced to a concept called "indexing." Effective in 1985, the tax-rate brackets will be revised annually to reflect the percentage by which the Department of Labor Consumer Price Index has *increased* over a one-year period ending September 30 of the previous tax year. The $1,000 exemption and zero bracket amounts will also be indexed.

The Consumer Price Index (CPI) at September 30, 1983, will be the base-year index for future computations. For example, the personal exemption will be adjusted for each taxable year by multiplying 1,000 by the cost-of-living adjustment. Therefore, if the cost-of-living factor is 12 percent, each personal dependent would be calculated as $1,120 (1000 + 120 = 1120). The cost-of-living adjustment will be determined by the CPI for the preceding calendar year. The CPI for any calendar year is the average CPI for the 12-month period that ends September 30. Indexing will help soften the phenomenon that pushed you into a higher tax bracket after a pay raise. This is known as "bracket creep" and has been a devastating tax burden for the taxpayer.

HOME SALE

For those of you who are contemplating selling your residence, you now have up to two years to replace the one you sold for a new principal residence without incurring an immediate tax liability if there is a profit on the sale. This will allow you to defer a portion or all of the tax that would normally have been due, if you had incurred a gain upon completion of the sale. In order to defer taxes altogether, you would need to purchase a home for a greater price than the one that was just sold. If you purchase a new home for less than you sold the previous house for, you will incur some tax consequences on the difference.

As stated earlier, if you are over 55 years of age and have lived in your house for the last three years prior to selling, you will be entitled to a one-time $125,000 tax-free gain from the sale of the residence.

BUILDING REHABILITATION

The tax credits for the rehabilitation of older buildings has been somewhat modified. Under old law there was a 10 percent investment tax credit for expenditures to rehabilitate nonresidence structures. Under the new law there is a 15 percent credit for buildings anywhere from 30 to 39 years old, 20 percent for buildings in excess of 39 years of age, and 25 percent for buildings that are certified historical structures. In order to qualify for this credit, you must spend a minimum of $5,000 over the original purchase price of the building in a rehabilitation effort, excluding land cost. For those of you who are interested in restoring old buildings, especially those that qualify for the National Register, this particular tax credit could be very lucrative. With many changes regarding investment tax credits (particularly tax consequences upon sale) of any structure using same, you must deal with a tax professional familiar with this area. When tax credits are derived from older buildings, the original basis (purchase price) will be adjusted by a reduction to the depreciable amount. If you are contemplating placing moneys in an older building, make sure you get adequate tax counsel.

STOCK OPTIONS

If you are employed by a company that offers stock options, these could be very attractive in long-term planning. The new tax act reinstated the capital gains treatment for stock options that meet certain conditions. When the options are granted or exercised, they will incur no tax consequences unless sold within one year; and if the employee finally elects to sell them after one year, she will enjoy a capital gains treatment on whatever gain there is at the sale. Again, because of the continuing changes in tax laws, make sure that appropriate tax advice is sought.

INTEREST

Beginning in 1985, all taxpayers will be allowed to exclude 15 percent of interest income to the extent that it exceeds nonmortgage and nonbusiness interest deductions up to a maximum inclusion of $450 for singles and $900 for joint filers.

GIFTS AND THE MARITAL DEDUCTION

If you are in a position to give gift money, you should also know that the Economic Recovery Act increased the amount one can give to another exclusive of the gift tax. Beginning in 1982, you can give as much as $10,000 to as many individuals as you choose. A married couple can give $20,000 per year to a person without having to pay gift taxes. Also, for married couples there is a substantial change in the marital-deduction provisions on gift giving or the passing of property from the deceased spouse to the surviving spouse. Prior to 1982, the marital deduction was limited to $250,000 of the decedent's adjusted gross estate. Effective January 1, 1982, the Economic Recovery Act changed this provision to an unlimited estate tax marital deduction. This will result in substantial tax savings to surviving spouses.

In addition to the increased limit of the marital deduction, there is also a substantial change regarding gifts transferred three years prior to death. Under the old law these gifts were in effect recaptured into the value of the overall estate for taxation. The current law reverses this policy and does not include in the taxable estate any gifts made within three years prior to death. The major exception is that life insurance gifted within three years prior to death is included in the gross estate.

DIVIDEND EXCLUSIONS

The new tax act terminated the $200 exclusion for singles and $400 for joint returns that was in effect prior to 1982. In 1982 it still allowed a $100 dividend exclusion, which was not of great significance. Dividend-reinvestment plans, though, are something of greater interest. If you elect to purchase public utilities, you will be allowed to reinvest dividends up to $750 a year ($1,500 for a joint return). To be able to do this, you must actually have the stock registered in your name and instruct the particular company to reinvest your dividends. When you finally elect to sell the stock, the dividends you turned into additional stocks will be treated as capital gain. These new shares will have a zero basis (i.e., their total value will be considered a gain rather than just the increase over purchase price) and therefore will be fully taxable. But keep in mind that the maximum tax you will have to pay is 20 percent of the sales proceeds, when you do sell.

WITHHOLDING ON DEFERRED INCOME

Under the previous law, income tax did not need to be withheld on pension or annuity payments, but a recipient could choose to have tax withheld on annuity payments. Under the new law, payors must withhold tax from some designated distributions. Designated distributions are defined as the taxable portion of payments made from or under:

- A pension, profit-sharing, stock bonus or annuity plan.
- A deferred compensation plan in which payments are not considered wages.
- An IRA.
- A commercial annuity contract.
- A partial surrender of an annuity contract.

The nature of the distribution determines the withholding rate:

Periodic payments (usually annuity payments) are treated like wages received from an employer.

Non-Periodic payments: These usually are subject to some withholding.

A recipient may, however, choose not to have tax withheld and the payor must advise the payee of that right.

RETIREMENT DOLLARS

Another area to keep an eye on is retirement—specifically, the laws that affect where you can place investment dollars for retirement purposes and what economic conditions dictate how you should earmark money for those needs.

When social security began, in 1935, there were approximately 15 workers paying into the system for every one retired person collecting from it. With the increase in life expectancy since that time, however, the number of retired persons has increased considerably so that today's ratio of "paying" workers to "collecting" retirees is 4:1 and could decline to lower ratios if there are not some adjustments soon to both coverage and the amounts paid to recipients.

So, while taxpayers in the early years of the social security system mistakenly expected it to be the "final word" in retirement support, today's taxpayers realize they should definitely be considering and planning for alternative sources of income during retirement. I would recommend that anyone under fifty years of age seriously discount the funds anticipated from social security and look to herself for retirement funds.

IRAS AND KEOGHS

It seems that our Federal Government, in a moment of lucidity, came to the same realization. As a result, in 1982 over 115,000,000 employed Americans plus an additional 20,000,000 spouses, became eligible for coverage under IRA (Individual Retirement Account)—one of the best tax shelters that has ever been created for the average U.S. taxpayer. In addition, self-employed Americans may also place up to $30,000 a year in a Keogh plan. Any contributions you make to an IRA or a Keogh plan, if you are qualified, are deductible from your adjusted gross income. Under the old IRA plan, if only one partner in the marriage was working, you were allowed a spousal program that required you to contribute 50 percent to each account. Under the new plan you are still entitled to do a spousal account, which would add an additional $250 for a total of $2,250; but it is not necessary to divide the contribution equally. Also, you may do both the paperwork and the actual dollar contribution for your IRA up until the time you file your tax return for the preceding year. Keogh is a different case: you must have the paperwork completed by December 31 of the year, but you can make the contribution up to the time you file.

There is what can be considered a "kicker" in the IRA and Keogh section of the current tax law. If you are self-employed, you not only can begin a Keogh account, but you can also contribute $2,000 to an IRA. For example, let's assume you have gross revenues of $50,000 and, after all expenses, a net income of $30,000. Fifteen percent of $30,000 is $4,500. Therefore you could place $4,500 into a Keogh account and an additional $2,000 into an IRA account. This, of course, will not take into consideration individual losses or excess itemized deductions that you would normally take on your tax return. If you are married and your spouse does not work, you can add an additional $250. If you had $30,000 in taxable income and it was reduced by a $4,500 contribution to a Keogh account and a $2,250 contribution to an IRA account, you would have a remaining taxable income of $23,250 and a Federal obligation of $3,168. If you had not placed the funds into these various retirement accounts, your Federal taxes alone would be an additional $1,650. This, of course, does not represent a 100 percent tax savings, but it does represent a 24 percent tax savings on the actual dollars invested, as well as an ability to control where the funds are placed. If you earned enough money to make the maximum contribution of $30,000 per annum for a Keogh account, as well as the contribution toward an IRA, you could claim a total deduction of $32,250. The IRS at some point in time could challenge this loophole, but under today's law it is certainly permissable. Once you begin an IRA or a Keogh account, however, please be aware that you can neither use these funds as collateral nor borrow from them.

For those of you who are self-employed and have children, you might consider employing them in your business. A 10-year-old may be able to type up simple envelopes, empty wastebaskets, dust, assist in filing, and run errands. For this, he or she would be entitled to a wage. Under the current tax laws, there is no tax obligation if an individual has reportable income of $2,300 or less. You could then employ your children, pay them salaries, take the necessary deductions such as social security and disability, if applicable, but would not need to withhold on state or Federal if they earned less than $2,300. This, of course, would be an expense to your business; and the children, because they made less than $2,300 each, would not have to file a tax return or pay any taxes. They, in turn, could place $2,000 in an IRA account and accumulate money until a later time. If, for example, your child places $2,000 a year into his/her account and decides in eight years to go to college, he/she could terminate the plan and begin to withdraw funds. There is, of course, a penalty for such withdrawal. But for someone with minimal wages and minimal taxable income, the 10 percent penalty and declaration of the amount as taxable income may actually represent an insignificant payment. And remember that even though the new law allows low-income individuals such as the ones in our illustration to put almost 100 percent of their earnings into this deferral program, regardless of how much an individual earns, he/she can still place only $2,000 per annum into an IRA account. But whatever amount is contributed to an IRA is deductible from ordinary income.

There are a few other rules to keep in mind. First, although there is no minimum age for participation in an IRA account, there is a maximum age of 70½, after which you cannot contribute. In addition, you cannot withdraw any moneys without penalty prior to the age of 59½, with the exception of death or permanent disability. The penalties, as stated before, include a declaration of whatever is withdrawn as ordinary income and an overall 10 percent penalty on that amount. This penalty is not tax deductible (as is the penalty for early termination of a certificate of deposit) and is collected by the financial institution you deal with.

There are several areas in which you can allocate your IRA contribution. For example, you can put it into a bank or savings & loan and earn its passbook interest. It is highly recommended that you not take this as one of your options, since the only one who really wins (besides you in taking the overall contributed amount as a deduction) is the bank or savings & loan, which lends it out at a higher rate in its normal daily operations. Second, you might consider placing it in a time deposit with the same financial institution. Such time deposits come in all sizes, shapes and terms, and you should verify what interest they offer as well as what penalty they collect at early termination. A time deposit is a far better choice than a passbook. I would limit the duration of a time deposit to four years.

Third, you can place your funds in an annuity. An annuity is a program of the life insurance industry that allows you to accumulate dollars at a fairly high interest rate over a long period of time. If you elect this option, be sure to find out first if there is a provision in the annuity contract demanding a penalty payment for withdrawal or termination of the contract. If this is the case, it is likely that the penalty will decline over a stated period of time.

You might also place your money in mutual funds which have different objectives. One example is the money market fund. Money market funds only invest in money-related issues such as U.S. Treasury obligations, certificates of deposit, commercial paper and bankers' acceptances. Money market funds often offer substantial interest rates consistent with U.S. Treasury obligations and liquidity. Also, the money market fund does not charge a commission, although there is an ongoing administrative fee that is structured within it. Other funds may charge a commission as high as 8½ percent. Such a fund is known as a load fund. If you choose a load fund, be sure to verify what its track record is, since if you make a contribution of less than $10,000 it may take several years before you are able to offset the cost of the commission.

There are some advantages in participating in a no-load (no commission) fund versus a load fund (up to 8½ percent commission) for an IRA investment. If you assume an equal investment performance for each fund, i.e., a 15 percent-per-year increase, your retirement plan would be far better off in a no-load plan compared with one that charges you 8 percent. Assuming that you place $2,000 each year into a fund and you are now 25 years of age, you will see that there is indeed a difference in the accumulated total over the next 40 years.

	Load Fund with 8% Commission	No-Load
10 years	$ 42,962	$ 46,698
15 years	100,680	109,434
20 years	216,770	235,620
25 years	450,270	289,423
30 years	919,920	999,913
35 years	1,864,556	2,026,691
40 years	3,764,555	4,091,907

The above numbers clearly illustrate that a consistent contribution of $2,000 a year with a reasonable return of a minimum of 15 percent on an annual return will yield you a handsome nest egg. Just remember that if you choose to place your dollars into a money market fund it is important to keep track of what is going on in the interest-rates market. If interest rates decline substantially, then the yield on your money market funds will also decline, thus reducing your overall return.

If you choose to invest in mutual funds, it may make sense to select one that has a family of funds, i.e., money market funds, growth funds, income funds, bond funds, technology funds, etc. Mutual funds offer a large variety to choose from and they allow you to switch from one to another without incurring substantial costs.

Another area to consider for placement of retirement dollars is stocks and/or bonds. If you are adept at structuring individual stocks yourself, then you should use a discount broker. If you believe in the market but are not particularly good at selecting stocks yourself, then you may want to engage a stockbroker. Take into consideration that you will be paying not only commissions, but often a transaction fee every time you buy or sell. This is because in order to qualify as an IRA, the stocks must be governed by an independent administrator or trustee. This applies to all issues. But most mutual funds as well as banks and annuities have their own trustee, so the annual charge is minimal.

Although the tax act eliminated your ability to invest IRA dollars in collectibles such as stamps, gems, art, rare coins and the like, there are other ways to participate in this market. You can purchase stock in companies that deal in collectibles. (Sotheby Park Bernet, for example, is a large auction house that deals in collectibles.) If the company is profitable in its auctions, it should result in an increased value for its stock.

Another area for retirement-investment consideration is a limited partnership. There are several public limited partnerships that are designed solely for pension dollars. These, as a rule, offer a minimum annual percentage return plus a substantial portion of the profit when the inventory property is sold at a later date. In effect, what the limited partnership does is to act as a bank. The funds are raised through the partnership, the partnership loans them to the manager for the purpose of mortgaged money, as in a real estate limited partnership, the manager in turn purchases the property, using the funds and paying the partnership ongoing interest in the form of mortgage payments. When the property is sold, the partnership receives a significant portion of any profit. Since a pension account cannot take depreciation and operating losses, a contract is usually worked out with the managers or the general partners of the limited partnership by which they will personally declare such losses. If this is the case in the partnership you are exploring and if you feel that real estate will continue to appreciate over the next ten to twenty years, the limited partnership may merit your attention. But I recommend that you first check the track record of the operator or general partner, that you make sure you will receive at least 75 percent of the profits upon sale and that you get all excess income after operating expenses.

Because IRA investments in these areas are fairly new, the track record of the operator or general partner may not be readily available. In this case, you will have to go back and look at the management's overall record in the real estate partnership area. Public partnerships such as the one we are talking about readily print the results of past sales of projects in their prospectus, which may be obtained through brokerage firms across the country. If the prospective general partners or managers don't have such a prospectus, then I would recommend you avoid participating until they establish one. The real estate limited partnership is only one example of what I refer to in Life Phase 3 as an "economic opportunity." Regardless of how your IRA dollars are placed, the account will be valuable to you in the long run. Remember that the amount compounds and can grow substantially over a period of time. If you merely earned 8 percent on a $2,000-a-year contribution, over a 30-year period of time your hard dollar contribution would be $60,000 and its overall value would be approximately $245,000.

You may have seen ads stating that you could be a millionaire in 35 years if you earn 12 percent on your IRA contribution. This is indeed the case, but unfortunately if we continue to have 12 percent inflation year after year, your dollars will be continually eroded and you are going to have to do even better. With the growing concern over the social security system, IRAs are considered a must for your current investment and retirement plan. Every working person under 70 years of age should begin an IRA *this year*. And, in fact, the earlier in the year you commence it, the better. The tax code allows you to do all the paperwork and make your contribution up to the time of tax filing, which is normally April 15. If you file an extension, which on the first request grants an additional 120 days, you would have until August 15 to open your account and make your contribution.

Many of us have become apathetic and lazy about planning for tomorrow. In fact, it will probably be a miracle if 30 percent of the eligible men and women actually participate in IRAs or Keoghs. Make sure you are not in the other 70 percent. If you are qualified to contribute to an IRA, do it. If you have the opportunity to participate in a Keogh plan, do that also. There are significant advantages in investing early in the year in IRAs or Keogh accounts. So, if at all possible, make your contribution at the beginning of the year, or even consider making an installment contribution. This will increase the amount of your retirement fund significantly over a period of time. For example, the table below shows an IRA investment for an individual, one for a working couple, and one for a married couple with one working spouse. Using a $2,000 per year investment and a constant annual interest rate of 12 percent compounded daily over a 30-year period, you can see that the accumulated amount for the January depositors is significantly greater than that for the December depositors.

Annual Investment	January Deposit	December Deposit	Difference after 30 years
$2,000 for individual	$653,312	$579,047	$74,264
$2,250 for married couple 1 partner nonworking	$734,976	$651,429	$83,546
$4,000 for couple both working	$1,306,624	$1,158,096	$148,527

What if you don't have enough money to make the full contribution? For example, you have saved only $1,000. Consider taking out a personal loan of $1,000 and investing both amounts in the IRA. The interest you will pay on the loan is tax-deductible and your contribution to the IRA or Keogh compounds tax-free until you begin to withdraw at a later date. If you are in the 50 percent tax bracket, every $1,000 you contribute to a retirement plan will save you $500 on the Federal level. If it costs you 18 percent to borrow, your after-tax cost is 9 percent. If your Keogh or IRA plan enjoys earnings of 12 percent per year, you will actually make 3 percent on the spread. This, over a period of time, can build into a reasonable return.

Let's assume you are thirty-five years of age and are currently in the 30 percent tax bracket, which represents taxable income of $23,500. You set up an IRA and make your contribution of $2,000 a year for the next 30 years—$1,000 of earned money and another $1,000 borrowed at an average interest rate of 18 percent on a monthly basis. The illustration below also assumes that you will repay the $1,000 loan within a year. According to the table below, at the age of sixty-five you will have accumulated $525,060.01. If, on the other hand, you had contributed only the $1,000 of earned money, you would have accumulated a total of only $278,581.69—a difference of $246,478.32.

Years to Retirement	Age Now	Accumulate w/$2,000 Investment*	Accumulate w/$1,000**	Net Difference (Borrowing vs Not)
30	35	$525,060.01	$278,581.69	$246,478.32
25	40	$280,353.38	$153,553.09	$126,800.29
20	45	$143,703.89	$ 82,553.07	$ 61,150.82
15	50	$ 68,672.89	$ 42,362.29	$ 26,310.60
10	55	$ 29,126.82	$ 19,913.97	$ 9,212.85
5	60	$ 9,011.87	$ 7,181.22	$ 1,830.65

* Contribute personal $1,000, borrow $1,000, repay loan monthly.
** Contribute personal $1,000 only.

TAX SHELTERS

Unless you go through life simply paying a minimal tax rate, you will probably at some time or another participate in a tax shelter. Even though the primary purpose of a tax shelter is to provide tax write-offs, you should never enter into them unles there is also a chance of making money. Otherwise, you will be far better off to make a sizable contribution to charity, receive a 100 percent deduction, and sleep well at night.

If, however, you do wish to put money into a tax shelter—these are also known as tax incentive investments—you can find one through any reputable major brokerage firm as well as through private syndicators. Brokers and advisers who sell shelters often receive a handsome commission. You should be aware that a deal offering commissions from 9½ percent to 16½ percent of the actual unit size can attract participants of questionable character. So investigate carefully before committing your funds. You will notice that there are many advertisements for tax shelters and tax reduction-type investments at the end of the year. Just remember that, as a rule, 99 percent of the quality investments are offered in the *beginning* of the year. Also, if you have made use of the opportunity to invest in an IRA, Keogh, or other reputable investment account, you should not feel "under the gun" to eliminate your tax burden at the end of December. In the best of circumstances, tax shelters can supply tax breaks substantial enough so that tax-pressured individuals will focus only on the plusses and ignore the drawbacks. In the area of tax shelters, *Caveat emptor* ("Let the buyer beware") is certainly an appropriate piece of advice.

Tax shelters are not low risk, and, as is often the case, one can lose her entire investment. Although tax shelters have been called loopholes in the tax law, they really are not. They are merely a way of compensating an investor for her willingness to undertake a specific risk. Before you place any of your funds in an investment that offers tax benefits, you must ask how much you are willing to risk, what your individual tax needs are, what other options are available to you, and finally, what the merits of the specific investment area are.

Prior to 1976, individuals who participated in tax shelters could have enjoyed anywhere from two-to-one up to a ten-to-one write-off of original dollars invested. With what are called "at risk" rules, such write-offs are now considered dangerous. "At risk" rules basically mean that you can get no more than a one-to-one write-off. If your deductions in the first year exceed your original investment, it is highly possible that the IRS will question whether you are entitled to those benefits. With the 1981 tax act, excessive write-offs are no longer so valuable to you because of the reduction in the individual personal tax bracket. In addition, income that could be produced from a successful shelter will be taxed at a declining rate. Therefore, it is probably more profitable for you to invest in a financially sound project that will produce both income and growth than to place your dollars at risk for a current tax write-off.

There is no question that the IRS is focusing on tax shelters. Partnerships are being examined more closely, and losses you claim on your tax return may trigger an audit. Individuals who have participated in previous multiple write-off deals may be requested to sign a waiver of the statute of limitations. If they don't, they can face an immediate disallowance of the questionable deduction. This does not mean you should avoid what looks like a worthwhile tax benefit venture for fear of a tax audit. Just make sure you keep accurate records and that the person or company managing your particular investment uses a reputable accounting firm that will validate the various tax benefits.

If the particular partnership you have invested in goes through an IRS audit and some or all of the deductions are disallowed, you could face a 20 percent interest charge on any delinquent taxes due. This is up substantially from the former 12 percent interest charge.

As a rule, a tax shelter is presented in the form of a limited partnership, and there could be one or several general partners who manage it. The offering may be public or private. There are pros and cons to each.

Private partnerships are limited to 35 partners with capital contributions of no more than $150,000 each. Partners who can place amounts of above $150,000 are not included in the count. Units can sell for as low as a few thousand dollars each. Private partnerships may also be funded in stages. For example, let's say a unit sells for $50,000—$15,000 this year, $10,000 the following year and $25,000 the third year. In private partnerships you often know where the money will go (for example, into one building in a real estate offering), and it is often easy to get a reading from the managing general partner or operator as to the estimated current market value of your investment. One of the drawbacks to a private placement is that if something critical happens to the person managing the project, the partnership could be forced into a dissolution.

On the other hand, in a public program, there is no restriction on the number of partners. As a rule, most of these investments are offered in units of a minimum of $5,000. Public offerings are regulated by the Securities Exchange Commission and often by the individual states in which the units are sold. Because an offering is registered in a state and SEC-regulated, this does not mean it is approved or that you have a guaranteed deal. It merely indicates that certain disclosure requirements have been met. In fact, there are many large public offerings that have been fully funded and in a few months go under totally because of gross negligence and mismanagement by the operator. On the other hand, one of the advantages of the public partnership is that there are usually several layers of management. In case one of them becomes unable to tend to business, another will be able to step in with no significant changes. In addition, public offerings are often quite large, carry substantial reserves, and are usually more diversified than private ones.

In either type of partnership, limited partners will generally deduct losses up to the extent of their investment. If they are required to make additional contributions in the form of a non-recourse loan (one in which there is generally no liability beyond the security initially offered), then that too may be deductible. In the case of real estate, non-recourse is also considered to be deductible.

Some limited partnerships, such as equipment leasing and oil-and-gas partnerships, may require what is called a letter of credit. A letter of credit is a bank's guarantee that an individual is basically "good" for a loan. That letter is issued from one bank to another on behalf of the limited partner and it allows for the second bank to draw funds, if necessary. This means that the individual partner is at risk for the amount of the letter of credit and could have a loan the following day with the bank that issued it if the corresponding bank elected to draw down on the letter of credit.

One of the attractions of investments that use letters of credit is leverage. This means that you may put up a small portion of an investment unit in cash and supply the remainder by a letter of credit. Let's say you are interested in putting $25,000 into an oil-and-gas venture that requires a $5,000 cash deposit and a $20,000 letter of credit. Although you may have only $5,000 of cash in it, the investment will indicate that you have $25,000—thus, the deductions you receive for it will be based on a full $25,000 investment, not just the $5,000 cash you have put in. How does this help? Well, when you have significant tax obligations, write-offs for a larger dollar amount will be more beneficial to you and, in fact, in some investments such as oil and gas and equipment leasing, the write-offs can be significantly larger than the actual cash deposit.

If you are responsible for a letter of credit, this doesn't necessarily mean that you will be allowed tax deductions or write-offs in excess of your initial cash deposit or contribution. The IRS now states that it is necessary for a taxpayer to put up cash as collateral for a letter of credit in order to be truly "at risk" in their eyes.

A typical shelter will generate losses through various areas such as offering expenses, mortgage payments and depreciation. Of course, it is necessary to offset any revenues that are received. The excess amount will be allocated to investors per their percentage ownership of the partnership, and they in turn will report them on their tax return. A loss from a partnership is used to reduce adjusted gross income.

Shelters usually have two types of risks. One is tax risk, the other investment risk. In the area of tax risks, there is always a possibility that the tax savings projected by the syndicator will not occur. What could cause this? Well, tax laws change. The IRS could come back and rule that the deductions you took really weren't valid, or that the anticipated losses to various start-up costs and/or reduced revenues are offset by an actual increase in revenues for the particular investment.

Risk in the investment area has several aspects. For example, you might anticipate a fixed income and find that it is actually much more—or less—than you expected.

Limited partnerships as a rule are highly nonliquid. There are only a few programs that actually offer to buy partnership units out. One is The Liquidity Fund which is located at 1900 Powell Street, Emeryville, CA 94608. This fund is interested in just about any public partnership that has a three- to five-year track record and some cash flow. At this writing, the fund is not interested in buying raw land or in special purchase projects such as recreation facilities, programs that have a minimal appreciation potential and/or business opportunities, such as a mom-and-pop-type store. Be aware that if The Liquidity Fund does buy, it may offer you much more or less than you put in. If you are in a partnership such as those described in this section (real estate, oil and gas, equipment leasing) and wish to get out for any reason, you may want to contact this fund. The Liquidity Fund will consider buy-outs on a one-by-one basis, as it is not necessary for everyone in the partnership to want to sell their particular partnership unit.

Many of the limited partnerships on today's market currently offer income either on a monthly or quarterly basis. As a rule, these are far less risky than shelters that offer substantial write-offs. If you are thinking about investing in a shelter that offers a substantial write-off (which in my opinion should be considered extremely speculative) you should be in a high tax bracket—at least 48 percent if you are single (a taxable income of approximately $55,300) and a minimum of 49 percent if you are married (a taxable income of $109,400). If there is any possibility that you will need the sheltered money within a few years, don't invest in it, regardless of the write-off.

Shelters can have many functions. One is deferral. These particular limited partnerships are designed to hold taxable income and are actually considered more suitable for investors who expect their taxable income to decline substantially after write-offs have been taken and income starts to come in. An example is equipment leasing. Normally, write-offs are taken for the first three to five years and income is reported in the later years. Write-offs for the first year will range anywhere from 40 to 100 percent of the cash put in. In addition, if your shelter requires a letter of credit and you have it backed by the appropriate cash, you can get an even greater write-off.

Another function of tax shelters is equity building. Instead of the shelter's incurring a substantial write-off at once, write-offs are spread over several years, and at some point even tax-sheltered income may be distributed to each limited partner. You may receive, for example, anywhere from 15 percent to 30 percent of your write-off annually over a few years. In the third or fourth year you may actually receive income, but because of depreciation, most of it will be sheltered.

These particular limited partnerships allow a substantial write-off well in excess of your original cash investment because of such things as real estate non-recourse debt. In real estate, as a rule, the actual debt or mortgage on the real property is much greater than the amount of cash originally invested. Over a period of time, the interest payments, expenses and depreciation may substantially exceed the original cash-in. When you have non-recourse debt, the limited partner will not be obligated for the actual mortgage if it goes into default. Although he enjoys the excess write-off if the property is sold and not enough funds are received to pay off the debt, the lender will either have to take the loss or, if allowed, may have some recourse in obtaining the deficit amount from the general partner or manager. These limited partnerships are designed for investors who will have a very high income for several years. Cash flow is minimal, if it exists at all, and profits may come many years later when the property is sold. Housing subsidized by the government is another example of a partnership that allows a write-off in excess of the amount originally invested.

Although few of us have crystal balls, it is important to try to consider what the long-range economic environment will be when deciding on a particular investment. It makes sense to be skeptical when you are evaluating a tax-shelter proposal. You should probably sidestep any syndicators who offer substantial write-offs and almost guarantee phenomenal returns in addition to your initial capital. Read the offering memorandum or prospectus that should accompany any tax shelter proposal carefully. If there is no such document, don't get involved. If you are considering one, there are several questions you may want to ask:

1. *What is the objective of this particular investment?* I often tell clients that if the partnership's objectives don't match their own personal goals, then it doesn't make sense to waste any more time reading what may well turn out to be the all-time cure for insomnia. Assuming, however, that the objectives match yours, proceed to analyze the use of proceeds. As a rule of thumb, a maximum of 25 percent of all funds raised should go for organizational costs, commission and reserves. A minimum of 75 percent should actually go into the property. If you use these figures as a guideline, you can eliminate many prospectuses that come your way.
2. *Has the general partner successfully managed and operated similar investments?* If possible, compare the current offering and tax-break projections with the projections and actual performance of past programs. Public programs include a history not only of ongoing operations but also partnerships that have been completed. This track record will give you a good idea of how the managing general partner may actually negotiate a sale in the end.
3. *Is there enough reserve to handle any negative cash flow and are expected operating costs realistic?* In the case of real estate, the Institute of Real Estate Management in Chicago publishes an annual analysis of various real estate operations across the country. This will give you a reading on how a proposed manager handles operating costs and expenses. For

example, you may be considering investing in a small apartment unit in the Sacramento area. You should look it up in the Institute's guide and get a reading of what the high, medium, and low vacancy rates are, as well as what the high, medium, and low operating expenses are. These, of course, are averages. The financial projections that should be included with your prospectus will help you to determine whether the proposed operating expenses are in line with previous reported averages. There are, of course, no guarantees, but it is nice to have some guidelines.

4. *If it is necessary to come in with additional funds in later years, even though this is not originally stated or required in the prospectus, would you be willing to do so?* If the economy runs into a bumpy time, it may be necessary to invest additional funds because of some unforeseen reasons—cash flow has decreased or a mortgage has come due that must be renegotiated at a substantially higher price.
5. *How is the general partner being compensated?* As a rule, the bigger the stake the general partner or partners have, the more carefully they will monitor the partnership. Always be suspicious of heavy prepayment services to the general partner or affiliates. In my opinion, compensation should be based only on performance. For example, once the limited partners receive their funds back and have achieved a certain annual percentage increase, then the general partners should be entitled to a certain percentage of the profits. Be wary of any general partner who will not only get a percentage of the profits in the end, but also receives a front-end development fee, consulting fee, and a commission for selling the investor units to each of the limited partners. If the only front-end fee charged to the partnership is in the area of 10 percent of the total funds raised, then this would be acceptable. It would not be acceptable if in addition to a front-end fee the general partner also received a commission for selling the units and if, as in the case of real estate, he or she would receive a sales commission on the property that is being bought or sold. Most general partners normally will build in a fee, such as the 10 percent amount referred to above, that will allow him or her to pay finder's fees or a commission to others in selling the units. Be wary of anything over this amount. It is quite com-

mon to be a managing general partner and receive some ongoing fee such as 5 percent of the gross revenues on a continuing basis. This should cover not only staff time but also copying, postage, phone calls and other related items that are incurred on behalf of the partnership.

Other questions include the following: *If the investment is offering projected tax benefits, are they based on current tax law? In the opinion of the investment adviser, financial planner or accountant, will they stand up in court? Does the investment look valid or is it merely put together for tax write-offs?*

In a public partnership, it is extremely difficult to determine whether or not the particular item is being offered at its fair market value or at an inflated price. Normally, in a public offering, a partnership may purchase anywhere from eight to 15 shopping centers, commercial buildings, and/or apartment houses. It is highly unlikely you will have contacts in the various states where these acquisitions are being made. In the case of a private offering, however, you will often be able to make simple inquiries to real estate brokers in the area and thereby determine if this particular acquisition is being offered at fair market value. I also recommend that if the building is being purchased for the partnership, you include in the offering memorandum a copy of the deposit receipt as well as a statement of any loans or notes, their interest rates, and their length or term.

Quite often, when the partnership is first put together, some fees will be involved. Commissions in public programs will average approximately 8 percent. In private programs the average is about 10 percent. In addition, there is often a one-time organizational fee of anywhere from 1½ percent to 3 percent. These fee percentages could be considered reasonable and would be used to pay for the printing of the offering material, postage, appropriate staff necessary to complete the formation of the partnership and possibly initial accounting and legal expenses.

I strongly recommend that you consult your financial adviser before placing your dollars in any investment. There appears to be a trend among accountants and attorneys to recommend specific deals from which they get some reimbursement. In my opinion the primary function of an attorney or accountant should be to answer legal and financial questions: Do the numbers make sense? Are the tax projections feasible with current law? If a particular partnership investment gets into trouble and you go back to the accountant and/or attorney for a recommendation as to whether there was negligence, mismanagement or misuse of funds, you may encounter a conflict of interest if he/she in fact received some reimbursement for getting you into the partnership. In addition, anyone who receives a commission for recommending a specific deal will have a strong economic incentive to analyze the investment in a favorable manner. If you feel this is the case but also feel there is strong merit in your particular investment, do yourself a favor and round out an analysis by getting the opinion of an independent financial adviser. This could prove invaluable. And keep in mind that although your financial adviser may be quite competent to analyze various tax consequences, his or her experience on the business side may be limited in regard to the particular partnership you are exploring. Consult with a person who is experienced and knowledgeable in the specific business of the partnership.

QUIZ

You have been audited for three years on your job-related deductions. Each year, after spending much time and energy to validate your deductions, you have cleared the audit. In this morning's mail you receive an envelope marked "U.S. Treasury." Upon opening it you find that the IRS is asking for verification of the same expenses. You should:

(a) Burn it and pretend you never received it.
(b) Call the IRS and blow a whistle into the mouthpiece.
(c) Make an appointment to meet with the IRS again and go over the deductions.
(d) Call your accountant and tell him/her to deal with it.

Answer: If you answered (d) you are correct; (c) is not correct because the IRS cannot audit on the same issue repeatedly when you have already received clearance in prior years.

Afterword

"It takes little talent to see clearly what lies under one's nose, a good deal of it to know in what direction to point that organ."

—W. H. Auden

THE key to your financial success lies only with you. Laws change, the economic environment changes and you must have the tenacity and experience to flow with these changes and turn them to your advantage. Your hope for a successful financial future depends upon your ability to educate yourself in life, set goals, be resilient when you make mistakes and use them as part of your ongoing education, and then implement what you have learned and turn it into a more lucrative reward.

Index

accountants, 228–29
accounting, 117–18
  annual reports and, 163–64
  changes in, 164
  FIFO (first in, first out), 164, 172
  LIFO (last in, first out), 164, 172
Alliance Capital Reserves, 65
American Express, 54
annual reports, 163–68
  accounting changes and, 164
  balance sheets in, 165–66
  CPAs and, 163
  earnings per share in, 165, 167
  footnotes in, 164, 165, 167
  "generally accepted accounting principles" and, 163–64
  income-and-expense statements in, 167
  liabilities in, 165–66
  nonrecurring revenues in, 165, 167
  outstanding shares listed in, 165
  quick ratios from, 166
  sale of division and, 164–65, 167
  top management letters in, 165
annuities, 38, 44, 156, 170–72
  benefits of, 156
  FIFO vs. LIFO accounting for, 172
  as IRAs, 215
  liquidity of, 173
  "normal" life span and, 172
  premature withdrawal from, 172
  principal maintained in, 156
  return from, 171
  taxes on, 171–72, 177
  withdrawals from, 171–72
antiques, 72–73
assets:
  break-even point for, 35–36
  cash, 146, 158, 170
  evaluation of, 26–27
  inflation and, 27
  listing of, in wills, 133
  marriage and, 31–32
  out-of-state, 133
  taxes and, 160–62
attorneys, 74, 173, 228–29
  estate-planning, 148, 160
  incorporation and, 119
  power of, 162–63
  tax, 44, 143, 161–62
  wills and, 133–34
audits, by IRS, 43–44, 221

banker's acceptances, 67–68
bankruptcy, 137, 140–41, 166–67
banks and bankers, 42–43, 53–54, 70–71
  borrowing from, 53–55, 59, 71–72
  in life phase 2, 88
  in life phase 3, 135
  lines of credit from, 121, 143–44
  as trustees, 185–86
  value of having more than one, 88
bonds, 83, 136–40, 173, 216
  bankruptcy and, 137
  with callable features, 140
  capital gains on, 139, 140
  corporate, 173
  discount, 137, 146–48
  interest rates on, 136–37, 140, 146–148
  junk, 137
  municipal, 37, 147, 158, 177, 179
  "at par," 137

premium, 137
prices of, 136–37, 140, 146–48
quotations for, 138–40
reasons for offering of, 136–37
repurchase of, 148
sale of, at a loss, 147–48
short-term market for, 147–48, 179
swapping of, 147–48
tax-exempt, 170, 173

bond trusts, 158

bookkeeping, for own business, 117–118

borrowing, 52–62, 71–72, 75–76
from banks, 53–55, 59, 71–72
from brokerage firms (margin accounts), 57–59
without credit rating, 53–54, 59
credit ratings and, 52–54, 62, 75–76
from credit unions, 53, 57, 59, 135
from financial thrift institutions, 57
inflation and, 18
interest rates for, 57–60
payment problems and, 54
from savings and loans, 55–57
sources for, 55–58
unsecured line of credit for, 121, 143–44
see also loans; mortgages

break-even point, 35–36

Bridwell, Roger W., 111

brokerage firms 44–45, 163
borrowing from (margin accounts), 57–59
information from, 48–49, 89, 101
limited partnerships offered by, 141
money market funds of, 65, 69
see also stockbrokers

broker's call rate, 57–58

businesses, ownership of, 116–21
background information for, 117
bookkeeping for, 117–18
capital gains tax and, 145–46
children in, 213–14
costs of, 116
emotional involvement in, 119–21
expansion and, 145
experience and, 116–17
hobby-related, 170
incorporation of, 118–19
in life phase 4, 158
owner compensation and, 119
selling of, 145–46
tax deductions from, 118, 200, 204
tax write-offs from, 170

capital, net working, 166

capital gains and capital gains taxes, 145–46, 204
on bonds, 139, 140
business ownership and, 145–46
depreciation and , 151–52
gifts and, 145, 179
on incentive stock options, 114
incorporation and, 118
long-term, 102, 145
mutual funds and, 102
on real estate, 148–52, 168, 179, 208–9
short-term, 102
on stocks, 160–62

Capital Preservation, 65

careers, 81, 171
see also, businesses, ownership of

car loans, 59–60

carry-back financing (carrying back paper), 169

cash flow statements, 27–31, 49, 52–53

CBOE (Chicago Board of Options), 95, 101

CDs (Certificates of Deposit), 18, 68–69, 179
as collateral, 55–57
premature termination of, 83

Certified Public Accountants, *see* CPAs

Chapter 7 (bankruptcy), 167

Chapter 11 (bankruptcy), 137, 140–141, 166–67

checking accounts, 50–51, 54, 70–71

children, 81, 159, 170
in college, 157
credit ratings for, 61–62
as employees, 213–14
home ownership and, 148
IRAs for, 213–14
joint ownership with, 162–63
life insurance and, 86–87
loans to, 174–75

children (*cont.*)
tax credits for, 206
wills and, 131–32, 134
closing costs, in real estate, 161, 193
collateral:
annuities as, 156
for banker's acceptances, 67–68
CDs as, 55–57
real estate as, 55–57
collecting and collectibles, 72–73, 216–17
commercial paper, 67
commodity markets, 142
community colleges, 117
Complete Money Market Guide, The (Donoghue and Tilling), 70
Consumer Price Index (CPI), 15–16, 208
contacts, 40–48
corporate bonds, 173
cost basis, 160
CPAs (Certified Public Accountants), 43–44, 74, 119, 143, 162, 163
credit cards, 51, 54, 60–61
credit ratings, 52–54, 61–62, 76
credit-reporting agencies, 53
credit unions, 53, 57, 59, 135

deductions, tax, *see* tax deductions
deeds of trust, 57, 103, 168–69
depreciation, 38–39, 122
accelerated, 151–52
recapture and, 151–52
of rental property, 38–39, 122, 148–52
straight-line, 151–52
Desautels, Paul E., 72
disability insurance, 41, 62, 84–85
amount of, 84–85
cost of, 85
purpose of, 84
Disaster Relief Act (1974), 205
dividends:
stock, 92, 115, 153–56, 177
tax-exempt, 177, 211
divorces, 143
Donoghue, William, 70
Dreyfus Liquid Assets, 65

Economic Recovery Tax Act (1981), 122, 180–81, 190–93, 204, 207–229
education, 48–50, 201
cash flow analysis in, 49–50
free seminars as, 48–49
investment courses as, 49
educational loans, 60
E. F. Hutton, 65
entrepreneurship, *see* businesses, ownership of
equipment leasing, 127
equity, stockholder's (shareholder's), 166
equity buildup, 106–7, 168, 225–26
estate-planning attorneys, 148, 160
estates and estate planning, 112, 173
executors of, 131, 134, 181–84
gifts and, 179
invalid claims against, 184
joint accounts and, 162–63
marriage and, 131–32, 173, 180–181
taxes on, 181, 184
see also wills
executors, of estates, 131, 134, 181–184

families, *see* children; marriage
finance companies, 59
financial inventory, 27
financial planners, 42, 46–48, 74, 143, 162
compensation of, 47–48
financial profile, 26–35
assets evaluated in, 26–27
cash flow statements in, 27–31
net worth statement in, 27, 31–34
foreclosure proceedings, 57
Franklin Money Market Fund, 65
futures, 129, 142

gambling, 176–77
Gem Kingdom, The (Desautels), 72
gems, 72
gift and gift taxes, 145, 158–59, 185, 187
capital gains tax and, 145, 179
loans as, 174–75
marital deduction and, 210
in wills, 159, 179
GNMA (Government National Mortgage Association), 158

hard expenses, 122
High Tech: How to Find and Profit

from Today's New Superstocks (Toney and Tilling), 111
High Tech Investing (Bridwell), 111
holographic wills, 132–33
home ownership, 76, 81–82
  children and, 148
  equity in, 106–7, 168
  mortgage refinancing and, 107–9
  rental vs., 102–7
  tax benefits of, 121, 193–94
home sales and purchases, 102–10
  capital gains and, 148–52, 168, 208–9
  closing costs and, 161
  leveraging and, 148–49
  "loaning in" and, 168–69
  tax bracket and, 102–6
  timing of, 168
  underlying notes and, 103

IBM (International Business Machines), 152–56
incentive stock options (ISOp), 114, 135–36
income, 20
  adjusted gross, 60, 195
  alternative minimum taxable, 114–115
  interest, 210
  in life phase 2, 82–83
  in life phase 3, 123
  in life phase 4, 147, 172–73
  in life phase 6, 175–79, 187–88
  marriage and, 31–32
  phantom, 127–28
  reporting and taxable, 37, 82–83, 187
  tax-deferred, 38, 187, 211–12
  tax-exempt, 37–38, 177–78, 187
  tax-sheltered, *see* tax shelters
  types of, 37–39
income averaging, 82–83, 143
incorporation, 118–19
inflation, 15–20
  asset value and, 27
  borrowing and, 18
  compounding factors for, 22
  CPI and, 15–16
  implications of, 15–16
  income and, 20
  investment break-even point and, 35
  IRAs and, 218
  life insurance and, 85
  money market funds and, 66
  mortgages and, 170
  rate of, 15–16, 18
  stocks and, 168
inheritance taxes, 184
Institute of Real Estate Management, 226–27
insurance, 62–63
  automobile, 62
  casualty, 41
  cost of, 62–63
  disability, *see* disability insurance
  homeowner's or renter's, 63
  life, *see* life insurance
  in life phase 5, 173
insurance agents, 41–42, 85, 143
interest rates:
  on annuities, 156
  on bonds, 136–37, 140, 146–48
  broker's call rate as, 57–58
  for loans, 57–60
  on money market funds, 65–66
  1981–82, 42
  prime, 143
  Regulation Q ceiling on, 66
  rental property and, 152
  on savings accounts, 21, 64
  on second mortgages, 169
  tax bracket and, 59–60
  on Treasury obligations, 157
International Association of Financial Planners (IAFP), 47
investment advisory letters, 101
investment counselors, 48
investment tax credits, 125, 207
IRAs (Individual Retirement Accounts), 23, 38, 63–64, 76, 79, 144, 212–20
  borrowing for, 219–20
  for children, 213–14
  inflation and, 218
  in life phase 2, 111
  in life phase 3, 135, 141
  in life phase 4, 157, 159
  in life phase 5, 175
  in life phase 6, 176, 178, 188
  limited partnerships and, 217–18
  liquidity of, 83
  opening of, 218
  placement of, 63, 135, 157, 214–18
  premature withdrawals from, 172
  state taxes and, 193

IRAs (Individual Retirement Accounts) (*cont.*)
as tax shelter, 121, 213–14
timing of deposits to, 218–19
IRS (Internal Revenue Service), 38–39, 75, 82, 161–62
audits by, 43–44, 221
business ownership and, 118–19, 170
incorporation and, 119
T-bill futures and, 129
ISOp (incentive stock options), 114, 135–36

joint ownership, 162–63, 180

Keogh accounts, 63–64, 157, 176, 178, 212–20
premature withdrawals from, 172
kiss-off funds, 94, 98–99, 112, 138

lawsuits, incorporation and, 118
letters of credit, 223
leveraging, 148–49
life insurance, 41, 44, 62, 85–87, 158, 173, 210
amount of, 86–87
cost of, 85–86
inflation and, 85
personal vs. group, 86
proceeds from, 158
replacement goals for, 87
life insurance companies, 156
life phases, 21–26, 37
1 (ages 18–25), 23, 37, 39–80
2 (ages 25–35), 23–24, 80–111
3 (ages 35–40), 24, 111–41
4 (ages 40–50), 24–25, 141–59
5 (ages 50–65), 25, 159–75
6 (ages 65 and over), 25–26, 175–188
limited partnerships, 49, 63, 77–78, 123–30, 221–29
for equipment leasing, 127
IRAs and, 217–18
letters of credit required by, 223
liquidity of, 173, 224
losses and gains of, 125
oil-and-gas-drilling, 125–26
phantom income and, 127–28
private, 141
public, 42, 44, 77–78, 172
public vs. private, 77–78, 222, 228
for research-and-development, 126–27
tax write-offs from, 124–27
venture capital and, 141
liquidity, 72–73, 75, 83, 168
amount of, 83
of annuities, 173
defined, 83
of IRAs, 83
in life phase 3, 135
in life phase 4, 158
in life phase 6, 175, 188
of limited partnerships, 173, 224
of money market funds, 66
Liquidity Fund, The, 224
living expenses, 50, 81, 147, 157
loans:
banker's acceptances as, 67–68
credit cards as, 60–61
educational, 60
as gifts, 174–75
rating of, by net cost or gain, 56
to relatives, 174–75
repayment of principal for, 103
see also borrowing; collateral; mortgages

margin accounts, 57–59
marriage, 81
assets, income, property and, 31–32
estates and, 131–32, 173, 180
joint ownership and, 180
in life phase 4, 141–42
separation of assets in, 31–32
tax deduction for, 208, 210
Mary Kay Cosmetics, 95–100
Memorex Corporation, 137–38
Merrill Lynch, 45, 65, 69
mid-life crisis, 141, 159
Money, 79
money market checking accounts, 70–71
money market funds, 65–70, 77, 80, 168, 179, 215
general-purpose, 69–70
history of, 66
interest rates on, 65–66
investments by, 67–70
liquidity of, 66
maturities and, 70

minimums for, 65
types of, 69
mortgages, 42, 62, 103–9
assumption of, 168
equity buildup and, 107
inflation and, 170
refinancing of, 107–9
second, 168–69
taxes and, 82, 102–9
term of, 169–70
underlying notes as, 103
moving, wills and, 134
municipal bonds, 37, 147, 158, 177, 179
mutual funds, 42, 63, 83
capital gains treatment of, 102
commissions of, 101, 188, 215–16
for IRAs, 215–16
"no-load," 76, 101–2, 188, 215–216
personal, 179
progressive growth, 101
trading value of, 101–2

net working capital, 166
net worth, 81
chart for, 32, 53
corporate, 165–66
growth of, 20–21
negative, 50
statement of, 27, 31–34
NOW accounts, 51

oil and gas drilling, 125–26, 177
opportunity costs, 75
options, *see* stock options

partnership, limited, *see* limited partnerships
passbook accounts, 55–57, 64, 214–215
pensions, private, 175–77
phantom income, 127–28
Pizza Time Theatre, 88–89, 93
planning, 20–36
break-even point determined in, 35–36
financial profile in, *see* financial profile
goals of, 20–21
life phase identified in, 21–26
life phase 2 and, 81–82
yearly financial inventory in, 27
power of attorney, 162–63
private syndicators, 109
probate, *see* wills
profit potential, 160
profit-sharing accounts, 177
property:
marriage and, 31–32
rental, *see* rental property
property managers, 46

real estate, 94, 177
capital gains on, 148–52, 168, 172, 208–9
as collateral, 55–57
in life phase, 6, 179, 188
limited partnerships for, *see* limited partnerships
taxes on, 104, 150–52
value appreciation of, 52, 106–7
see also home ownership; home sales and purchases; rental property
real estate brokers, 45–46
real estate commissions, 161
recapture, 151–52
record keeping, 28, 196–97, 200
Regulation Q, 66
rental property, 110, 121–23, 204–5
cost of, 122–23
depreciation on, 38–39, 122, 148–152
hard vs. soft expenses for, 122
interest rates and, 152
as tax shelter, 121–23
tax write-offs from, 150–52
value appreciation of, 123
reorganization, corporate, *see* bankruptcy
research and development, 126–27
retirement, 171, 212
risks, 5, 160
in tax shelters, 221, 224–25

savings & loans, 55–57, 70–71, 170
savings and savings accounts, 16–18, 21, 51, 54, 65, 81, 109
see also passbook accounts
second businesses, 111–12

ABOUT THE AUTHOR

Judith Briles is a Certified Financial Planner and is president of Briles & Associates, a corporation that does management consulting, teaching and financial planning in Northern California's Bay Area.

Ms. Briles received her M.B.A. in 1980 and plans to complete her doctorate in business in 1985. She is a frequent lecturer on money management and instructs classes in numerous colleges, universities and high schools throughout the Western United States, including the University of California campuses at Berkeley and Santa Cruz and the University of Hawaii extensions.

She is the Managing General Partner of multiple limited partnerships and is on the boards of directors of several corporations and the advisory boards of the National Association of Female Executives and *BusinessWOMAN* magazine. She is the editor of *More Money* newsletter, a nationally distributed letter on current financial issues, and has contributed articles to *Working Woman, Self, Executive Female, New Woman* and *Savvy* magazines. Among her professional affiliations, Ms. Briles has served on the advisory board of the Western Women's Bank (of which she is a former director), is a founding member of The National Speakers Team, and is listed in *Who's Who of American Women* and *Who's Who in Finance and Industry*.

Her 14 years of experience has also included appearances on *Good Morning America, Hour Magazine* and *The Mike Douglas Show,* as well as local television and radio exposure.

Judith Briles is the author of *The Woman's Guide to Financial Savvy,* which was published in 1981. *Money Phases* is her second book.